Praise for Mia Birk and *Joyride*

Mia Birk's story is inspiring and entertaining[...] hope, change, and the fact that it's okay to be [...] eventually the world catches up. Mia proves [...] and the ability to herd cats can eventually trump the car-centric status quo. *Joyride* is about making our world a better place, one bike lane at a time.
> — *Jonathan Simmons,* Boston Globe

Birk leaves cyclists giddy.
> — Calgary Herald

Fierce advocate. Thanks to Birk, we're all feeling the love.
> — Fitness Magazine

Capably balances personal anecdotes with sharpened sustainable-transportation policy arguments. Keeps both the average reader and policy wonk engaged.
> — New Urban News

A much livelier read than a polemic or wonky policy paper... *Joyride* artfully mixes personal history and facts to create a candid, compelling memoir...clear lessons for anyone who wants to foment change.
> — Willamette Week

A breath of fresh air. Timely.
> — Huffington Post

Mia Birk's *Joyride* is a delightful read and a must-have book. It weaves together illustrative stories that are useful problem solving exercises. *Joyride* is timely, provocative, entertaining, and informative.
> — *Charles A. Flink, author,* Trails and Greenways for the 21st Century

Required reading. Engaging narrative. Feels like your friend retelling war stories over a couple of beers at your favorite bar.
> — Momentum Magazine

A witty, poignant, and often funny memoir detailing how Birk persuaded politicians, city bureaucrats, and average citizens that bikes are a perfectly sensible form of transportation. You don't need to ever mount a bike yourself to appreciate this story, which is really for anyone who ever wanted to understand how to make things happen in a modern American city, suburb, or small town.
> — *Jeff Mapes, author,* Pedaling Revolution: How Cyclists Are Changing American Cities

Anyone interested in changing their life or community for the better is going to love *Joyride*. It tells the story of how we transformed Portland into a livable, thriving cycling mecca. Mia Birk is the right person to tell this story.
> — *Earl Blumenauer, Member of Congress (OR-03)*

Part history lesson, part memoir, and part how-to guide, *Joyride* entertains and inspires.

> — *Jessica Cassity, Fitness Editor,* Prevention Magazine,
> and *author,* Better Each Day

The world's climate change problems can be affected by forward-thinking leaders like Mia Birk. Her painstaking research of European bicycle transportation solutions and daring application to Portland, Oregon, and other cities offer lessons for all us.

> — *Ellen Pope, Former Director of Comparative Domestic Policy,*
> *The German Marshall Fund of the United States*

Mia's work strikes at the heart of what it means to make cities healthy and rewarding places to live, create, and thrive. Students and professionals will find both practical knowledge and inspiration in this important new book.

> — *Ethan Seltzer, Director, Toulan School of Urban Studies*
> *and Planning, Portland State University*

The Association of Pedestrian and Bicycle Professionals (APBP) was proud to award Mia Birk the 2007 Professional of the Year Private Sector Award for her force of nature leadership in creating more bicycle- and pedestrian-friendly communities, bringing back bicycling and walking to schools, and advancing the professional capacity of the planning and transportation field.

> — *Kit Keller, JD, Executive Director, APBP*

Tremendously captivating personal stories filled with passion and intrigue. The message that anyone can help build a more livable community with clear vision, personal commitment, and the right coalition-building skills leaves us cheering for more.

> — *Cascade Cycle Club, Seattle, Washington*

Joyride is a great chronicle of the vision and tenacity that it takes to transform a city's mindset and infrastructure, and is a great handbook for those of us who want to bring change to our own cities.

> — *Angela Hunt, city councilwoman, Dallas, Texas*

Mia knocked it out of the park. She brought the right tone, mix, and personality to the various events throughout the day, and folks were universally impressed with her style and content.

> — *Bob Ferris, Executive Director, RE Sources for*
> *Sustainable Communities*

Joyride gave our trails group the get-up-and-go inspiration we've needed for quite some time.

> — *Moses Lake Parks and Recreation (Washington State)*

Joyride

Pedaling Toward a Healthier Planet

by Mia Birk

with Joe "Metal Cowboy" Kurmaskie

THE MOUNTAINEERS BOOKS

THE MOUNTAINEERS BOOKS
is the nonprofit publishing arm of The Mountaineers,
an organization founded in 1906 and dedicated to the exploration,
preservation, and enjoyment of outdoor and wilderness areas.

1001 SW Klickitat Way, Suite 201, Seattle, WA 98134

© 2012 by Mia Birk

First edition published by Cadence Press, 2010. Second edition, 2012

Manufactured in the United States of America

Cover Design: Karen Schober
Interior Design: Anne Bothner-By
Layout: Peggy Egerdahl
All photographs by the author unless otherwise noted

Cover photograph: Deborah Moon

Library of Congress Cataloging-in-Publication Data
Birk, Mia.
  Joyride : pedaling toward a healthier planet / by Mia Birk with Joe
"Metal Cowboy" Kurmaskie. — 2nd ed.
    p. cm.
  Originally published : Portland : Cadence Press, 2010.
  ISBN 978-1-59485-760-7 (pbk) — ISBN 978-1-59485-761-4 (ebook)
  1. Cycling. I. Kurmaskie, Joe. II. Title.
  GV1041.B54 2012
  796.6—dc23
                              2012029407

ISBN (paperback): 978-1-59485-760-7
ISBN (ebook): 978-1-59485-761-4

SUSTAINABLE
FORESTRY
INITIATIVE
Certified Chain of Custody
Promoting Sustainable Forestry
www.sfiprogram.org
SFI-01268

SFI label applies to the text stock

For Skyler and Sasha

Table of Contents

❁❁❁❁❁

Section IV: Plant Seeds and a Garden Will Grow 133

Section V: Spreading the Love 173

Section VI: A Long and Winding Path 213

The Making of *Joyride*

Mia Birk

One evening, I was downtown watching a bicycle race with my mentor and friend, the Honorable Earl Blumenauer. He'd been my boss when I was the City of Portland Bicycle Program Coordinator in the 1990s. Much more, though, he was a man who had seen a vision of the place we could become and who had imparted this vision on both a city and points beyond.

"So, how are you?" asked Earl in his disarming style—innocuous, polite, and full of intention.

Suddenly, I was choking back tears. "I'm just so stressed, Earl...I'm busy all the time, and my head is bursting." For many years, I had lived and breathed every battle, public meeting, behind-the-scenes roller-coaster debate, and city council hearing, cataloging our progress, celebrating our successes, bemoaning our failures. I told these stories in my classes at Portland State University (PSU), where I taught bicycle and pedestrian planning. At the same time, I was working nationwide creating more bicycle-friendly communities through my rapidly expanding firm, Alta Planning + Design. Over and over, I heard from students, staff, clients, and colleagues about how my stories affected them in a positive way.

Turning these stories into a book seemed the next logical step. But, between parenting two kids, working more than full-time growing Alta (I was both the COO and CFO at that point, plus managing numerous projects), and teaching at and founding PSU's Initiative for Bicycle and Pedestrian Innovation, among a few other things, I couldn't see how writing a book was in the cards.

Earl locked my eyes with his usual intense gaze. "You need to write it, Mia. Now. It's our excellent story of hope and change. Believe me, people want to hear it. And Barack Obama is going to win. I want to get our story in the hands of Obama and every congressperson. The time is now. Stop whining. Start writing." (How many of you have been ordered to stop whining by your congressman?)

But it wasn't just the Portland story I was trying to tell, it was the story of our country, of our movement away from auto-dominance, and the hundreds of communities taking their first steps with a bike plan or trail or Safe Routes to School program. Transportation is at the heart of every society and is deeply intertwined with our lifestyles. But the impacts of our overdependence on the automobile have been nothing short of disastrous: $150 billion spent annually on the horrific health impacts (e.g., asthma, type 2 diabetes, high blood pressure, strokes, even cancers) of sedentary lifestyles; livability and safety problems; stress; lost productivity; and costly, unacceptable levels of noise, water, and air pollution.

Too often, solutions have consisted of simply more of the same: building more roads and parking, maintaining low fuel prices, and buying more cars. The stark reality: it is impossible to resolve our problems and sustain economic vitality by focusing investments on personal auto-based systems. Portland's story shows what we gain with a holistic, progressive approach.

Every project itself is a story with characters and drama—like the incredible pressure faced by the folks designing Portland's Steel Bridge Riverwalk when they had but forty-eight hours to finish the project with ten years of work on the line; shepherding San Francisco's Shared Lane Marking study through layers of analysis and bureaucracy; delicately negotiating between trail proponents and hard-nosed railroad lawyers and engineers determined to protect their turf; returning to and finding positive hope and energy in my hometown of Dallas. And every story yields lessons.

Having taken Earl's pushy admonition to heart, I started writing. My goals were to inspire folks to take those hard first steps, to keep up the momentum, to overcome the seemingly endless stream of obstacles thrown in our paths; to reach beyond our teeny audience of the already enlightened to political leaders, health care officials, environmentalists, casual and fitness riders, bike racers, even mainstream North America; to enlighten readers to the nuances of transportation—similar to the way *The Omnivore's Dilemma* or *Fast Food Nation* opened our eyes to the food industry. I imagined my thoughts and observations would seemlessly weave with technical information, like President Obama's lovely wandering style in *Dreams of My Father*. And with a compelling plot distilled into bite-size chapters, readers, I envisioned, would devour it, bring it to their book clubs, propel it to the best-seller list!

I'd like to think my naïveté was cute. More likely it was pathetic.

A few months later, I rode over to a coffee shop in North Portland with my first draft, which I slapped down on the table in front of best-selling author/performer Joe Kurmaskie, aka, the Metal Cowboy. It took him no time at all to pronounce that I had some good material, but working alone I was going to need on the order of ten years to complete the task at hand. His words conveyed the brutal reality that my painfully boring tome had completely missed the mark of intent.

"Uh-uh brother," I shook my head. "The time is now. Earl said so. I want this done in a year."

"It might take two," laughed Joe. "But I'm your man!"

Joe agreed to guide me, to help turn my technical diatribe into a work of art. For months we met weekly, usually with two, three, maybe five kids running around, jabbing lightsabers, begging for snacks. We swapped stories, laughed ourselves silly, and then I would rewrite a chunk at a time.

Joe Kurmaskie: Collaborator, Publisher of the first edition

Mia had one helluva a story on her hands, and from the beginning I knew she was smart, driven, and mission-oriented, but writing a book, any book, worthy of serious attention is similar to trying to take up brain surgery after watching a few *NOVA* specials on PBS. Bad books are like binge-drinking college students—an embarrassing mess, and the only ones laughing are the drinkers and a few "friends" who didn't have the courage or heart to stop them.

But Mia didn't need stopping, and this wasn't some ego-boosting vanity project. What would become *Joyride* was a life-affirming, community-changing, meat-of-life story that needed to find its shape and texture and tone.

The structure of *Joyride*—along with practically every word, story, and character—is intentional. We start at the global level with the crushing weight of the world's problems, deeply rooted in our unsustainable addiction to driving. But we don't dwell in misery for long. We didn't want to add to the voluminous "World is going to hell—went there yesterday, in fact" literature that crowds our bookshelves, evening news, and morning shows. We wanted to tell a positive story, which starts with Mia, once a typical overweight American who opened her eyes and embraced a healthier, safer, saner, sustainable, and more prosperous path from the seat of her bicycle. Everyone has a story—that's why happy hour was invented—but the Aborigines of Australia believe that if sung at the right frequency, detailed with enough truth and vision, a good story will produce harmonies that can lead us where we need to go.

Mia Birk

Joyride Section I sets the stage for the battle over the future of our parochial stumptown Portland. At countless meetings across the world, people have said to me, "Oh, you're from Portland! I love Portland. What a great city! And it's so bicycle friendly! We could never be like that...I mean, it's so...Portland!" But this is a myth.

Once, Portland was polluted, degraded, and near-abandoned, miserably in lockstep with the rest of North America. But we chose a different path, and today are simply ahead of many North American cities in a long journey toward more balanced, sustainable transportation systems. We too have felt an inferiority complex, in our case relative to our European counterparts in cities like Copenhagen and Amsterdam, "They're so bicycle friendly! We can never be like them!" But this too is a myth, for they are also on a journey, having battled their own auto-addiction demons.

In Section II, the battle lines are drawn as we both plan and begin retrofitting Portland's auto-oriented transportation system with bikeways on our roads and underused urban spaces. Only in hindsight can we truly appreciate the battles for what they were: the first salvos in a revolution to bring humanity back into core of the North American transportation system.

Section III takes us deeper into transportation reform as we learn that it is not just excellent bikeway networks that create lasting change, but the evolution of our maintenance practices and building codes. And to accomplish that, we have to retrain every single human involved in urban transportation, no matter how esoteric or minor his or her role.

And at the same time we are creating the infrastructure, reformulating the systems, and retraining the humans, we—all of us—have to reform our own behavior. There's no time to sit back and wait for our friends and colleagues and neighbors to discover that new path, bike lane, or rack and decide to give it a try. We have to bike and walk for more trips—now— no matter where we live or work, no matter how many kids we have or obstacles we perceive. And we've got to think not just of ourselves but of the next generation, instilling in our kids an expectation that bicycling is simply how we get around. This, then, is Section IV's takeaway: Given the right impetus, we—society—can and will change our behavior.

Behavior change is deep stuff. Section V takes us beyond Portland to the national level as I shift jobs to then-tiny Alta Planning + Design. As of this writing, Alta has expanded to sixteen offices and hundred-plus staff dedicated to creating active communities where bicycling and walking are safe, normal, healthy, and fun daily activities. My colleagues and I take on reform of national standards, mores, methodologies, models, and guidelines. We're in the suburbs, rural areas, and in the heart of Car Culture, U.S.A. Despite infinite challenges, hope springs eternal as we implement thousands of bikeway and walkway miles, touch hundreds of communities, and enhance the health and daily lives of millions.

The lesson: Wherever you are, that's where you start. Neither Copenhagen nor Portland nor Vancouver, B.C.; New York, Chicago, Seattle, San Francisco, Washington, D.C., Cambridge, Berkeley, nor Boulder changed their transportation system and culture overnight. It takes time, is a struggle, and is worth it.

Section VI takes us back to Portland to find that meaningful change takes time. New battles begin, richer still than those of the previous decade, and we learn that we have only scratched the surface of what we can become.

Mia and Joe

We are grateful for the overwhelmingly positive response to the first edition of *Joyride* and to all the communities who hosted *Joyride* events, readers who told us their own stories of change and hope, and groups who used *Joyride* to inspire and engage staff, advocates, and leaders.

With this second edition, you'll now find embedded throughout the book **Fifty keys to transforming communities and empowering people**. An expanded list of these keys is now included at the back, along with an updated resources guide, and a new author interview.

The proceeds of *Joyride* continue to be directed toward nonprofit organizations working to create sustainable transportation.

Enjoy the ride!

FOREWORD

America is undergoing a bicycle renaissance. From coast to coast, bicycling is no longer the province of spandex-wearing triathletes or occasional recreational riders. Although these cyclists continue to be an important part of the movement, the profound changes in the cycling movement have come from Americans who are rediscovering the bicycle as the most efficient form of urban transportation ever designed. Since more than a third of all trips in America can be made in less than twenty minutes on a bike, cycling has become a godsend for Americans concerned about traffic congestion, their personal health, and their household finances. At a time when we are concerned about not just reinvigorating our neighborhoods but literally protecting the planet, burning calories instead of fossil fuel has a great deal of appeal. Bicycling enables us to become healthier and be better environmental stewards while we improve the livability of our communities.

Today, when economic concerns abound, bicycling is also extraordinarily cost-effective. A bike costs less than a dollar a day to maintain; annual operational costs for a car approach $8,000. For the cost of a single lane of urban freeway, an entire city can be outfitted with safe and accessible bike connections. You can park fifty bikes in four car spaces.

Bicycling has also become an economic engine: Bike tourism is exploding all across the country, pumping millions of dollars into rural communities; sales, service, apparel, and manufacturing are growing exponentially as well. As the Portland, Oregon, commissioner of transportation I made bicycling one of my top priorities—and have since seen cycling blossom into a $100-million-a-year enterprise employing one thousand people as it makes a dramatic difference in the city's physical and cultural landscape.

These things don't happen by accident. In Portland, we poured a lot of hard work and dedication into making the changes needed to quadruple our cycling share to one of the highest of any major city in the country.

One person was at the center of that work, pushing on the policy, addressing the politics, and fine-tuning the details to make it all happen. That person was Mia Birk—a dedicated and savvy individual who learned how to pull it all together and make it happen. The most important thing I did for bicycling in Portland was to hire Mia.

Bikes make a lot of sense, especially in these times of economic upheaval and increasingly urgent environmental concerns. But of all the facts, the figures, and the trends, the most critical component of making any change happen is having strong advocates who can develop plans, make the case, and build public support. Mia not only played a key role in Portland's bicycling success, she built on her experiences there to become a nationally sought-after consultant, professor, speaker, and CEO of a leading bicycle and pedestrian planning firm. Today, Mia is one of the most influential leaders in America, a woman whose fingerprints are on transportation plans from coast to coast.

Joyride captures the enthusiasm and insights of a free-spirited, open, and thoughtful advocate as she generously shares her passion for bicycling with planners, city officials, advocates, family, and friends.

As our national bicycle renaissance grows and flourishes, Mia will continue to be one of its prime movers. *Joyride* explains why.

Congressman Earl Blumenauer (OR-03)
May 2010

PROLOGUE

Nine Brothers in a Box

Thanksgiving 1995, Dallas, Texas

"Now Honey, your dad told me you were doing something involving, let's see, what did he say? Oh yes, bicycles. Now, what's that about?" I'm cornered at a packed Thanksgiving party. She's a friend of my father's. Her name escapes me, but not that laugh, which sounds like a mischievous hyena.

"Does it have to do with Greenpeace, Honey? Why did y'all have to blow up that boat?" She means well, in a twisted way, warm in her Southern tone that belies the undertext of her question. In this world, the acceptable career boxes are medicine, law, or business. In the room are my three blood brothers and four of my stepbrothers (from Dad's remarriage); all are highly successful with impressive mainstream careers. My other two stepbrothers, an architect and a teacher from Mom's remarriage, also fit the bill. In case you've lost count, that's nine brothers.

My one stepsister, on Mom's side, is in pharmaceutical sales. In this day and age, we all understand that one. I get no relief from this side of the family either. My stepfather, Tommy Thompson, a good ol' boy native of the oil-rig land of East Texas, is hobby-loving, friendly, kind, and generous and loves to get my goat with choice but affectionate words like, "Why Mia, yer jest a young uppity flamethrower. This environmental crap is for y'all hippies. You don't understand a thing about the real world" (i.e., making money). (I respond that he is a stubborn, close-minded ol' fart.)

While I take a deep breath and chant inside my head, "Serenity now," Dad's friend jumps ahead. "Oh, and you remember my Laura. She's a wonderful mom." She pulls out the pictures of her grandkids.

It's only about the zillionth time I've been dismissed by well-meaning friends, not just in my hometown but everywhere I go. Standard one-liners (often accompanied by eye-rolling) include:

"OOOH, how neat! You get paid to ride your bike?"

My biological brothers and me. Left to right: Russell, Bruce, Glenn

"Oh, *that's* a good use of taxpayer dollars."

"You're trying to do what? Get people to ride bikes? Ha, ha, that's a good one. Come check out my new car."

Truth be told, I'm leading a revolution, savoring every battle scar and getting back up each morning to pick up the charge again. We are engaged in a large-scale social experiment to see if we can transform a large, auto-oriented American city—Portland, Oregon—into one in which bicycling is an integral part of life. The results will determine the quality of life for generations to come. Win or lose, it's a universe away from here. How does one explain this in cocktail party conversation?

"Do they, um, pay you for that?" She pats me on the arm, as if she's very sorry I have such a pathetic job. Maybe I should say "no" so she'll offer me money?

"Didn't you hear? She's going biking with the President!" On each side of me, Tweedle-Dee and Tweedle-Dum, aka brothers Bruce and Glenn, are grinning ferociously, delighted at the opportunity to see me agitated.

"She gets paid by the pedal stroke. That's why she's always spinning her wheels." That's Bruce, the jokester.

Glenn, a button-pushing Michael J. Fox look-alike, jabs, "Seriously, Sis. When are you going to get a real job?"

I stammer huffily, "Well, thanks, Brother. Always the nice one, aren't you? I consider it a pretty important job."

If I succeed, Portland is going to become a city where people choose bicycling as a normal everyday means of transportation, maybe not for every trip but for many trips. I am trying to realize this for city councilman Earl Blumenauer, a bow-tie-wearing intellectual who is leading a livability insurgency and has hired me to be his field general. This is because bicycling is a win-win solution for our growing energy, environmental, livability, and health problems. In a not-too-distant future, I hope, many of us will live a car-free or car-light existence. This will mean, as I myself discovered, personal empowerment. We will be fit and healthier, with more money in our pockets. Our kids will arrive at school by foot or bike, energetic and ready to learn. Our stress levels will drop, and we will be freer.

Glenn wants to let us know, "You know what I think when I see bicycles on the road? Fifty points! No, that's too much, it's too easy to hit 'em."

He turns his imaginary steering wheel toward me, grinning. "Boom...Gotcha!"

Oh boy, this is not going to be easy.

For one hundred years, we have planned and designed our cities around personal automobile travel. We have cemented our auto addiction through our land-use practices, management of traffic, use of publicly financed space and layout of our buildings. We have gotten so used to driving everywhere for every trip that we have forgotten how to use our bodies to fulfill our basic transportation needs. All of us are creatures of habit, and bicycling seems so out of character, so odd, really, that we cannot imagine a lifestyle in which we hop on our bikes to get where we need to go. These habits I am trying to change, through provision of bikeways and bike parking, and through events and activities to encourage people to try it. Because just like me—once a car-addicted chubster—once people try bicycling, they really like it.

I try a last-ditch effort at explanation. "Have you ever been to Copenhagen or Amsterdam? More than a third of daily trips are made by bicycles in these beautiful, cosmopolitan cities."

Dad's friend eyes me closely. "Amsterdam...I've heard about what they smoke there." She backs away, tracks down my dad, and whispers, "David, we need to talk. I think your daughter's in serious trouble."

Maybe I am, or maybe I'm onto something. Only time will tell.

SECTION I

Training Wheels

Set off in the early morning dew on the Lincoln Street Bikeway and you will be in good company. Follow a line of blinking red lights to downtown. Cross one of our renovated bridges, marvel at the floating path on the Willamette River, then park your bike in one of thousands of covered, secure racks. Walk into a meeting holding your helmet and not one person will snort in amusement or derision. They've probably biked in themselves, if not today, another day. If not yet, soon. Take a deep breath, let your pulse rest, and know that you've started the day healthily, economically, safely.

It would be easy to think that the Portland, Oregon, we see today has always been the nation's #1 bicycling city. Easy, but wrong. It didn't just happen. We made it happen. And it wasn't easy. The fifteen-year battle to evolve our auto-dominated transportation system started practically from scratch.

CHAPTER 1

Reality Check

1993

My first day as Portland's Bicycle Program coordinator finds me slotted into a meat-locker-sized, burnt-orange cubicle, identical to the ones on my right and left. Natural light does not penetrate this part of the building.

One cubicle over, a blond man is yelling in a faux-Australian accent into the phone. Apparently yesterday's rugby match was highly entertaining. "No, mate, he din't break his collarbone, just dislocated his bloody shoulder! Popped the sucker right back in!"

I'm working my way through an inch-high stack of forms. Suddenly, a woman with short spiky hair and flowing fire-engine-red dress is in my space. She is communications director Loretta, sent to tell me that a local advocacy group, the Bicycle Transportation Alliance (BTA), has filed a lawsuit against the city. She barks at me, "I'm telling you right here and now. Whatever you do, do NOT speak to the media!"

"Um, OK," I respond. Since I have no idea what she's talking about, it seems wise to agree.

I stick out my hand. "I'm Mia Birk. Nice to meet you!?"

She explains that the bicycle group insists that bike lanes—marked bicycle-only lanes on streets—are required by law. The city, my employer, has refused to mark bike lanes on a road adjacent to the prominent new Portland Trail Blazers basketball arena.

Since my job is supposedly to improve conditions for people who ride—or want to ride—bikes, I ask innocently, "Why aren't we installing bike lanes?"

She glares at me and tattoos her phone number on my hand. "They talk to me, not you, got it?" Clearly a command, not a question. She storms out, sending my stack of paperwork flying. I quietly gather the raining paper. Heads pop up from the surrounding cubicles.

"She's high-spirited," notes the rugby player. "You don't want to get on her shit list."

"Great," I think, "just great. One hour on the job and already floundering."

"Ready to ride?" Rob Burchfield asks a few days later. Skinny as a stick and sharp as a tack, Rob is the city's lead traffic engineer. He often rides his bike to work 15 miles (24 km) one-way from his farm in rural Washington County, where on the weekends you'll find him behind the wheel of a tractor or fixing the chicken coop.

"Always!" I grab my helmet in excitement.

He's taking me on my first Portland bicycling adventure. I'm lucky it wasn't my last.

We wait under the portico of the government-function Portland Building, whose front door is protected by an enormous statue of a ready-to-attack warrior goddess holding a trident. It's hard to imagine that this building's design—swaddled in blue tile and a big red bow, making it resemble the inside of a gift-wrapped restroom—was award-winning at the time.

The Bicycle Program's stalwart, Jeff Smith, joins us. A slender but towering man, Jeff's a cartographer by training, calm as a morning in the country, and a take-no-prisoners croquet player.

We roll out for North Portland, an annexed suburb characterized by wide, flat streets and an older, working-class population. We ride into a four-mountain day—Mount Hood to the east, and St. Helens, Adams, and Rainier to the north—all demanding the attention of us city dwellers. We set off on reasonably calm downtown streets. I feel like I'm on holiday, with these million-dollar views and a light breeze in my face.

The narrow but functional sidewalks of the Broadway Bridge take us to the east side, where we take two right turns onto Interstate Avenue heading north. That's when things get interesting.

A couple miles of this gritty, high-speed road and my nerves are starting to fray. Then Jeff and Rob stick

Traffic engineer Rob at home on the farm with his son Cody

out their left arms to indicate we're turning onto a
steeply ascending four-
lane highway.

"Are you kidding?" I
think, as they make a
break for it, quickly merg-
ing into the left lane. I nervously follow their lead.

Grunting our way up
North Greeley, we hug
the edge of the road and
slow to 6 or 7 miles per
hour (10–11 km/h). Like

A typical Portland road in the early 1990s

a swimmer flailing in a powerboat wake, I grasp my handlebars to steady
myself from 18-wheeler wind blasts.

After the crest, we execute another left-turn-across-traffic maneuver
onto Willamette Boulevard, a quiet street lining a bluff overlooking the
Willamette River's shipyards. I breathe a little easier, sip from my water
bottle, let my shoulders relax.

The all-too-brief mile of calm is replaced five minutes later by a solid
line of traffic as we approach the University of Portland, home to one of the
country's top women's college soccer teams. I wonder if the players' biggest
concern is crossing Willamette to get to practice.

"Willamette is a very popular road for touring cyclists," Jeff explains
as we stop for a break. He and Rob have been trying to add bike lanes in
response to a cavalcade of complaints about safety.

"Students and local residents in particular are demanding improvements."

"As they should be," I concur.

"But it's been hard," he sighs. "Folks around here don't like the idea of
bike lanes at all."

I look up the wide, straight expanse of asphalt. "I don't understand.
Just narrow the existing lanes. Or remove one side of parking. Looks like
no one parks here anyway. Isn't it a no-brainer?"

Rob and Jeff shake their heads, and Rob's bony shoulders slump in wea-
riness. "It's not about brains, it's about emotion. You'll see at the public
meeting next week."

Jeff gets up off the grass. "Let's keep riding."

We squeeze along parked cars. Motorists impatiently hover behind us,
then gun it to pass. We reach a narrow two-lane bridge, with not an inch
of space for bicyclists or pedestrians. It's been stressful until this point.

Now it's white-knuckle terrifying. The bridge dumps us onto a bona fide industrial highway where no one drives below sixty.

I've been gritting my teeth, trying to be brave, but I can't take it anymore. I let loose.

"What is this? You call this bicycling? We're going to die out here!"

Rob looks back to see if something has happened to me.

"Where is the trail? The bike lanes? This is crazy! In Washington, D.C., I biked on a path in Rock Creek Park, not on highways with eighteen-wheelers." My ranting gets their attention, and we stop. Trucks and cars fly by in a steady stream.

Jeff and Rob look at each other. "Um.... Well, yeah," Rob says. "This is why we hired you." He tries a gentle smile and touches my arm with long piano-playing fingers.

By the most generous accounting, Portland at the time has but a few dozen miles of disconnected bike lanes, green Bike Route signs on a few neighborhood streets, dead-end paths, highway shoulders, and way-too-narrow bridge sidewalks. Better than most cities, but nowhere close to where we need to be. Nothing resembling an attractive bikeway network. It's like so-called roadway networks from the late 1800s—unpaved, unsafe, incomplete, dysfunctional. If my job is to fix this, I've sure got my work cut out for me.

I spew profanities. They wait me out. I turn my bike around.

"I've seen enough." I sound like Ebenezer Scrooge to the ghosts in *A Christmas Carol*. "Let's go."

What was I thinking? That Portland was already like Amsterdam or Copenhagen? Bicycling conditions are deplorable, scary. I wouldn't send my worst enemies onto these roads.

Back at headquarters, I try to shake it off on my way to a promising-sounding meeting. Rob leads me through the cubicle maze to a small windowless conference room, where we join engineers Stephen, Mike, and Ben. They roll out maps and pass around data sheets.

"Four streets are under consideration." Rob begins. "Beaverton–Hillsdale Highway, Southeast Seventh, Northeast Broadway/Weidler and downtown Southwest Broadway."

One of these could be the first major roadway in Portland retooled with bike lanes. I'm practically jumping up and down in my seat with anticipation.

"Well, we definitely can't do Broadway/Weidler," Mike states. He rolls out a map. The bulk of each one-way street has four lanes plus on-street parking on both sides. He launches into a speech about traffic "capacity," levels of congestion, peak-hour flow, and the like. I understand almost none of it, but I get that it means keeping car traffic moving is very, very important.

Stephen chimes in. "The businesses aren't going to like it, especially if we touch their parking."

Wow, eight lanes of travel and four lanes of parking. Seems like an awful lot of space for cars. But what do I know? I keep my mouth shut.

Northeast Broadway, 1993 (compare with photos on pages 73 and 92).

"Let's move on to Southwest Broadway downtown." Rob unrolls another map. "It's on the paving list, so that would be an opportune time to install bike lanes."

He pulls out a ruler and measures. "Fifty feet. Eight feet of parking on each side, three twelve-foot-wide travel lanes. Pretty tight. Not sure how we could squeeze in a bike lane."

Ben shakes his head. "No way. We've already got traffic signals timed for a slow speed. Bicyclists can just ride in the middle of the lane."

"Excuse me," I interject. "Ride in the middle of the lane? Isn't Broadway a little steep? I'm pretty fit, but I can't keep up with the signals."

He looks at me for a long moment.

"The downtown businesses will hate it," he says. "See these hotel parking zones? See all these driveways?" He points to half a dozen parking garages. "You can't expect motorists to yield to cyclists when they turn into a parking garage. This is a nonstarter."

We then dismiss another road, Southeast Seventh—four lanes plus parking—as similarly problematic and controversial.

Ben turns our attention to Beaverton–Hillsdale Highway. "This one is doable," he states emphatically.

It only needs a marked fog line to create a shoulder that can double as a bike lane. No parking need be removed on this puppy. Motorists turning across the bike lane into driveways and onto side streets don't bother him this time. Neither does the fact that we'll have to drop the bike lane where the highway divides, forcing cyclists to merge left across fast-moving traffic.

They quickly reach consensus that this is the best choice because no inconvenient trade-offs for the motoring public are required. Who cares about a few safety trade-offs for bicyclists? They high-five each other and walk out cheerful.

I, on the other hand, leave confused and glum. It's better than nothing, I console myself. Then why am I not satisfied? Three perfectly good candidates for bike lanes were dismissed. Besides Rob, do any of these men ride a bike? Loretta's warning about the Bicycle Transportation Alliance lawsuit floats into my head. No wonder they're suing the city for refusing to put in bike lanes.

My impression had been that the bulk of the job would be convincing a skeptical public that bicycling is a viable means of transportation. Apparently, my job is also to evolve the bureaucracy, which, like every American transportation department, is almost entirely dedicated to moving and parking motor vehicles.

On our way to the Willamette Boulevard public meeting, Jeff and I retrace our North Portland bike-route ordeal.

It isn't any more comfortable the second time.

At previous meetings, Jeff and my predecessor Krys Ochia had tried to explain that bike lanes would reduce travel speeds and improve safety. Opponents had shouted them down.

A series of negative letters and editorials in a neighborhood newspaper decried the bike lanes under the guise of safety concerns related to the relatively high driving speed of 35 to 50 mph (56–80 km/h). In response, Jeff and Krys suggested bundling the bike lane proposal with speed bumps to reduce travel speeds to 30 mph (48 km/h). This infuriated residents even further.

Opponents formed a group called Save Our Boulevard. Their flyers compared the bumps and lines of the city's proposal to the barbed wire of the Berlin Wall and labeled the city as a communist regime intent on commandeering people's cars. Tonight's public meeting is an attempt to clear the air and combat the misinformation.

Crystal Atkins, one of my new colleagues, meets us at the door of a fifty-person classroom she's emptied to accommodate the expected crowd. Redheaded, solidly built, she is a hard-working horse farmer in her private life, which is fitting as her work life consists of corralling a wickedly diverse herd of opinionated residents. On the one hand, Crystal, a so-called "traffic calming specialist," fields a never-ending stream of requests for speed bumps and circles to slow auto traffic on neighborhood streets. On the other hand, she calmly absorbs fervent opposition to the city's attempts to rein in unsafe driving habits. I'm grateful she's here. Her horse-whisperer skills will help us rein in the wilder broncos.

It's a fact: The faster we drive, the more dangerous our daily existence. And unless we're forced to slow down, we don't.

Crystal, Jeff, and I position ourselves around the room. I stand by a poster showing photos of bike lanes filled with happy pedaling people. Fire captain Dave Bellucci arrives and introduces himself to Crystal. They chat for a few moments, and he parks himself at the door.

Newspaper headlines express the state of progress at the time.

Crystal whispers to me, "We're in trouble."

"What do you mean?" I whisper back.

She nods over to where Dave is standing with a woman my age who looks like she is about to cry. In a flat, somber tone she explains: "The Fire Bureau doesn't like this project."

I shimmy close to the door. A young woman pushing a two-year-old in a stroller stops at the sign-in table.

Dave leans in close enough for her to smell his breath. "Do you know it only takes two minutes for a house to catch fire?"

"Excuse me?" The woman looks up to see a clean-shaven, buff, uniformed man with fire in his eyes.

"Where is your child's bedroom? It takes us another forty seconds to reach his room." He clears his throat.

"These speed bumps will slow down our response time. Your child's life is at stake."

My mouth drops open in shock. This guy works for the city, right? Aren't we on the same team?

The mom picks up her toddler and cradles him close to her heart. The tyke struggles to get down to the plate of cookies on the table.

I follow the woman to one of the posters and engage her in conversation. "Speed bumps and bike lanes will bring travel speeds down below 30 mph," I explain. "This will significantly reduce the number and severity of auto crashes."

I want to tell her that the Fire Bureau spends the bulk of their time as first responders to traffic crashes, not fires, but I never get the chance.

She looks at me like I have a communicable disease, turns on her heel and, after stopping to shake Dave's hand, flees the premises. Crystal, Jeff, and I watch, embarrassed and aghast, as Dave swoops in like a bird of prey pecking at people's worst fears.

The mood gets darker as the night wears on.

A thirty-something man with a long brown ponytail grabs my arm. "You're going to have to pay me for the damage to my motorboat," he warns.

"Excuse me?"

Before he can answer, an elderly couple lambasts us as hippies. Next up, a man dressed like a lumberjack hisses that we'll have to pry his cold, dead hands from his steering wheel before we'd see him on a bike. And if he sees any of us riding on his Willamette Boulevard, he's going to run us down with his two-ton pickup truck and no one will care, because everyone in North Portland, including the cops, hates cyclists and all that we stand for.

I argue back, "Sir, we stand for clean air, fitness, health, safety, and mobility. Surely we can find common ground."

He leaves the meeting even angrier than when he came. "Well done," I mumble to myself.

I can see why Krys had gotten worn out and tired of this negativity. No wonder he expressed relief when transferred to make room for me. People are so incensed, you would think we're kicking them out of their houses or confiscating their cars.

After the meeting, I ride home slowly, tired, defeated. Back in the office, the fallout is clear. The project is put on hold.

The string of reality checks doesn't end in North Portland.

"When is this silliness going to stop?" demand business and community leaders. "Bike racks? You want us to put in bike racks? What's next? Are you going to require us to put in ski racks or toy chests too?"

Next stop: the police bureau. After a series of unnecessarily aggressive police actions that result in dozens of pricey tickets to cyclists, I arrange what I envision as a cordial discussion about enforcement of cyclist-related laws. This, I am sure, will end with a common understanding and new-found close partnership. We'll walk in strangers, and walk out friends.

Once the donuts are consumed, I pass out a one-page summary. A nano-second later, an officer cuts me off with, "Under whose authority do you speak? Are you a lawyer?"

I hold my smile. "Well, no. I'm the bicycle coordinator. I am very familiar with these laws, and..."

A low moment, caught on camera during the early days of my tenure at the City of Portland

He raises his hand in protest. "We are sworn to uphold the law. Your personal interpretation means nothing." A few seconds later, I am staring at an empty room.

"Ah, yes," I think, "that went well." Chalk one up for utter naïveté.

In a few short months, I've discovered how far we have to go within my own agency, other city bureaus, the business community, and the public at large. Nothing but challenges, day in and day out.

Back in my cubicle, surrounded by mounds of paper, the buzzing fluorescent overhead lights flicker against the orange cubicle walls.

My phone rings. "How's your dream job going?" asks my mom.

I cradle my aching head in my hands, moaning.

I've come such a long way.

I have such a long way to go.

CHAPTER 2

Cleopatra Opens Her Eyes

My formative years were spent in Dallas and Richardson, Texas, where we drove everywhere, always.

Until puberty, I was relatively active, playing soccer and softball and doing gymnastics. By age twelve, I was sedentary and depressed. My body hit a size 14, way too fat for Texas, where popularity was gained in direct proportion to one's looks as defined by Barbie. Intelligence, athletics, and good works all took a back seat to beauty.

By fifteen, I was a soccer-sister chauffeur with a license and a car. Job #1: cart around my three little brothers to ball games and doctor appointments. (Our mom had four kids in three and a half years. As a mother of two born over the same time span, and a third born a decade later, I believe she was borderline insane.)

I'd turn on the AC and let it idle for a while, until the seatbelt buckle was no longer scorching to touch. Then, we'd drive across the street to the grocery store. No, across the street isn't code for "5 miles away." I'm talking directly, right-over-there across the street. We'd shop, then get back in the car, turn on the AC, idle some more, then drive home. Perfectly normal. A way of life shared by everyone not just in Dallas but all points beyond. This, along with a zillion hours watching *Gilligan's Island* while snacking on Dunkin' Donuts under the ceiling fan, offers a reasonable explanation for my generous size.

Pre-bicycling teenage chubster

I have but two childhood memories related to bike riding. Neither is good.

First, when I was six, a high-spirited black Labrador startled me to the pavement on a steep driveway. It wasn't serious, but it freaked me out. (Jumpy dogs still alarm me.) Second, denied a lift to a friend's house, I set off on brother Bruce's ten-speed Schwinn and crashed into a fire hydrant. This incident is immortalized in my tenth-grade high school photo. An inch-thick layer of pancake make-up covering the scratches on my face, frizzy over-permed hair, overweight, oily skin, braces: not the best look. After that, bicycling was eliminated from my list of to-dos.

And then, as I was packing for a move to Washington, D.C., where I was starting the second year of graduate school at Johns Hopkins Paul H. Nitze School of Advanced International Studies, Bruce made an innocuous suggestion.

"Take my bike."

"Need I remind you of what happened the last time I tried to ride your bike?" I shuddered at the memory.

"You mean when you crashed into that fire hydrant? Yeah, that was funny." He amused himself by punching me in the shoulder, hard.

"It *was* a sharp corner, you know."

"Whatever. You said you can't park a car on campus in D.C. You said your house was too far from school to walk or take the Metro. Here's a thought, Miss Environmentalist: get off your lazy ass and ride a bike. Maybe you'll stop complaining about being so fat."

Nothing like a little sibling heckling to get the blood flowing. He was right, I had packed on twenty new pounds during my first year of grad school. Heck, how could I not? I was in Bologna, Italy, and my roommate Edoardo hailed from a family of southern Italian caterers. His papa and Zio Alfonso would show up at our apartment, unannounced.

"What are you drinking?" Alfonso would demand.

"Vino." The cheap kind.

"Give it to me." He would sniff it, recoil in disgust, and dump it in the sink. Then he would haul in two demijohns of homemade wine, seven thousand pounds of pasta, a dozen loaves of bread, and fifty different kinds of cheeses, olives, olive oil, salami, and sweets. Life was good.

For breakfast, I dipped biscotti in a bowl of caffe latte. For lunch, we ate either a huge cheese-laden sandwich or an entire pizza. Dinner was late-night pasta. So yeah, I had gotten a bit chunky.

He was also right about the environmentalist part, as my studies were focused on the connection between economics, energy, and the environment. I had crafted this concentration after reading an *International*

Herald Tribune article about the economic implications of ocean pollution, which sickens coastal populations, taints food, spreads disease, destroys medicinally valuable native species, and adds enormous costs to law-abiding nations' budgets.

The article's message penetrated to my marrow, delivering a wallop of an "aha" moment and provoking reform of my lackadaisical study habits. At the University of Texas, we had been required to read something like a book a class per semester. I easily coasted, doing minimal work, scoring consistently high grades, and graduated with honors in three years.

Now I was supposed to not only skim but actually digest several books per week, per class. I quickly got into tsunami-sized trouble, grades-wise, and was close to slinking back home in failure when that article snapped me out of a deep inferiority funk. While my fellow students had been busy at work at Chase Manhattan or the U.S. Agency for International Development, or just come back from a Peace Corps stint in Burkina Faso, or spent their childhoods moving from country to country as the offspring of Foreign Service officers, I had been dressed as Cleopatra in a toga and snakes, serving cocktails, and singing goofy songs at the Magic Time Machine restaurant to put myself through public university, where tuition was a princely $500 a semester. I developed a theory that they accepted me at Johns Hopkins because they were seeking geographic diversity— after all, Texas is sort of like another country.

Once I had a clear purpose, though, I was able to shake aside the insecurities about my youth and unimpressive background, focus my energies, and earn decent-enough grades. Now I was heading to D.C. to complete my studies and start a career in environmental activism.

"Practice what you preach," Bruce goaded. So I strapped that old bike on top of my Honda Civic and headed north.

Day one in D.C., I pulled out the Schwinn, loaded my books in a backpack, and set off for school. The first bit, a steep but short hill, necessitated pushing, but the rest was an easy 2-mile (3 km) coast down Eighteenth Street to Dupont Circle.

I parked my bike in the courtyard in a little metal slot meant to be a bike rack. My bike was alarmingly lonely; its only companion was the sad remains of a pilfered frame locked to the adjacent slot. Long gone were the wheels and seat. A rusty chain lay on the ground. Probably the student was long gone as well.

"Will my bike be OK out there?" I asked a security guard.

"Dunno," he shrugged. "We don't get too many folks parking here."

I smiled nervously, and he promised to keep an eye on it.

Of course, a downhill one way means an uphill the other.

Not a bad way to put myself through college, really

Out of shape, not having ridden a bike since that fateful day in high school, my pace was slower than my eighty-year-old grandfather on foot. The insufferable D.C. humidity added to the misery. It was like pedaling in a sauna on a stationary bike directly in front of a giant hot-air-blowing fan.

"Come on, sister, you can do it," yelled a sympathetic pedestrian. I dug for a little more strength and made it home.

I rode my bike the next day, and the next day after that. After a week, that hill didn't feel quite so big. After two weeks, I had lost eight pounds. A few weeks later, I had to buy a whole new size-8 wardrobe. My hair, which I had been perming to required Texas height since I was a teen, grew long and Breck-girl luscious.

Now that I was bicycling every day, I didn't have to worry about what I ate. My body naturally craved healthy food.

And oh, the energy surging through my body and soul! Not only could I bike to and from school and work, I could study, entertain a houseful of people, then walk down to the Kilimanjaro reggae bar, where we would dance until the wee hours. And still I would happily bounce out of bed the next day, bike to school, and absorb the complexities of the never-ending conflict in the Middle East.

Fellow student John Beebe asked if I wanted to go on a longer ride. He made killer chocolate-chip cookies (the secret is to soften the butter in advance) and had simply gorgeous legs. I would have ridden any distance with him. We rode about 25 miles (40 km), down the Mount Vernon Trail past Ronald Reagan National Airport to Alexandria, Virginia, and back. I felt like I was flying. At the end, I was exhausted and exhilarated. At that moment, bicycling found its way into my marrow. It became my passion, pleasure, and career.

Like so many of us, I had spent a small fortune on gym memberships, aerobics classes, and Jane Fonda videos. Each of these was like forcing yourself to go on a date with someone you don't really like and is not a good match. Plus you're stuck with the bill. None lasted long.

Bicycling struck down all my mental barriers; it didn't feel like exercise since I was actually getting where I needed to go. Once I got a routine

On the path to fitness, having ridden about fifty miles from Washington, D.C., to Harpers Ferry, West Virginia

down, I started riding everywhere: between work and home, and to friends' houses, bars, and meetings.

For days on end, my car would sit, forlorn and neglected, begging for attention, which, as it turned out, it received in spades from an exuberant crew of parking enforcers. Their bosses must have been awful pleased with the windfall they got out of me. A spendy breakdown in a not-so-good neighborhood sealed the deal. Given the tightness of my budget, on a fresh-out-of-school nonprofit salary, the universe was clearly sending me a message. I sold the bugger and shifted to a car-free life.

In 1992, boyfriend Ned and I moved out to Takoma Park, 8 miles (13 km) as the crow flies on busy roads or 14 miles (22 km) through beautiful Rock Creek Park and the U.S. National Mall over to my office at Union Station. One hundred weekly pedaling miles sculpted my calves and quads into Tina Turner-esque things of beauty. I could hardly believe they were mine! I looked good. I felt even better. The insecure young woman who had so struggled with her weight and body image felt like a ghost of the past.

While bicycling for daily transportation shaped my body, it also informed my professional view. For four years, I researched transportation issues for the International Institute for Energy Conservation (IIEC). In growing Asian and Latin American cities, I saw thick congestion and increasing health and safety problems, coupled with massive investments in road building.

"How can it be possible," I wondered, "that in places where almost no one can afford to own a car, the only solutions under development are infrastructure, policies, and pricing directed at motor vehicle ownership and operation?"

Unfortunately, the excitement of connecting with transportation leaders worldwide was tainted by the toll on my health. On each trip, I got ridiculously ill. Dehydration, Montezuma's revenge, sinus infections, hives, asthma attacks. All trips left me malnourished and scrawny. Each time, bicycling was my salvation, my steadfast and faithful partner in building back emotional and physical strength. My 28-mile (45 km) round-trip commute felt like a godsend.

The coup de grace was getting stuck for several hours in a cloud of dust and diesel by a stalled train in Varanasi, India. My sinuses went haywire and asthma flared. Back at the hotel, I used my inhaler over and over, and it didn't make a difference. When I started blacking out, a colleague called for a doctor who immediately diagnosed the severity of the situation. I was in real danger of joining the multitudes that come to this ancient city by the Ganges to die. Worse still, the doctor couldn't get a lock on any of the small, rolling veins in my arms.

Seconds turned to years as he poked in vain. Slim rivulets of blood ran down my arms and onto the floor.

"Hold her down," the doctor ordered, and stabbed a vein in my foot. The epinephrine kicked in almost instantly. My lungs relaxed and sobs racked my body as air flowed into my lungs.

Independence has been instilled in me since I was a baby. I was taught to be reliant on myself, and to be strong, no matter what. In that moment, I just wanted to crawl into my mom's arms. I wanted to go home. I wanted to be in a place where the air is clean.

"How many people across the world experience similar harmful effects of polluted air?" I wondered. Something shifted in me that day, pushed my psyche to a visceral daily commitment to ensuring that the air we breathe is as pure as the water we drink (or should drink).

The more I traveled and learned, the more I felt like I was a preacher with no moral ground on which to stand. The United States accounts for less than 5 percent of the world's population but close to a quarter of its oil consumption; our transportation sector alone consumes about 16 percent of the world's oil.[1] Our Middle East policies are integrally linked with this insatiable oil consumption. How could I be explaining to developing-country officials how important it is to consider investments in bicycling, walking, and transit when we have failed to do so ourselves?

The last straw came at a United Nations meeting in Göteborg, Sweden, where I was invited to help draft an action plan solidifying international commitment to the principles espoused at the 1992 U.N. Conference on the Environment and Development in Rio de Janeiro. Göteborg is a beautiful city, the second largest in Sweden after Stockholm. Its transportation system is centered on bicycling, walking, and transit; its cobblestone plazas and clean air, a blessing.

The four-star hotel was by far the nicest place I had ever stayed. A lively opening dinner featured flowing alcohol and a top-notch speaker. The next day, we were to start working out our action plans. One by one we introduced ourselves, about fifteen men and women from Africa, Latin America, the Middle East, Europe. And then there was me, representing Asia. It was a mistake, I was sure. Where is the Chinese delegation? Where are the Thais, Vietnamese, Singaporeans, Indonesians? How could I, an American woman, age twenty-four, be

---

[1] Information from U.S. Energy Information Administration, Independent Statistics and Analysis.

responsible for fair representation of the entire continent of Asia, population two billion? The exalted U.N. didn't bother to find a single Asian to speak intelligently about transportation? What a farce.

I stayed up all night with Stephen Karakezi of Kenya, the only other native English speaker, writing a report encompassing transportation-sector energy conservation strategies for every region in the world. That report undoubtedly ended up in the U.N.'s circular files. At least I didn't get sick.

Returning to my job in body but not spirit, I spent a day at the office in contemplative silence, then rode down the Mount Vernon Trail to a field near National Airport and watched. Plane after plane packed with diplomats, consultants, government officials, and agency representatives flying around the globe, talking about the world's problems, swooping in for a day or two, coming back, writing reports about complex things that could neither be fully captured nor affected from an office in Washington, D.C.

I didn't want to do it anymore.

I wanted to make a tangible difference on the ground, for people at a local level, and needed to see, taste, and feel the fruits of my labor. And if I wanted to accomplish that, I had to change my own life first.

CHAPTER 3

Breaking Away

Flying into Portland that clear April day was like floating in a recurring-dream memory of the Beartooth Mountains, where the clean air had caressed and healed my lungs after the near-death asthma attack in India. In Montana, I had fallen deeply in love with the stunning mountain beauty in my own country. Now, the snowcapped Cascade Range shimmered in the sun, with flat-top Mount St. Helens asserting that Mother Nature is alive and well and blows her stack from time to time. A lush blanket of green gently warmed the city's half-million residents. It was just a fact-finding mission, a series of lunches and meetings, but my heart fluttered like a promising first kiss.

In its early history, Portland's developers and city leaders had laid out streetcar tracks to connect residents to housing developments. Post–WWII, the auto age came to Portland in full force. Streetcar tracks were paved over or ripped out, and freeways and suburbs were built in all directions. Portland was harmonically in tune with the rest of the country, heading downhill fast.

Neighborhood streets were choking with traffic, housing prices declining, and the number of auto-involved crashes and fatalities soaring. By the 1960s, Portland's air was foul, and its downtown degraded and declining. Businesses fled to the suburbs. Parents followed suit, with Portland's public schools emptying of middle-class families.

To the east, Mount Hood, Oregon's most popular destination, rises to 11,249 feet (3,429 m). She is home to four world-class ski resorts, twelve glaciers, and hundreds of miles of hiking/bicycle/cross-country ski trails. The driving route to get there from Oregon's largest city is not ideal, somewhat circuitous, and frequently congested. Thus, planners conceived of the Mount Hood Freeway, which would have wiped clean the Clinton Street neighborhood.

Mount Hood looms brightly to the east of Portland's downtown.

Originally settled by Italian immigrants, the connected grid of tidy, one-thousand- to two-thousand-square-foot homes allowed for easy walking access to streetcar stops and locally owned business clusters. By the 1970s, it was downtrodden and neglected, thanks to many decades of a promised government buy-out to make room for the freeway. Nothing like an impending forced evacuation to dampen enthusiasm for home repair.

But this time, having seen the long-lasting negative impacts of destructive freeway construction, residents revolted. Under the name STOP (Sensible Transportation Options for People), they declared war on the Mount Hood Freeway.

STOP volunteers teamed up with leaders like Mayor (later Governor) Neil Goldschmidt and State Representative (later city councilman) Earl Blumenauer, fought hard, and won. The Clinton neighborhood was saved. Instead of the Mount Hood Freeway, Portland got its first light-rail line (MAX). A downtown parking garage was replaced with a town center, Pioneer Square, that lunching workers and a mix of programmed and spontaneous entertainment keep lively year-round. To top it off, leaders turned half of river-hugging Harbor Drive, a clogged, ugly highway on the eastern edge of downtown, into Waterfront Park, whose popular summer events infuse tens of millions into the local economy.

It is not possible to overstate the impacts of these transformational projects on the culture and economy of Portland. Downtown businesses saw the light, taxing themselves to upgrade the look of downtown and discourage suburban flight. Another key moment came when city leaders placed a cap on the number of downtown parking spaces and prohibited new surface parking lots to encourage transit use—thereby reducing air pollution—and preserve developable land.

Regional leaders got into the act too. They adopted an "urban growth boundary" outside of which farmland was preserved and development prohibited, in order to contain suburban sprawl. They drew up plans for both expanding MAX and encouraging development along MAX lines, while another group of forward-thinkers developed a concept for a connected system of green spaces and trails. Together, leaders and residents researched and debated and grew solid in their mutual understanding that land-use—the places people live, play, and work—goes hand in hand with transportation. ⚷

Portland's waterfront, aka Harbor Drive (left, circa 1965) was transformed into Waterfront Park (right) in the 1980s.

⚷ **Combine investments in bicycling with compact development, transit, and walking.**

All this I had learned through my D.C.-based transportation policy work. I figured that if Portland was so progressive in transportation and land-use policy, they were probably aces in bicycle transportation too. Not so, I quickly learned, not so at all.

"Well let me tell you, there's a lot going on right now," stated the city's Rob Burchfield, after we had placed our order at the Harborside restaurant on the Willamette River. This was my fourth or fifth such networking meeting as I looked into thus-far mildly intriguing job possibilities with various environmental and energy conservation groups and government agencies.

"Since the federal transportation spending bill passed," he explained in the tone of one who is under tremendous stress, "we've been under a lot of pressure to make Portland more bike friendly." He grimaced and stroked a short beard that matched the remains of his thinning strawberry-blond hair.

The 1991 Intermodal Surface Transportation Efficiency Act (ISTEA) was the nation's first transportation spending bill with provisions for spending on bicycling and walking. Its passage is what prompted me to entertain the notion of becoming a city bicycle coordinator, preferably in Portland. The year of my bolt from D.C., though, only a handful of such jobs existed nationwide. The odds of getting one weren't real good. The odds of getting the already-occupied Portland position were less than zero.

"Have you gotten any of the federal grant money?"

"Yes. We've got money to attach a bike/pedestrian path on the Steel Bridge. That's the one four bridges to the north." He pointed; I craned my head toward the river, but the Steel Bridge was out of view.

"We're also working with the county," he added, "which owns most of the other bridges, to make them more bicycle and pedestrian friendly too." He became more animated, gesticulating with his hands.

"We're converting an abandoned railway—the Springwater Corridor—into a sixteen-mile paved multiuse trail. My group is responsible for designing the intersections where the trail crosses the roadway. We've also got money for a bicycle parking facility called Bike Central. We're envisioning indoor bike parking, showers, lockers, and bike repair."[2] He stopped to eat; my salad sat untouched as I absorbed his words.

He told me about Earl Blumenauer, the politician who helped stop the Mount Hood Freeway and was pushing for transit and neighborhood livability. What a combination of forces were at work! They had community

---

2   Nowadays, many of these are developed under the trademark BikeStation.

activists through the newly formed Bicycle Transportation Alliance, what sounded like a decent amount of funding, senior staff like Rob, and political leadership in the form of Earl. I wanted to be part of it, with all my heart.

I babbled for too long about life in D.C., my travels and reports, my grandiose ideas for applying the concepts of energy conservation to transportation. We walked out and I grasped his hand between my two.

"It would be an honor to work with you, Rob. I think I'd be a perfect match for your program. I know you already have a bicycle coordinator, but I am ready and available if a position comes open."

"You know, it's not all that easy or fun here." He looked down and shuffled his feet. "The advocates are breathing down our necks and pressuring us to go faster. It's pretty stressful."

He hinted that they might be adding or shifting staff soon. I didn't put much stock in this; I knew how slow government typically moves.

I returned to D.C. and submitted a letter of resignation. I figured I would dust off Cleopatra and go back to waiting tables, or maybe write grants for one of the nonprofit groups. Whatever. I just wanted to be in Portland. One night, I arrived home famished as usual from the long ride. I inhaled a banana, greeted Eric,[3] a new friend visiting from Portland, and sat down to open my mail. "City of Portland" proclaimed the envelope's seal.

> *Dear Mia,*
>
> *It was nice to meet you last month. I am pleased to offer you the job of bicycle coordinator. Please contact me at your earliest convenience.*
>
> *Sincerely,*
> *Robert Burchfield*

 Key human elements: strong local politicians, effective community advocates, and well-trained and supported city staff.

---

3   Eric and I were married from 1995 to 2007.

The paper fell from my hands. Mouth agape, like a fish gasping for air, I explained to Eric that I had just been offered the job of my dreams. What alien force had possessed Rob, on the basis of a one-hour lunch, to offer me this position? Was he Zorro, slicing through red tape with a beautiful sword?

I took it as a gift from on high, a clear sign. I was on my way.

CHAPTER 4

Go Like Hell

Earl Blumenauer wheels his mountain bike into the elevator at city hall. A few months on the job getting schooled in Portland's transportation history and system, and I'm well aware of the enormity of the task at hand. I've also come to understand that what we are trying to do is unheard of. No large American town or city has yet made much progress in becoming bicycle friendly. I need guidance, and Earl's the man to give it.

Wearing a yellow and red polka-dotted bow tie over a white button-down shirt, Earl doesn't just enter a room, he takes it over. He lays his bike helmet on his desk and doesn't bother to take off his pant-leg strap. Small and wiry, steadfast and confident, Earl's slightly uneven, slightly awkward smile and raccoon eyes convey an intel-

PHOTO: OFFICE OF EARL BLUMENAUER

The Honorable Earl Blumenauer

lect so ferocious that he was first elected to the state legislature at the tender age of twenty-three. Since then, his leadership in transportation, planning, environmental programs, and public participation have helped Portland earn a well-deserved international reputation as one of America's most livable cities.

He stashes his bike in the corner and waves me into a chair. A bright yellow rain jacket hangs on a hook in the corner next to a poster (depicted on the next page) from the Netherlands showing the same number of

This famous poster dramatically demonstrates the difference in street space allocation among different modes of transportation.

people in four contrasting traffic situations: all driving cars, on a bus, walking, and on bikes.

"Mia, we have an enormous opportunity. I want us to be the country's most bicycle friendly city." Recently back from a European study tour, he's got a vision.

For a second, he looks at me so intently, I think he's going to reach out and place his fingers on my forehead, thumb and pinkie on my cheeks, in a Vulcan mind-meld, so I can see for myself the image in his head: women in skirts and fashionable boots, each pedaling along with two or three children in a specially made Bakfiets cargo bike. Throngs of kids arriving at school by foot or bike on safe neighborhood streets. Men in business suits riding on protected bikeways on major roads. Thousands of bikes lined up at transit stations.

The negative impact of the post–WWII auto boom on the environment, livability, and culture of cities like Copenhagen led to mass revolt. Business owners in Amsterdam told the government that their livelihood was threatened because delivery trucks couldn't reach their stores. Buildings that had stood for hundreds of years started to blacken with tar. These governments slammed on the brakes, reversed course, and invested in public transit, bikeways, and walkways while reining in the auto through taxes on gas, purchase price, parking, and registration.

"I hear ya, Earl," I concur, "but let's get real. The only real examples are in Europe or small, flat college towns like Davis, California. I've spent the last few months running smack into opposition both outside and within the city government. How are we going to do this?"

He asks, "Did you hear about the Neighborhood Traffic Congress?" I shake my head no.

"We invited everybody who had a gripe about traffic to the Convention Center—we figured it was the only place big enough." He comes out from behind his desk and paces.

"Out of that day-long effort, we found over one hundred volunteers who have been working with us to redesign the city's traffic program. We call it 'Reclaiming Our Streets.'"

I like the sound of it and agree to connect my efforts to theirs. He suggests I attend the Portland State University Traffic and Transportation class.

"We pay residents' tuition for a semester-long class to learn about—and help solve—the city's biggest transportation problems. We want Portland-ers to engage, to be part of the solution, not just complain." The class, he suggests, would be a good way for me to meet more positive-minded residents and leaders.

"Look," he states, "you have my support for however long I'm commissioner. And you have my confidence."

I sit still, taking it in, waiting for more. He stares intently, as if to say, "What are you waiting for? We need a plan. Make it so." He points his index finger at the door. Move it, girl. Engage.

I grab my new commuter bike—a Trek 7500—and head up to Washington Park. (10,000 miles [16,000 km] had thrashed both Bruce's Schwinn and my first commuter, a Giant Innova hybrid.) I pass the Multnomah Athletic Club, which hosted Portland's early bicycle racing clubs back in the 1880s.

Up from the MAC are road segments so steep I have to stand up to crank, even with my bike in granny gear. I plant myself on the terrace above the Shakespeare Garden, which honors the Bard with roses named after characters in his plays. My back leans against a brick wall featuring Shakespeare's image and a quote: "Of all flowers methinks a rose is best."

With Earl's words ringing in my head, I catalogue the situation. We have a crummy bikeway system and are in a legal dispute with the group that should be our closest ally. Recent attempts to put in bike lanes have stalled due to neighborhood opposition. Projects to reduce congestion on neighborhood streets have burnt staff to a crisp in long, heated public battles.

Our transportation officials are almost exclusively trained in motor vehicle infrastructure construction and management, and are decidedly uninterested (at best) in bicycle transportation. Emergency services are focused on the needs of motorists.

The public, at least in part, puts bicycling on par with root canals, while business leaders view bicycling as childish play.

I pull out my notebook, and make a list.

Politics is politics, and leadership requires leaders. Before Earl came, Portland did not have a solid champion. Look where that had gotten us. What would happen post-Earl? After all, he won't be on city council forever. I need to go as fast as I can, as hard as possible, for as long as I can.

I write, in big bold letters, "Go like hell! Til you can't go no more."

And then... off to the races I go.

SECTION II

Build It and They Will Come

Step #1 in creating livable, bikeable communities: bikeways. People will not drive into the river where no bridge exists, wait by the side of the road for a nonexistent bus, or walk on streets lacking sidewalks. Similarly, few people will bike where no bikeways exist.

The question is: Can we retrofit our large, auto-oriented streets toward bicycle transportation? Who will fight? What trade-offs will be required? What impacts will that have? How can we convince the right people to accept the proposed changes?

No one has succeeded before.

Can we?

CHAPTER 5

Wheel-and-Pony Show

Well, all right, Earl, I'm gonna go like hell. Hmm...what does that mean exactly? I don't have a clue how to do a bike plan. Where do we start?

For weeks, I ride around my new hometown, gaining courage, and mentally cataloging the opportunities and constraints. The flatter eastside neighborhoods, easy to navigate until you hit a seemingly insurmountable freeway crossing. Small towns, rural roads, and lush vineyards of the surrounding counties. Busy, scary suburban highways and bridges.

One twilight, I'm lost in thought as I blast down a steep road through a wispy fog on the hilly westside. Out of the surrounding forested park, an enormous elk materializes and bounds across the road. An elk? In the city? Am I dreaming? As if to answer my query, he slows, then pauses.

I slow too, carefully gripping my brakes as I gape in awe at the majestic creature, who turns and fixates me with an Earl-like stare.

"Yes," he conveys with soulful eyes. "I'm real."

I smile and bow my head in respect. A second later, he's gone and I'm standing by the side of the road, my heart racing. Suddenly, I know what to do. The more Earl had talked to folks, the more he had found people frustrated with status quo—traffic clogging their neighborhood streets, declining air quality, increasing stress. That connection with the public made it easy for him to advance his ideas.

I'll engage residents in a community conversation about bicycling. I'll look people in the eye, share my experiences, listen to their fears and frustrations, and capture their vision and ideas. Then, I'll create a plan.[4] 0—⊤

What the heck, it's worth a shot.

0—⊤ Develop a robust, visionary, comprehensive bicycle plan.

---

[4] Nowadays, plenty of cities have Bicycle Transportation Plans. I've personally been involved in hundreds. Each is a blueprint for how to make those communities more bicycle friendly—a recipe, if you will. You get the ingredients together (bikeways, parking), mix them up just right (create a balanced plan), cook it (build the network), decorate (signs), and enjoy (encourage people to use it). Back then, few cities had even considered such a thing. We were inventing as we went. For guidance, see the Resources section at the back of this book.

⊕⊕⊕⊕⊕

We advertise a series of public meetings about the future of bicycle transportation. First up: funky inner southeast, where I live. It's a stormy night, and I have no idea what to expect. Will people show up?

I stand by a table of treats near the high school cafeteria door. Rain is coming down in sheets. In walks Jim Ferner, a carpenter from the suburbs. A few years prior, in the dark, rainy, dead of winter, he was denied a bus ride with his bike. He turned his outrage into a petition drive, ultimately convincing the transit agency to put bike racks on a few buses; this led to the formation of the Bicycle Transportation Alliance.

Other like-minded folks sporting yellow, mud-splattered jackets start trickling in. Here's architect Rick Browning, bike shop owner Sherman Coventry and engineer Ron Kernan. These three were deeply involved, from their positions on the city's appointed Bicycle Advisory Committee, in pushing Rob to replace tired-out Krys. In part, I owe them my job.

In short order, we've swelled to about sixty largely familiar faces who devour the cookies and grapes, drain six carafes of Starbucks coffee, and form small groups at circular tables. Most are in their twenties to forties. A quick head count reveals but a handful of women.

Showtime. I click through two trays of slides about the benefits of bicycling. It's a lovefest with a revival feel. Any second now, someone is going to raise hands in the air and cry, "Amen, Sista! You tell it!" Finally, someone is speaking their language.

Left to right: Bicycle Advisory Committee members Ron Kernan, Rick Browning, and Sharon Fekety

I ask, "How many of you own a bike?" All hands go up.

"How many of you regularly ride? To work? All year round, rain or shine?" The room is full of dedicated, opinionated cyclists. They ride despite the miserable infrastructure conditions, stoically slogging through the gloomy, dark, drizzly winter months. They are the pioneers of transportation pedaling, and they know every square inch of our fair city, blindfolded.

A hundred pages of notes capture their ideas and complaints, from the maddening—a path that dead-ends in a homeless camp, a bike lane that ends just before a heinous intersection—to the mundane—cracked pavement, glass on the road, slotted drainage grates, and railroad tracks that catch bike tires.

We roll out big maps that, within seconds, look like a Crayola-factory explosion. Big red circles note trouble spots, bright blue and yellow lines delineate desired routes, and handwritten notes in green, black and purple explain

Not-too-useful "bike path" (compare with the photo on page 98, depicting the same location a decade later).

the micro-details of daily bike commuting in today's Portland. The colorful collages would make a preschool art teacher proud.

Among these people, I feel at home. They get that bicycling is a good thing. They all want what I want: a cleaner, greener world. They're thrilled to pieces that the city is stepping it up a notch and are more than happy to give up their evenings and weekends to help us get there.

I pack up my bike trailer, pull on my rain pants, cover my hair with my hood and tuck it under my helmet, click on my blinkie lights, and head out into a dark drizzle. Clumpy wet leaves make for a slow, slippery ride. Brain still buzzing with bike-talk, I slow as I approach a stop sign, look both ways and roll through.

"!@#$% cyclist!" yells a motorist out his window, snapping me back to the daily reality outside the warm receptive audience by whom I've just been embraced. The norm is not these fabulously fearless freaks in nuclear-waste handler outfits, but the people of North Portland, for whom speed bumps and bicycle lanes are a declaration of war on their way of life, along with business people who regard bicycles as toys, engineers for whom bicycles are an impediment to traffic, and police officers who perceive all bicyclists to be scofflaws.

It hits me: If I spend my time preachin' gospel to the choir, the bicycle revolution isn't going to spread very far. The vast majority of Portland is not in our camp, and our army is too puny to penetrate public consciousness.

It's time to go on a recruiting mission.

Loading up the wheel-and-pony show

A few weeks later, I load up a bike trailer with two trays of slides and projector, plus bike maps, surveys, and brochures, and head east to a Denny's 5 miles (8 km) out and a world away.

Dressed in black pants, low-heeled sandals, and a short-sleeved, cream-colored button-down blouse, I'm trying to model that cycling for transportation isn't about Lycra shorts and clicky shoes.

A couple of teenagers toss an empty Coke can in my direction and yell, "Get off the road!" I say a little prayer before barreling through a nasty freeway interchange and fight off the urge to quit my job and go back to waitressing.

"Less stressful...give up..." says the little creep on one shoulder.

"Make a difference. Save the world. Keep going," argues the purple-winged fairy on the other. An early arrival gains me a few minutes to get my wits back in order. A little touch of mascara and lipstick—both stashed in a little handlebar-mounted accessory bag—do the trick.

I seat myself with some folks at a circular table, eat a plate of ravioli, and take in the discussion about Joan's mom's fight with lung cancer, Fred's new car, and the trouble Jack is having at his furniture store with his stock boy not showing up on time.

Lions Club Grand Poobah Chuck Smith, a jovial Jiffy Lube franchise owner, finishes his cigar, chocolate cake, and coffee and stands up to introduce me.

"Good afternoon, friends. It's great to see you all. First, I want to congratulate Paula on raising $250 through sales of her knitted booties and hats. All the proceeds will go to our youth mentoring program." Paula stands and acknowledges the applause.

Chuck continues, "Reminder that we're having poker night on Friday, and George, listen, please bring some money this time. Can't loan you another dime, but do come!" The men chuckle at George's expense.

"Next, I'd like to introduce our speaker, Mia Birk. She is the..." he stops to squint at his note card, frowns, then continues, "hmmm... it says here, 'Bicycle Coordinator' from the City of Portland. She's here to talk to us about, well, bicycles." He hands me the microphone.

"Thank you so much for inviting me to speak today. I work for the Office of Transportation. My job is to develop bicycling as a transportation option. Let me start with a question. How many of you bicycle on a regular basis?" Not a single hand goes up.

"How many of you own a bike?" About half the audience nods.

"Do you use those bikes occasionally?" A few hands go up.

"Let me ask you this. What are the reasons you don't use those bikes?" The silence is deafening.

"Come on," I urge. "Don't be shy. How many of you biked as a child?" This time, most of the room nods.

"I did too. But then I stopped, since everyone in Texas, where I grew up, drives everywhere. I was out of shape and overweight then, for a long time, until I started bicycling for transportation."

I launch into my slide show, describing the incredibly rapid rise in obesity rates, resultant health care costs, and the simple fact that bicycle transportation is a win-win solution for our health, environmental, congestion, economic, and livability problems. I stop for a question.

"Yeah, say, why are you here and what the hell are you talking about?" asks George, the popular poker player. He's in a business suit, arms folded under his chest.

"Chuck, did you invite her?"

I gauge the mood of the room and sense confusion. I seem to have landed from Mars, onto their planet, and am speaking Martian about a topic that could not be less important.

I try to inject humor into my slide show with cartoons like this one. Admittedly, it doesn't always go over that well.

All across the country, thousands of miles of paths inject local communities with pride and tourist dollars and provide healthy places to gather and exercise. They reduce crime, particularly nuisance activities (drug use, graffiti, dumping) that are typical of neglected corridors such as abandoned or active railways. They increase property values and safety. The evidence in favor of paths is overwhelming.[5]

From his seat, Chuck reminds folks to be polite. "It's not like she's trying to take away our cars." He guffaws with a big booming laugh and shoots me a warning glare, adding, "I'd like to see you try!"

"Ah, no, Chuck, I'm not." I respond through clenched teeth and a faux smile.

"Go ahead, little lady." He waves at me to continue.

Serenity now, I remind myself.

"The real question is, how can we make our city more bicycle friendly so that folks like you dust off those old bikes and start riding? What we need is a comprehensive, connected bikeway network that is comfortable, convenient, safe, and gets you from where you are to where you want to go." I click through a series of slides.

"Let's start with off-street paths. We also call these shared-use paths, multiuse trails, off-street trails, and bike paths. Has anyone here ridden on the I-205 bike path, or along Waterfront Park?" A few heads nod.

Develop a network of connected, comprehensive, low-stress bikeways.

---

[5] Many helpful resources are available through the Rails-to-Trails Conservancy: www.railstotrails.org.

"In an ideal world, we'd put paths all around the city, next to the rivers, on our abandoned and active rail corridors, near highways, or wherever there's a strip of available land, just so long as the path is separated from the road."

"What are you, crazy?" Paula angrily wants to know. "That I-205 path is dangerous. Some kids got killed trying to cross at Southeast Foster."

I know exactly the location she's talking about, and she's right, it is dangerous. Local lore is that the state highway department ran out of money and eliminated the bridges and/or tunnels that would have separated this and other tough crossings. They still built the path, but users have to cross freeway off-ramp traffic.[6]

"You are absolutely right. Paths can and should be designed better than that!" The screen flashes with examples from Boulder and Seattle.

The trade-off: cost and complexity. At $200,000 to a million dollars a mile and fraught with challenges like property acquisition and roadway crossings, they're neither cheap nor simple. But compared to the $50 million a mile it costs to build a freeway, they're a bargain.

"Let's move on to on-street bicycle lanes. Usually located on busy roads, they offer direct and fast connectivity. Relative to off-street paths, they're dirt cheap at less than $20,000 a mile."

George interrupts angrily. "Who is paying for this? It's us, isn't it? Why should we pay for you bicycle riders? Bicyclists don't pay taxes! F***ing government, wasting taxpayer dollars on *road lice!*" He storms out of the room.

I plead my case. "We all pay for our transportation system, no matter how we get around. Most cyclists own cars and pay the same property and income taxes. The truth is that gas taxes do not cover the full cost of driving."

The crowd is on the verge of anarchy. It's like I'm trying to tell them that red is, in fact, black. The more I try to convince them otherwise, the angrier they get. I'm offending their American ideals by suggesting they don't pay enough.

We pay less for gas than we do for bottled water. The price of gas in real terms is less than

On any given street, we need at least 10 feet (3 m) for bike lanes—5 feet (1.6 m) in each direction. For comparison, a typical motor vehicle lane is 10- to 14-feet (3–4 m) wide.

---

6   Later, the Oregon Department of Transportation improved most of the heinous crossings.

Fahrradstrasse *(bicycle street) in Germany.*

Motorists must turn while cyclists continue through this intersection on Southeast Lincoln Street, Portland's most popular bike boulevard.

it was in 1919. It's a deal that's too good to be true.

Few are willing to accept that driving is massively subsidized, and that our paltry gas taxes and registration fees cover but a small fraction of the full cost of driving—not the emergency services, not the environmental impacts, not the contribution to the impacts of sedentary lifestyles on health, not even the direct costs of infrastructure. Various scholars estimate that gas is underpriced by about five dollars to fifteen dollars per gallon.[7]

The Europeans have got it figured out: In Copenhagen, gas is more than five bucks a gallon and the tax on car ownership 100 percent of the sales price. It's not coincidental that two-thirds of their daily trips are by bicycle, foot, or transit, and that this cosmopolitan city is green, prosperous, healthy, safe, and livable.

"Look, folks, I've got just a few more slides, and then I'd like to invite you to help shape our future. Shall I continue?" A few heads nod. Most want me to be done so they can get on with their lives.

"Another option in our toolbox is bicycle boulevards.[8] In the Netherlands, such streets are called *woonerfs* (living streets), in Germany *Fahrradstrasse* (bicycle streets). Basically, it's a residential street on which we've done various things to prioritize the movement of bicycles over cars."

---

7 Victoria Transportation Policy Institute and International Center for Technology Assessment are two of many organizations that have researched this topic.
8 For more information, consult the *Urban Bikeway Design Guide*, published by the National Association of City Transportation Officials (NACTO), 2012.

I show a necked-down intersection that allows motorists to exit, but not enter, the street.

"I don't get it." Paula is confused. "You block off the street? How do I get to my house?"

"Good question. As a resident, you might have to go a block out of direction to get home, but in exchange, you get less traffic. We also put in speed bumps and mini-traffic circles, things that reduce driving speed, making it safer for everyone."

Paula nods her approval. "Seems safer for me and my kids. Cars go 40 mph down my street."

I nod back. "Bicycle boulevards are very family friendly." I advance slides of kids biking around planted mini-traffic circles.

"But," I admit, "they are not a perfect solution. In neighborhoods like yours, the streets aren't as connected, so it's hard to find a good route. Also, it can be tough to cross major streets, so we have to mark cross walks, add signals, and try to shorten long crossings. Not super-cheap at $200,000 or more a mile."

Vancouver, B.C., has many excellent bike boulevards.

Starting in 2010, Portland has rebranded its bicycle boulevards as 'neighborhood greenways,' reflecting the broader benefits of safe, green, calm neighborhood streets. Features include park-like drainage areas called 'bioswales,' shared lane markings, excellent signage, stop signs turned to favor continuous bicycle travel, intersection improvements, and devices to reduce motor vehicle speeds and volumes.

I wrap up with the importance of teaching bike safety and installing bicycle parking. Chuck hauls himself up to turn on the lights.

"Now, before you go, each of you gets to help. I'm giving you each a fictional $100 to spend on bicycling. The question is, how would you divvy up the money? You can spend it on bike lanes, paths, boulevards, parking, or education. Go ahead, knock yourselves out." Soon, I have their guidance: bike lanes first, then paths and boulevards with a splash of change reserved for everything else.

Chuck thanks me with a certificate and Lions Club T-shirt, and most people run for the doors—and their cars. "Phew," they sigh in relief as they caress the dashboard. "That crazy woman was trying to get me to give you up, my precious..."

But, a few people linger. Jack, the furniture store owner, tells me that his doctor says he needs to get more exercise to help with his high blood pressure. He asks where he can get his bike tuned up. Another few individuals sign the mailing list and leave with bike maps.

And then there is Paula. She waits patiently, looking sad. She's built frail, dressed plainly, with short blond hair and cracked hands from daily hard work. Her face reminds me of Carmela Soprano, a tough woman who has seen her share of hard times and will defend herself and her family with all her heart and soul.

"My son," she quietly tells me, "was badly injured in a car accident when he was in high school and, well, he's never been the same again."

"I'm so sorry." I reach out to touch her arm.

"It was his friend who was drinking and drove the car off the road. I knew he was running with a bad crowd, but..." Her voice breaks just a little. The load of guilt she carries on her shoulders bears down harder.

"Listen," she says, "my grandkids are starting to ride their bikes around, and it's just not safe on the road. I want to know where they can ride and where they can learn bike safety. I want to keep them from driving as long as I can." I fix her up with bike maps, bike repair coupons, vouchers for free helmets, and safety information.

I bike away with a light spirit. In this group, four out of twenty had taken the time to talk to me. I've got more than sixty more wheel-and-pony shows scheduled. If every group I talk to has twenty to fifty participants, and two or three or even ten open their minds to bicycling as a result, that means I am influencing 10 to 20 percent. If these folks start bicycling, and their friends see them getting healthier and fitter, and then their kids start biking...I seem to be on the right track. Better keep going.

CHAPTER 6

Viva la Revolution!

From the lush, affluent West Hills to the hip inner city, I spread the word to business groups, ethnic groups, neighborhood associations, school groups, churches—pretty much anyone who will listen. Thousands contribute ideas and comments. With unanimous city council support, we adopt a vision of a 630-mile (1014 km) connected network of bikeways. Our goal: make the bicycle an integral part of daily life.

And now, with our marching orders in hand, we've got to go like hell, 'til we can't go no more.

First order of business: fix the bridges. Basically, they all stink from a bicyclist's perspective. And in a town with a river slicing through the middle, if you can't get across the bridges, you're not going to bike much. It's that simple.

We load up the first cannon: marking bike lanes on the highly visible six-lane Burnside Bridge, a major portal connecting the eastside to downtown. Bicyclists have two choices: squeeze with pedestrians on narrow sidewalks or hug the curb in car-packed travel lanes. Most select door number three: leave the bike stashed in the garage.

It's time to be bold, decides Rob Burchfield. With the support of Earl and officials from Multnomah County, which owns the bridge, he proposes trading off one travel lane for two bike lanes. This will mean two car lanes in one direction, three in the other. Lose one auto lane, gain two bike lanes. It looks good on paper.

It's reality he's worried about: Will it work, or will gridlock ensue? Will we spark a counter-revolution of negative media attention and angry motorists?

Commissioner Blumenauer and posse are undaunted.

"This isn't a stealth operation." Earl declares. "It's a celebration of our first decent bikeway in downtown Portland! Let's do it with style." 0—⚡

0—⚡ Embrace the role of encouraging people to bicycle as a core part of the task at hand.

City staff, led by communications director Loretta, hire a band and food vendors, rent porta-potties, and advertise "BikeFest on the Burnside Bridge."

"The bridge will be closed to auto traffic!" we warn people. "Don't worry! You can still use the other downtown bridges."

We expect a few hundred people and brace for public outcry over the changes.

The night before BikeFest, the striping crew comes out and quietly repaints the lane lines. The fuse is lit. There's no turning back now.

By 6 a.m., we're up on the bridge marveling in true geek fashion at the fresh asphalt and new lines. At 8 a.m., the sun rises on a crisp and windy day. Groups of riders start to show up. The first is Sharon Fekety's group from the West Hills. Sixty years old and fit as a fiddle, she beams a huge smile as they ride back and forth, whooping and hollering. Six more groups arrive. Individuals and families slowly file onto the bridge. Festive balloons, banners, and signs dance in the wind.

On the stage, a marimba band entices people to form a snaking conga line. Next up, Nike, Columbia Sportswear, and the Bike Gallery parade models across the stage in all manners of bike gear—polka-dotted bike helmets, wind-resistant fluorescent vests, fleece jackets, Burley rain jackets and pants. We raffle off the clothes and a high-end racing bike. Toward the bridge's east end, a stunt team on teeny kid bikes wows the crowd with aerobatic tricks.

Cheerful volunteers pass out bike maps. Police officers direct kids through an obstacle course. Traffic engineer John Bustraan demonstrates that to get traffic signals to turn green, you have to place your bicycle on a pavement "hot spot." Transit agency staff train people to load bikes on new front-mounted bus racks.

Rockin' and rollin' on the Burnside Bridge

The bridge groans in ecstasy. It has never before been massaged by 20,000 feet. The added pressure, like strong palms kneading tight spots in your back, feels like heaven.

No one complains. The cannon shoots not bombs but fireworks. It is a glorious start to the revolution.

CHAPTER 7

Ask for Forgiveness

Burnside is salvo number one on our list of bridge upgrades. The rest are going to take a while, but the ball is rolling. In the meantime, we've got other fish to fry. The public wants bike lanes, pronto.

Only problem is, just like the Burnside Bridge, every bike lane means a trade-off with motor vehicle space. And frankly, when it comes to the details of reallocating roadway space, I'm a neophyte as green as a brand-new bean shoot.

"Question for ya," I say one day to the paving crew head, the fit and amiable Rod Yoder. "How do we stripe bike lanes, exactly?"

"Why don't you come along and see for yourself?" Rod invites.

After a few weeks of watching them in action, removing and replacing old lane lines and crosswalks, or grinding up the roadway surface, laying out fresh asphalt, and marking new lines, I realize that it's going to be a whole lot easier and cheaper if we include bike lanes during repaving projects. Otherwise, we have to grind off the old lines with a beadblaster (sort of like a ray gun, very spacey), leaving a visible and shallow indent that pools in the rain. Also, it seems pretty inefficient to repave a street, put in fresh lane lines, and then, a year or two later, burn off the now-old lines. Far better to do it right the first time.

"Say, Rod," I ask. "I was wondering if, when you're getting ready to repave these streets, you could let me know? I would truly appreciate it."

I feel buoyed by the fact that he rides a bike from time to time.

"Well, Mia, lemme see here," he looks at me quizzically, with a Billy Crystal question-mark grin. "You want me to do what, now? Bike lanes? You've got some ideas in your little head, dontcha? Lemme see what I can do. Thanks for stopping by."

One Saturday morning, Rod calls. "Mia," he says. "We're about to repave Southeast Seventh. I'm looking at your bike plan, like you asked me to, and I need the striping plan so I can add the bike lanes."

First reaction: joy. Someone listened to me! Second reaction: shock. Striping plan? Huh? I'm quite certain that there is no striping plan in existence.

"What do you mean?" I ask.

"I mean I need the striping plan," says Rod, uninterested in teenage stall tactics. "By noon. Or no bike lanes. *Capisce?*"

My brain spins into problem-solving mode. Let's see, can I make up a striping plan? Nah, I'm not a traffic engineer. Clearly, I need reinforcements.

I track down the home number of traffic engineer Doug McCollum and pray he's not river-rafting with his best buddy, Lewis Wardrip, next on my list of potential victims.

Thankfully, I find him at home with his kids. "Hi, Doug. Sorry to call you on a Saturday."

In many cities, traffic engineers are an obstacle to creating safe and convenient pedestrian and bicycle conditions. This is not because they're bad people or idiots, it's because their education, training, and management direction are all solely focused on moving motor vehicles. As I've already learned, if engineers do not themselves ride bicycles, nor have they ever experienced a truly bicycle friendly city, their ability to grasp cycling issues is going to be highly constrained. Lewis and Doug, though, are mold-breaking rarities: traffic engineers who ride a bicycle for daily transportation and who embrace the task of improving bicycling conditions as a core part of the job. Without them and Rob, I'd be hosed. ⚷

When I ask Doug to give up his Saturday, he doesn't hesitate. "You bet! I'll be there soon."

⚙ ⚙ ⚙ ⚙ ⚙

This isn't our first bike lane project, though. By shaving a few feet off each travel lane, we've striped dozens of miles of bike lanes already. We call these the "low-hanging fruit."[9] No longer are bike lanes seen as a novel concept. Many staff and public objections have melted away as the scary concept has become a concrete, comfortable reality. ⚷

Southeast Seventh, on the other hand, hangs a bit higher up in the challenge tree. Running through a busy industrial/commercial area, it's got four already-svelte travel lanes and two lanes of parking. It wasn't but a couple years ago that it was rejected as too tricky in our first round of demonstration

---

⚷ **Get your traffic engineers on a bike as part of their job.**

⚷ **Start with the low-hanging fruit: easy-to-implement projects.**

---

9   North Smith, North Ida, Southeast Flavel, Southeast Duke, Southeast Hawthorne (Grand to 12th), parts of Northeast Broadway and Weidler, Southeast Division (east of 72nd), Southeast/Northeast 122nd, Southeast/Northeast 148th, Southeast 92nd, Southeast 102nd, much of Southeast Woodstock and Southeast Bybee, among others.

This bike lane on Southeast Madison was one of our early successes.

projects. Like the Burnside Bridge, we'll have to trade off a travel lane to get in bike lanes.

This kind of change is called a "road diet." It's kind of like Weight Watchers, whereby you focus your eating on small but healthy portions of food. In street lingo, you trim the excess space from wide travel and parking lanes. Or you take it a step further, tighten your belt a few more notches, and trade off travel or parking lanes. The chub is reallocated to healthy infrastructure—bike lanes, sidewalks, median islands, curb extensions, planter strips, etc.... Now it's a balanced meal, a "complete street."[10]

Doug and I meet Rod at the corner of Southeast Seventh and Clay. Doug's already drawn up the new three-lane cross section. A slim W.C. Fields with gray hair and a crooked smile, Doug's pranks liven up my cubicle existence, particularly when he lobs a perfectly aimed rubber band over our shared wall when I'm engaged in a heated discussion with a pissed-off motorist.

"We've had quite a history of crashes on this stretch," he notes. "This is our opportunity to make it safer for everyone." On Southeast Seventh, like many four-lane streets, motorists tend to smash into those waiting to turn left.

"You know it'll be controversial." I want to take the words back as soon as they come out of my mouth. Despite the fact that Southeast Seventh is part of the Bicycle Master Plan as well as a central-city transportation plan, I worry about the lack of notification. Words in a long-range plan sitting on a shelf at city hall are one thing. Altering reality on a weekend is quite another.

I hold my breath. Will he do it? If it goes wrong, we'll both be in major hot water.

"Yeah, I know," he admits with an impish grin. "But if we don't do it now, I'm not sure we ever will." He hands Rod the striping plan.

---

10 For more information, visit the website of the National Complete Streets Coalition: www.smartgrowthamerica.org/complete-streets.

Typical "road diet." Above, before: four lanes. Below, after: three lanes plus bike lanes.

Monday morning comes, too soon and not soon enough. Business owners and employees show up for work and go into shock.

Earl calls. "Mia what the heck is going on? I've had seven phone calls this morning from businesses along Southeast Seventh."

"Yeah, about that, Earl. We made a few changes this weekend. Don't worry. It'll be fine."

I apologize repeatedly—to Rob, his boss, and his boss's boss as well. "Yes, we did restripe Southeast Seventh this weekend. No, we didn't notify each of the property owners in advance. You see, we didn't know that the street was about to be repaved until Yoder called. Yes, I realize people are upset. Don't worry! I'm on it!"

Better late than never, I personally visit each property owner with a note stating, "The City of Portland Office of Transportation is pleased to have been able to fulfill our adopted Bicycle Master Plan and Central City Transportation Management Plan by implementing the approved modifications of Southeast Seventh. Look, I know change is hard, but the sky will not fall. Bicycling is good for our world, and you should be pleased to have bike lanes on your street. Deal with it, would ya?"

Psych! The note really says, "We apologize for any inconvenience this may cause you. Please call me if you experience any problems or have any comments or concerns."

We receive about a dozen calls, none of which has much to do with the bike lanes. A neighboring trucking company regularly blocks a driveway.

There's still plenty of traffic capacity on Southeast Seventh, and a more balanced, safer situation all around.

The signal timing makes it hard to turn onto Southeast Morrison. How does one get a loading zone signed? Etc. The simple provision of a phone number seems to provoke folks to complain about long-simmering issues.

On Southeast Seventh, safety improves for motorists and cyclists alike. Traffic congestion does not noticeably increase. Cycling noticeably increases. The fervor dies down, and we zoom around, striping bike lanes at a furious pace, riding the wave of Doug's lesson: Sometimes it's better to ask forgiveness than permission.

CHAPTER 8

All News Is Good News

I open the paper one day to the Metro section, where a sad man gazes wistfully onto a busy intersection from the window of his popular lunchtime eatery.

"Uh oh," I realize. "We're in trouble."

The intersection—a complex location on Southeast Sandy Boulevard where six streets converge—is part of a project to complete the new Southeast Seventh Avenue bike lanes. Although the crash history is not alarming, Chad, the restaurant owner, sees a lot of near-misses from his vantage point.

"The people in the bike program here have been fanatical about throwing down bike lanes based on greed instead of statistical analysis," Chad says in the article. "They've been slapping down bike lanes without any analysis of whether the street needs a bike lane."

I don't agree with his assessment, obviously. I guess we'll have to agree to disagree.

Instantly, bicycle advocates organize, hand out flyers, and show up en masse at public meetings. Opponents respond by bombarding the media, sending me hate mail, and banding together in an impressive show of determination. I will not be begging forgiveness this time. If they have their way, permission will be denied.

The battle rages for months. Taking note, the producers of *Town Hall*, a show early in the Geraldo Rivera–genre of low-level humanistic debate, invite me to make my case to about fifty thousand viewers. The point of the show is to foment controversy, to fan the flames of dissent. Bikes versus cars. It's a perfect battleground for the hearts and minds of Portlanders.

We are headed for a showdown.

Not knowing the first thing about a TV debate, I consult with my husband and friends in the environmental community. These are the people who shut down the Trojan nuclear power plant and led Portland's early battles on its transportation future. I am lucky to have access to these clever minds.

Piece of advice #1: gather your troops. I present the show's producers with a long list of thoughtful and articulate people. My list is far longer than the allotted pro-bike numbers, but I figure some won't make it.

Hanging out patiently in the TV station's parking lot that night is a peaceful posse of about fifty. I bike up in a black skirt, red silk blouse, and high-heeled waterproof boots, a classy look intended to boost my confidence. My entire invite list, it turns out, is here, plus a dozen more. All are eager to help.

I follow the perky producer, Chris, to the front of the TV studio and sit next to Chad in the "hot seat." He and I are rulers of the throne, on a stage a few feet above floor level. The swivel seats in front of us are laid out in an oval.

About thirty of my troops file in and take their seats to my right. I look to my left and see that Chad's side has but a baker's dozen. The phone calls— "Hey there, want to give up an evening with your family to fight against bicycle riding in front of a large TV audience?"—must not have gone well.

Producer Chris looks panicked. A half empty anti-bike side isn't going to look good.

"I think some folks are still in the parking lot," I suggest. "You could see if any of them want to come in."

She sticks her head into the cold January air and invites the remaining coffee-drinking crowd to come on in and fill any empty seat.

Local television personality Jeff Gianola wanders the room, Oprah-style. With perfectly manicured hair and a bright fixed smile, Jeff opens with, "Folks, we're here today to talk about bicycles. The City of Portland wants to get more people to ride bikes, but is it safe?" He is very serious, very concerned.

"Let's start with our guests in the hot seat. Chad, your business is located at a very busy corner, isn't it?"

"That's right. The stupidest thing you could do is put a bike lane on Sandy Boulevard. It's too busy. It's not wide enough, and the intersections are all blind. These city folks are trying to force us out of our cars for their own agenda."

"Now that's interesting," comments our host. "Mia, would you care to respond?"

"Sure, Jeff, thanks. Actually, I don't see this as being about bikes versus cars at all. Most of us own cars ourselves. We're not anti-car; we're pro-livability, pro-safety, pro-health."

Jeff smiles at the camera. "So, Mia, what you're saying is that bikes are good for Portland? Is that right? What about you all, does anyone disagree with that?" He turns to the anti-bike side. No one raises a hand. But Bicycle Advisory Committee member Sharon Fekety stands up. Jeff hands her the mike.

"I ride my bike every day all over town," she explains, "leading rides for the Portland Wheelmen Touring Club. I drive, too. I can tell you that when I drive, I'm thrilled when I have my lane, and bicyclists have theirs. And when I bike, I feel safer in bike lanes. The more we make Portland safe for bicyclists, the better our city will be."

I smile. This statement comes right off the cheat sheet I'd prepared for my posse, thanks to stellar piece of advice #2.

Next to her is another sexagenarian, Paul, who adds, "For a long time, we've built roads just for cars. It's time we allow people to choose other options."

Everyone seems to be agreeing with me. I imagine Chris whispering into Jeff's earpiece, "Jeff, for God's sake, liven it up a bit, would you?"

He nods slickly, then points to a man with a too-many-beers stomach encased in a white T-shirt proclaiming the American Automobile Club.

"Sir, what's your opinion on this?" Jeff has his concerned face on. "Do bicyclists have a right to the road?"

Mr. Auto Club hefts his weight into a standing position. We all wait for him to take the mike.

"Look," he starts, then pauses. Is he nervous? Revving up his energy for a salvo of anti-bike fury?

"I don't understand why we're here. I drive, and I also rode Seattle-to-Portland last year. Man, that was one long ride."

The crowd applauds. Two days, 200-plus miles (321-plus km) is a pretty mean feat no matter what condition you're in.

"What I want to know is, why can't we all just get along?" Phew. He is a gentle giant, his top-heavy frame a common one among the male long-distance bike-riding crowd.

Jeff gives up. The pro-livability forces, smelling victory, use the remaining time to detail our plans for the implementation of the Bicycle Plan. In this moment, I have an epiphany: Chad's rage and ability to garner media attention have helped engage far more people than would have otherwise taken notice.

The concept of the bicycle as not merely a toy but a vital—and extremely beneficial—means of transportation needs to be aired, discussed, analyzed, and confronted. No need to be afraid of the attention. My support team did me proud, too, for without them bicycle transportation is but another good idea lost in a sea of good ideas.

 Court the media; don't freak out over negative press.

The hotly disputed intersection now includes bike lanes, median islands, cross-walks, motorist turn lanes, trees, and signage, thanks in part to Chad's pressure. Guess what? It works much better for everyone.

For the grand finale, Jeff invites Chad and me to wrap up with our final salvos. Chad uses his time to rant about government intrusion into his business.

Then it's my turn. "Jeff, I want to share with the audience a vision of a brighter future. In this future, we will be fit and healthier, with more money in our pockets. Our kids will arrive at school energetic and ready to learn. Our stress levels will drop, and we will be freer. Does this sound like a vision you want for your kids? What if I told you that this vision is attainable within our lifetime? It all comes down to this: Invest in bicycle transportation, a win-win solution for our growing energy, environmental, livability, and health problems."

Jeff nods his approval and cuts to a commercial.

And for the moment, the debate is over.

CHAPTER 9

So, Sue Me Already

"I don't get it," I say to Doug McCollum one day as we lay temporary bike lane line markings on the pavement in advance of a marking crew. "We're striping bike lanes all over the place. Why is the BTA[11] still suing us?"

He rolls his eyes. "Don't get me started, please."

"Can't we just go ahead and put in the bike lanes?" The street in question, Northeast Multnomah, is about to be rebuilt.

"I'd like to, but the construction plans will have to be modified."

"So?" I probe.

By this point, all the streets earlier dismissed as too challenging or controversial, like Northeast Broadway, have bike lanes.

---

11 Advocacy groups like the Bicycle Transportation Alliance (www.bta4bikes.org) are critical to the evolution of every bicycle friendly community. The Alliance for Bicycling and Walking (www.peoplepoweredmovement.org) is your go-to organization to find the advocacy group in your area.

Rex Burkholder, cofounder of the Bicycle Transportation Alliance and an elected councilman for Portland's regional government, Metro.

"You gotta talk to Mike Bauer. It's his project."

Cue the dramatic piano music.

"The same Mike who dismissed every bike lane opportunity put right smack in his face? You're the one who approved Southeast Seventh. He wouldn't do it."

Always the optimist, Doug advises, "Give him a chance, Mia."

⚙ ⚙ ⚙ ⚙ ⚙

The Bicycle Transportation Alliance's complaint is that the city has violated the 1971 law[12] known as the Oregon "Bike Bill." The first of its kind in the nation, the law has two key provisions. One, at least 1 percent of transportation funding must be spent on bikeways and walkways. Two, bikeways and walkways should be part of all major road construction and reconstruction.

 **Set aside at least 1 percent of your transportation budget to get the ball rolling.**

---

12 ORS 366.514

Nowadays, this approach is called a "Complete Streets" policy, intended to ensure that streets are built with all users in mind. Back then, it was nothing short of revolutionary, an utterly bold statement from an Oregon lawmaker, Don Stathos, who was part of a richly progressive legislative era that led to the Bike Bill, recycling, and protection of Oregon's beaches and farmlands.

Through the 1970s and 1980s, Oregon's transportation departments ignored their obligation to build roads with bike lanes and sidewalks. What would our towns be like if we had started complying with the Bike Bill from the beginning? A whole lot more bicycle and pedestrian friendly, that's for sure. No question that it would have been cheaper, in the long run, to have done it right the first time.

A BTA founder, Rex Burkholder, became determined to change this pattern of noncompliance. He found a perfect test case when Portland staff refused to mark bike lanes on a street next to the high-profile new Trail Blazers Rose Garden Arena.

A Midwestern transplant with kind, anti-aging genes, Rex came to bicycle activism by trial and terror the day he took his adorable towhead five-year-old Gehron on a ride. The boy stopped in the middle of a busy travel lane to ask if he was going the right way. Rex decided that it just wasn't OK for streets to be deadly for all but the most aggressive or optionless citizens, and joined forces with a newly formed group of twenty ragtag cycling activists to push for change.

For two years now, the City of Portland and BTA have been going around in circles in court. In the meantime, I'm caught between my activist friends and my engineering colleagues, both of whom I need on my side.

✹✹✹✹✹

I ride out to the disputed road and lean my bike against a post. To the east is a modest street, nothing special, just two blacktop travel lanes leading into a prominent business district. Framing the area we've got the basketball arena, a new MAX light-rail line, and three imposing multi-story parking structures.

A fare inspector in a TriMet uniform walks over. "What'cha got there?" he asks politely.

I unroll a set of plans on the ground; he kneels to see how the new street will split around a cobblestone island.

⊶   **Adopt "Complete Streets" policies and/or legislation, then execute!**

"Looks nice!" he observes.

"Agreed. Only problem is that there are no bike lanes."

The fare inspector looks puzzled. "Bike what?"

"Bike lanes, you know, like a shoulder. They're separated lanes marked exclusively for bicyclists."

He looks confused. "No one is biking through here now. Why would we need bike lanes?"

"Well," I reply, "we're trying to get more people to bicycle for transportation, because it's good for the city and good for people. And we can't expect people to bike if we don't put in bike lanes."

"They're nothing but trouble anyway...getting in my way, riding all over the platform...." He takes a look at my bike and shakes his finger at me, as if just realizing that he is talking to an actual bicycle rider. (Common dualism in my world: There are no cyclists at all, so we don't need bike lanes, but wait...there are cyclists out there after all...and they're in the way.)

I roll up the plans and wish him well.

Back in cubicle land, I try to understand. "Mike, sorry if I sound dense. Can you explain to me again why we're not putting in bike lanes?"

Engineer Mike is a personable twenty-year department veteran famous for creating squirrely traffic patterns favoring motorists at the expense of pedestrians and neighborhoods. He smiles at me kindly, from his perch up at basketball-player height, as if I'm a little dense. "We don't have enough room for bike lanes. We need minimum thirteen-foot-wide lanes."

"Why can't we narrow the travel lanes, median or sidewalks? We only need a couple of feet on each side."

"Plus," he insists, "the bike lanes don't go anywhere. Just to the east, they'll drop. The law allows for an exception in the absence of need."

"But Mike," I counter, "we'll surely put in bike lanes in the future."

He shakes his head. "The plans are set, Mia."

On March 11, 1995, the Oregon Court of Appeals upholds the Bike Bill's intent. It doesn't really resolve anything. Technically, if the BTA wants to pursue the lawsuit further, they have to go back to court to explain how the city has failed to comply.

Nonetheless, they hold a press conference to declare victory. "We have set a precedent that jurisdictions must pay attention to the Bike Bill. They must take it seriously. It's been there since 1971, but it has no teeth,"[13] declares BTA director Karen Frost.

Suddenly, I've had enough. The BTA is my most important ally. Without their support, my job would be a million times harder. Being in an adversarial relationship with them feels wrong.

It's time for another showdown.

In a windowless, drab conference room I sit at the end of a rectangular table, like I'm the hostess of a dinner party. To my right sit Mike Bauer and Rob Burchfield; to my left, project manager Kevin Kohnstamm and Doug McCollum.

Putting on my best hostess smile, I welcome the parties to our little gathering. The appetizers will be congenial chit-chat, the main course a battle of words.

Doug and I suggest, oh-so-politely, that we modify the construction plans, shave a few feet off each travel lane and the median refuge, and put in the darn bike lanes. Then we can all go home and be done with this unpleasant chapter in our history.

"Come on, fellers," I urge. "Rob, you're leading the charge on bike lanes everywhere else...this is no different. Come away from the dark side; you know you want to...."

But no...a history I wasn't part of leads Rob and Kevin to dig in hard on the side of sticking with the no-bike-lane plans. "We had a deal! The BTA betrayed us! The bike lanes don't go anywhere! It makes no sense to put in bike lanes for a block!"

I am baffled by their stance, and sweet-talk isn't working. I can't rewrite history, and I've got no weapons to counter their stubborn emotional determination.

"Rob, Kevin, eventually we'll find a way to put in bike lanes on the rest of Multnomah. Come on, this is ridiculous! Whatever 'deals' were made are in the past. We're here, today, and bike lanes are the answer!"

Twenty minutes later, Rob and I are both red in the face. Our argument would have made better television than the *Town Hall* debate.

We reach an impasse: two on one side, two on the other. Some call this a tie, others a standoff.

Into the middle of this fracas, arms raised in a gesture of peace, wades Mike, shushing, "Children, children, get hold of yourselves."

---

[13] "Bicycle Enthusiasts Hail Ruling," *Oregonian*, March 11, 1995

Later, the city adds bike lanes to this, the last of the arena-area streets.

Then this old-guard traffic engineer pronounces, with great solemnity, "Now look. I developed these plans myself, but modifying them isn't that big of a deal. Times are changing. Even if the bike lanes only go for a block, it won't hurt. I agree with Doug and Mia. Let's put the bike lanes in."

Now I don't know exactly what motivated Mike to put aside his ego and car-centric thinking and defect to our camp. Perhaps he was swayed by our excellent arguments? Nah, that's just my own ego talking. Perhaps the fact that he is close to retirement led to a certain laissez-faire attitude? Hard to say. It strikes me, though, that old-guard engineers like Mike, given the right encouragement and respect, can and will cheerfully throw in the towel. I sure wish I could bottle his positive spirit; it would save me a lot of future aggravation. In the meantime, I'll take what I can get. Smiling, we walk out of the room, and head to the Lucky Lab brewpub for beers.

CHAPTER 10

No Free Parking

Notwithstanding a few skirmishes, by 1997 we've gained more than 100 miles (160 km) of bike lanes through the low-hanging fruit, Complete Streets road diet. The Bicycle Transportation Alliance drops its lawsuit.[14] Our engineers are mostly on board with the program.

Now we're faced with an opportunity to improve a short but critical link, Northeast Forty-Seventh Avenue as it crosses an interstate freeway. Low-hanging fruit it's not. Bike lanes can only be put in via trade-off of one side of on-street parking.

To pick this prickly pear, we are going to need some thick gloves. Even still, we may bleed. And based on what I've learned about people and their attachment to on-street parking, I may very well get booted back to Texas if we fail.

Back in the 1980s, my predecessor had proposed trading off one side of parking for bike lanes on Northeast Knott, a residential street with large driveways. City council got spooked by the ferocity of the opposition and voted it down. It was another blow to Krys, already under fire in North Portland. Since then, trading off parking has been considered a no-no.

It's been a decade, though, and times have changed. "We've evolved since then," I tell myself.

At least that's what I want to believe, that there is a widespread consensus that safely moving bicyclists is a better use of public space than parking cars, that driveways and garages can and should be used to park cars instead of store tools and camping gear, that residents accept, even embrace, that they may have to park in their driveways, across the street, or around the corner.

"You're delusional, you know that?" says Lewis Wardrip at the Lucky Lab, where a beer is helping soothe the thrash wounds he gained earlier

---

14 As Rex intended, the lawsuit set future precedents toward bike lanes. Oregon Department of Transportation (ODOT) Bicycle and Pedestrian Program Manager Michael Ronkin directed all agency staff that bike lanes and sidewalks are expected on all roadway projects, with rare exceptions. He personally reviewed state roadway plans and trained staff on the law's requirements. He notes, "The lawsuit was a turning point, helping me convince officials throughout the state, hey, this is for real." So far, there have been no additional lawsuits.

in the day from a group of residents who insist the city absolutely must not touch the on-street parking used primarily for upcoming Christmas parties. He shakes his gray lion's-mane of hair in disgust, and redraws the striping plan with the bike lane 7 feet (2 m) from the curb. (As expected, no one rides in the bike lane; they ride in the usually empty parking lane.)

In many European cities, public space in residential neighborhoods is considered too valuable for vehicle storage. Families either do without a private motor vehicle or get by with one ultra-efficient mini-car. Car-free business districts thrive, buoyed by exponentially higher volumes of customers than can be served if public space is gobbled up by parking.

It's a classic chicken-versus-egg argument. Whatever we do induces demand in that direction. If we provide on-street parking, people will park cars. If we provide a bike lane, people will bike.

I'm sympathetic, even empathetic, to the pain people feel over losing parking. It forces them to change their habits. It affects their lives. This can, of course, be positive.

It can also be frightening. And scared people are no fun.

"Yes, ma'am, I do understand that on-street parking is important to you," says Bicycle Program colleague Roger Geller, an urban planner who blew away more than one hundred other candidates for this position, on the phone to a resident on Forty-Seventh Avenue.

"Our parking study shows that the section in question has an excess of parking spaces relative to demand." His rational explanation, delivered with a serious and respectful look on his bearded face, sounds fine to me, but the more he explains, the more furious she becomes.

"We have eighty-four spaces available. Only 20 percent are in use 80 to 90 percent of the time." For this analytical explanation, he earns a formal complaint about his conduct. I swear to our boss that he was nothing but polite. The mere analysis of on-street parking demand raised this woman's hackles beyond rationality.

"Yellow alert, Captain," warns a Spock-like voice in the far reaches of my mind. We're heading for a bumpy ride.

We do our homework, talk to all the residents, and arrange a public forum. We are armed with information, analysis, and belief. That should do the trick. We're just talking about a few lightly used parking spaces, after all.

I walk through the halls of Providence Hospital, a major player on the street in question, to a basement auditorium and am greeted by a short, squat, gray man in a gray suit.

"Thank you for coming tonight," he welcomes the thirty or so residents. "Like you, I have been dismayed by the city's proposal to put in bike lanes at the expense of our parking."

Houston, we have a problem. The hospital is supposed to meet all its visitor and employee parking needs on its own property. Its enormous parking structures never reach capacity.

The blood in my face starts rising. He adds, "I encourage you all to voice your opinions here tonight and help put a stop to this outrageous proposal! And now, let me introduce Mia

The Bicycle Program team (back to front): Jeff Smith, intern Matt Arnold, Roger Geller, me, Barbara Plummer

Birk, from the so-called Bicycle Program, to tell you more about it."

"Thanks," I think. "Isn't your frickin' job to promote good health?"

Normally I can handle hostile questions and accusations. I'm a trained professional, after all! When motorists call to complain about cyclists who run red lights or get in their way, I don't argue. I just put on my headset, keep my hands busy sorting paperwork, and listen, while Doug or Lewis flings rubber bands at me.

"What is really going on in your life?" I always want to ask. "Having trouble making ends meet? Sick child? Relationship problems? Because if you're so on edge that seeing a bad-behaving bicyclist makes you want to scream obscenities at a complete stranger, well, something's going on."

After they run out of steam, I suggest they bring their concerns to Portland's Bicycle Advisory Committee and thank them for taking the time to express their opinion.

I even kept my cool the day a lady harangued me about how cyclists were the scourge of the earth. What provoked her? She witnessed an out-of-control motorist crash a car and three unrestrained children into a bridge sidewalk that happened to be filled with cyclists. (No one was injured.)

"Cyclists are the problem???" I wanted to scream back, but didn't.

I'd been called road lice, harassed to the point of filing a restraining order, and received letters accusing me of being a communist, hippie, piece of crap, and thief. So this negative set-up—an ambush, really—should be nothing I can't handle.

Wrong.

It starts well. I go through my slides, explain that this is a key segment in our bikeway system, and list the benefits of bicycle transportation. Slides of Roger's parking-demand analysis help bolster the recommendation that one side of parking be traded off for bike lanes.

From high in the back row, one man yells, "You f***ing cyclists think you own the streets. You can't take our parking!" The crowd eggs him on with a standing ovation.

I try to direct the conversation back to positive ground with, "I understand that folks have concerns about the parking removal..."

A sobbing woman interrupts. "If you remove the parking, my children are going to run into the street, and get hit!"

It's Julie, who has repeated this teary speech at every meeting for months.

"Well, I'm not sure it's our responsibility to keep your kids from running into the street," I mumble.

"I work night shifts," shouts a uniformed police officer, Michelle. "I need to park on street."

"Aren't your garage and driveway sufficient?" I ask. Not smart, Mia, not smart. Don't you know never to argue with a police officer? Red alert!

"No! I can't wake up my roommates in the middle of the night to get them to move their cars between the driveway and garage so I can get out."

I snap, "Perhaps you can walk all the way across the street to your house. It won't kill you, you know." I know, pretty pathetic.

The mood darkens from there. Face beet-red in frustration and embarrassment, I hand the mike to Roger and sit down.

Back in the office, I am in hot water. New transportation director Vic Rhodes, who apparently has had a little chat with our hospital friends, wants to see me. I sigh, and head through a friendly barrage of rubber bands to Vic's office.

Now, you have to understand that at this point, our level of bureaucratic and political support is a bit frayed. Earl Blumenauer is now a U.S. congressman. The passions of his city council replacement, Charlie Hales, lie in large-scale development projects and bringing back the urban streetcar.

Vic—intelligent, accomplished, and handsome in a Telly Savalas kind of way—is Charlie's handpicked transportation director. It's our first meeting, but he offers nothing in the way of pleasantries. Rather, he points a finger in my direction and demands, "Why can't we just allow parking in the bike lane?" I look around to see if I'm on *Candid Camera*, while searching for a polite way to express that if people park in the bike lane, it's not really a bike lane, and gosh darnit, do I really have to explain this? But apparently, we're back at square one. I feel very small and out of my league under his pointed questioning, which concludes with a thinly veiled warning about the future of the Bicycle Program.

The pressure starts to get to me. I waver, ready to give in. It's just one project, I rationalize.

"If we lose this, we lose a critical freeway crossing point," Roger angrily insists at the Lucky Lab, his distinctive silver hair standing in two tufts resembling Dilbert's boss or a *Wizard of Oz* munchkin. "The nearby crossings stink, and the next halfway decent one is a mile away."

"Stay strong," I whisper to myself, and conjure up an image of happy people riding in the new bike lanes by Providence Hospital.

❋ ❋ ❋ ❋ ❋

It's a rainy day when we head over to city council to ask for approval. Council chambers are housed in the building's rotunda, and they emanate dignity. The five councilors sit in an elevated semicircle against a backdrop of a relief of the city. Below and facing the councilors is an ornate dark-walnut table and three matching swivel chairs.

Viewers can watch from the floor or upper deck. There is little security. If you want to testify, you simply have to put your name on a list, and you get your allotted three minutes, no matter what.

I sit in one of the swivel chairs and, still chastened by the Providence Hospital blow-up, quickly, humbly, run through our slides. Commissioner Hales looks uncomfortable. Mayor Vera Katz, a tiny, assertive dynamo with spiky brown hair and a long history in state and local politics, flips through our report. Normally, her smarts and light-up-the-room grin remind me of my mother. Not today. Neither she nor the other councilors offer warm fuzzy thanks or smiles of encouragement. I move back to allow public testimony.

First up are two or three supportive cyclists.

"Have you tried to cross the freeway by bike?" asks BTA Director Karen Frost. "The crossing at Thirty-Ninth is a deathtrap. This is an absolutely critical connection."

Maybe she scored a few points, but I can't be sure.

Next up is Julie, who repeats her tearful warning about her children's safety, provoking sympathetic clucks from the audience.

Police officer Michelle then explains her car-shifting dilemma. "Hmm," the Mayor respectfully observes. "I can see how this is a problem for you."

I take a deep breath and try to stay positive, but involuntarily start to shiver as if Harry Potter's icy Dementors are sucking the life out of the room. The tide is turning against us, if it was ever with us in the first place.

Ken Wilhelm, an articulate, well-dressed businessman, is next.

"I conducted my own parking study," he explains. "My data shows a much higher level of demand than your staff purport we have. This proposal will harm our neighborhood. I have a petition from the residents on the street opposing the project. Vote no!"

The audience murmurs in approval. Charlie Hales rakes his fingers through his chestnut-brown hair and frowns. I close my eyes and sigh. Looks like we're hosed. Dang, another bike coordinator bites the dust, brought down by our ferocious addiction to on-street parking.

I want to scream, "Less than twenty affected households versus thousands of potential cyclists, people who will not ride unless we provide bike lanes! How can we become the best bicycling city in the United States if we won't sacrifice a few parking spaces?"

Wilhelm stands up and high-fives the gentleman next to him, a Mr. Fred Wilhelm, who states, "I conducted my own parking study. My data shows a much higher level of demand than your staff purport we have. This proposal will harm our neighborhood. I have a petition from the residents on the street opposing the project. Vote no!"

Mayor Katz looks puzzled. She peers over her reading glasses at Wilhelm #2. "Where did you say you live?"

"Out in Estacada." Since that's about an hour east of here, I can understand her confusion.

The clerk calls out the next name, Ms. June Wilhelm.

"I conducted my own parking study," reads June from a sheet of paper. "My data shows a much higher level of demand than your staff purport we have. This proposal will harm our neighborhood. I have a petition from the residents on the street opposing the project. Vote no!"

The Mayor removes her glasses, leaving them dangling around her neck on a beaded chain. June pushes her chair back.

"One moment, please," directs the Mayor. "Do you live in Estacada too?"

"No, Lake Oswego." Another suburb.

"Why are you here?"

"My son Ken asked me to testify." June smiles warmly at Ken.

The Mayor is not amused. "Mr. Wilhelm, I will consider your opinion sufficiently representative of your family." He looks away.

A surge of warmth envelops me. Perhaps all hope is not lost?

A young man in his twenties is last up. "Look, I do live in the neighborhood. If you remove the parking, I'm going to have to cross the street to get to my car."

"To go where?"

"Well you know, to the 7-Eleven to get pop and Cheetos and stuff."

"Isn't there a 7-Eleven two blocks from you? Why don't you walk?" The Mayor air-stabs her folded glasses in his direction.

He stares blankly at her, then turns to look at Ken.

That does it. The Mayor is fed up. This guy is so freakin' lazy, he won't walk a couple blocks to the store? No wonder obesity is replacing smoking as the greatest threat to our collective health. She calls for a vote. One by one, the councilors assert both their respect for the neighbors' concerns, particularly the policewoman's, and support for the bike lanes. No glowing speeches, just a quiet and unanimous vote of confidence that we are headed in the right direction, no matter how rocky the path. ⚷

⚷ **Backlash is normal. Expect it, prepare for it, but don't back down.**

CHAPTER 11

Painting the Town Blue

"Welcome home," beams Rob. "What'cha got for me?" I hand him a Swiss chocolate bar and my report, as he fills my pint glass at the Lucky Lab. Doug and Lewis join us not long after.

"Gentlemen," I start.

"Who are you calling a gentleman?" asks an indignant Lewis, chucking a peanut at my head.

"I saw a million things, some big, some small. If we were starting from scratch, I would want to make us like Houten, a place of supreme safety, radiant health, and wholesome calm. Its network of separated bicycle paths rarely interacts with streets. We would build a ring road around the periphery of Portland, and in the inner core, everyone would bike or walk or take transit."

Doug and Lewis look each other. "Earth to Mia," coaxes Doug. "Time to come home now."

Bicycle signal in the Netherlands. The number indicates time left to cross as well as time before the signal turns green.

I had just returned from a whirlwind investigation of eighteen bicycle friendly European cities.[15] The image Earl Blumenauer once tried to mind-meld into my head is no longer solely his distant dream. Now it's my marker of success.

"Yeah, guys, I know. We're not building a new town. So we've got to work with what we've got." I take a swig of stout and make a face. I don't much care for strong beer.

I pass around a stack of photos. "There are separate bike signals and wayfinding signs. Many bike lanes are connected to the sidewalk and protected

---

15 Trip funded by the German Marshall Fund Environmental Program. Cities visited: in Germany: Cologne, Bremen, Münster, Troisdorf, and Offenburg. In France: Strasbourg. In Denmark: Copenhagen, Odense, and Nakskov. In the Netherlands: Amsterdam, Groningen, Amersfoort, and Houten. In Switzerland: Geneva, Basel, Zurich, and Winterthur. In Belgium: Brussels.

Clockwise from upper left: Pavement color to delineate bikeways is a common European technique, particularly in conflict areas. Red in Luxemburg, Belgium; blue in Copenhagen, Denmark; green in Offenburg, Germany.

from turning cars. You can legally ride against traffic on one-way streets. Big bike markings tell motorists to share the lane where there are no bike lanes. At intersections, cyclists wait in front of motorists and go first when the light turns green. Colored markings to improve safety at conflict areas. Bike parking garages, safety education centers, hooks inside trains…"

"Hold it," admonishes Rob. "I told you not to come back here with a whole bunch of pie-in-the-sky ideas. None of these are in the Manual."

You may not have heard of the *Manual on Uniform Traffic Control Devices* (MUTCD or, simply, the Manual), but it is a major player in your daily life. The Manual dictates the signs, markings, and signals that govern your travel behavior. No matter where you go or how you get there, red always means stop, green always means go. Traffic engineers pull out the book for everything from signal timing to the width and number of traffic lanes. It is referred to as the traffic engineer's bible.

Unfortunately, very little bikeway design guidance is found in the Manual. For example, signals to help a pedestrian or cyclist cross a busy roadway from an off-street path are not "warranted" per its auto-oriented standards. Precisely zero of the techniques that make the eighteen cities on my tour supersafe, comfortable, and attractive are found between its covers.[16] Deviate from

---

[16] Its kissin' cousin is the *American Association for State Highway Transportation Officials (AASHTO) Guide to Bikeway Facilities*, which provides significantly more guidance but also lacks many forward-thinking treatments.

the Manual, we're warned, and run an increased risk of liability and maybe even lose our federal transportation funding. A complex set of committees approves new or innovative ideas only after many years of federally monitored experimentation, study, and analysis, if they approve them at all.

"Here's my read, Rob." I pull the good book out of my bike bag. "It's like we're trying to build a backyard fence with only a handsaw and drill bits. We can only make so much progress without a Skilsaw, drill, hammer, and screwdriver. So what to do? Go to the hardware store and get the tools we need. That European store I was just at has got one mighty fine set of tools. We're talking Craftsman quality. Not much point in letting them rust in the box. Let's get 'em out!"

Rob cocks an eyebrow and thumbs through the Manual, which I've carefully annotated with yellow and pink highlighting and sticky tabs. I can't tell if he's impressed or annoyed, so I keep talking.

"Color in bikeways is neither recommended nor prohibited. In fact, it's not mentioned at all. Therefore, I don't see why using color will be a problem." Oh yeah, once again, chalk one up for naïveté.

I pull out a map marked with spots where motorists are supposed to turn across bike lanes. At these challenging locations, where cyclists are most in danger, the Manual directs us to drop the bike lane, leaving cyclists twisting in the wind. In other words: cyclists, fend for yourselves.

The more we're striping bike lanes, and the more people are cycling, the more obvious this disconnect. Color will help, I'm sure.

Rob strokes his beard and scalp, grimaces, gulps half a beer, and then excuses himself.

"That went well," notes Doug.

"Deviation is not in Rob's DNA," explains Lewis.

Rob returns to our outdoor picnic bench, laces his fingers together, and looks down at his hands.

"Another beer?" I gently ask.

He murmurs, "Let's take this one step at a time. We need funding and a solid game plan."

It's a start, and that's all I need.

❁❁❁❁❁

"Blue," says the Federal Highway Administration (FHWA) official from his office in Washington, D.C. "You want to put *blue* on the pavement? Blue is for handicap parking stalls, not bikes."

I cringe at the flat, cold voice coming out of the phone.

Look to the world's best cycling cities for planning and design guidance.

"Yes, I realize that blue is used for marking disabled stalls in parking lots. I don't think that motorists will be confused and try to park in the middle of an intersection."

After a year of research and outreach, we're on the verge of marking Copenhagen-style blue at ten locations.[17] I'm trying to get "permission," which will, in theory, reduce our liability exposure should a cyclist get hurt.

"Ms. Birk," the official explains slowly, emphasizing each word as if he is speaking to a lower life-form. *"Blue is for handicap stalls."*

"Going out on a limb here...not loving it?" Officials, residents, and professionals alike, hundreds of folks with whom I consulted, overwhelmingly like the color concept. Blue is the preferred choice over green, red, and yellow, other colors I've seen.[18] Not for this guy.

Our FHWA application to experiment apparently is headed for the circular file. So much for seeking permission.

"Fine," I think. "Full steam ahead."

Next stop: the Bureau of Maintenance.

"Let me get this straight," asks Roger Talley, head of the markings crew. Looking down with disdain, he towers over me. "You want us to apply blue plastic around the city. Blue plastic? Yeah, that sounds like a top priority for us. I'll see if I can fit you in. How does 2025 look for you?"

Dang. After a year trying to figure out how to get the material, I've got a truckload of it, imported from Denmark, and am ready to go. But now I have to hire a contractor to apply and maintain the material? Oy.

Another few months go down the drain.

We issue a press release proudly announcing the impending blue bike–motorist zones, and are summoned to the editorial board of the state's largest newspaper, the *Oregonian*, expecting a lovefest of support for our low-cost safety improvements.

"$89,000...that's an awful lot of money for a bunch of blue paint," comments lead columnist Larry.

"Actually," I respond cheerfully, "considering that we're upgrading ten difficult intersections, conducting in-depth safety analysis and a public outreach campaign, presenting our findings at national

---

17 Grant funding provided by the Oregon Department of Transportation.
18 Two studies—in Copenhagen, Denmark, and Montreal, Canada—showed that blue improved safety. I could not find any documentation specific to red, green, or yellow. Trying to be respectful of the Manual had also led us to blue. Yellow, red, and green had specific traffic-related meanings (red = stop, yellow = centerline stripe, green = go), but blue was only used for the aforementioned off-street parking stalls.

conferences, and purchasing extra blue plastic for future use, it seems like a darn good deal."

Do they know how much motorist-oriented safety improvements cost? One signal = $250,000. One mile of freeway = $50 million. One interchange upgrade = $300 million. They're quibbling with me over $89,000? And it's not paint, it's long-lasting plastic. Did they read the press release?

"These so-called improvements seem like overkill." Larry leans forward and stares. I recognize this confused look from my wheel-and-pony show audiences. He asks, "Why not use the money to enforce the rules of the road? How about dotted lines through the intersection?"

I am starting to panic. Enforcement? The police won't even talk to me, let alone enforce every single motorist-turning movement. A single police officer's salary and benefits cost more than our whole project. Dotted lines? We're using the MUTCD-allowed dotted lines, and they don't do a dang thing.

"How much is one life worth?" I protest. An image of Keren Holtz, a young woman killed by a drunk driver earlier in the year, floats into my head. Keren's death ripped my heart to shreds. On the flat, straight road where she was killed, I'd spent countless hours cruising at 20 mph (32 km/h) or more on my Trek 1420 road bike, the shimmering water of the Columbia River to my left, a luminous Mount Hood straight ahead.[19] I feel more vulnerable now, more determined than ever to apply the lessons learned from our European colleagues.

I cry out. "What if a blue area wakes up one, just one, drunken or inattentive motorist? Would that be worth $89,000?"

My pleas fall on deaf ears. The November 15, 1997, editorial headline proclaims, "Over the Rainbow Blue Bike Lanes? C'mon, This is Portland, Not Oz. Blue, red, yellow? Why not purple, pink, or chartreuse?"

More negative press, hot on the heels of the Chad's Deli headlines and Northeast Forty-Seventh debacle. We want to make conditions safer. In eighteen European cities, colored bike lanes help. Why are we being criticized for trying to do the right thing?

"Buck up, Mia" encourages Rob. "They don't understand. How can they? You spent all that time in Europe. These guys have never even been on a bike. You've got to be patient. It takes time to change attitudes. We're on

---

[19] I still pedal on Marine Drive, still push my legs and heart against a stiff east wind along the Columbia River. I stop at the spot where, for many years, fresh flowers, ribbons, and photos reminded me that no parents should lose their child as Jane and Gerry Holtz lost theirs. I take solace in the tremendous gains we have made, for the city is safer and the road is not dotted up and down with memorials. 2008 brought the best safety record in seventy-five years. Thanks to Mothers Against Drunk Drivers, the Alliance for Community Traffic Safety, AAA, the BTA, and other groups who have pushed for stiffer penalties for drunk and negligent driving.

the right track." He coaxes a smile out of me with the promise of a beer and a bike ride.

"Yes, I noticed the blue, and I think it does improve safety," comments an enthusiastic cyclist in khaki pants and a green Burley rain jacket. I am standing on the east side of the Broadway Bridge just past a blue bike lane, surveying cyclists. With me is the well-respected University of North Carolina Highway Safety Research Center's William Hunter, who is helping us analyze the study data thanks, ironically, to funding from FHWA, the federal agency whose official declined our study.

We've already recorded bicyclist and motorist movements and interactions before and after the markings were applied. The surveys are added value, a barometer of opinion to go along with the technical results.

Blue markings at two of Portland's conflict areas: results positive!

"Yes, I noticed the blue areas," respond more than two-thirds of the surveyed motorists and cyclists, the bulk of whom are regular travelers on the routes in question.

Months later, Rob and I have William's data-intensive report in front of us. "He says here that there was a significant increase in motorists' slowing and yielding to cyclists. That sounds good!"

"Is it statistically significant, though?" Rob wants to be sure. He is, after all, on the hook to decide if the markings are a success or failure. This is the crux of the daily life of a traffic engineer, who approves signs, markings, signals, and roadway and intersection configurations. If someone is injured, the engineer has to be prepared to defend his or her decision. While Rob is willing to sign off on a carefully monitored, well-researched experiment with non-standard blue bike lane markings, he wants to be 100 percent sure the results show an improvement or at least a neutral impact. The last thing he wants to do is perpetuate the use of a less safe marking.

I read out loud: "'Significant behavior changes at a site were assessed by either an x2-statistic or a Fishers exact test when cell frequencies were too small. A Cochran-Mantel-Haenszel (CMH) x2-statistic was also computed to test for overall association across the tables.' Um, is this English? Let me get William on the phone."

He assures us in plainspeak that the results are derived from the best available statistical programs and tests and indicate a positive outcome. This gives Rob the comfort he needs to recommend blue markings be added to our toolbox.

The next winter, William and I stand in front of a packed room at the Transportation Research Board's annual meeting in Washington, D.C. This conference is a mainstay for the nation's transportation wonks, the vast majority of whom are concerned with the microdetails of pavement performance, signal systems, traffic flow theory, and intelligent transportation systems, a Jetsons-like concept for moving cars. In other words, no intelligence whatsoever will be required on the part of drivers, who will zoom around sipping jumbo Big Gulps like the oversized spaceship people in Disney's *WALL•E*. (To be honest, Intelligent Transportation Systems [ITS] also include useful concepts like signals that prioritize mass transit vehicles, real-time parking information, and variable message signs used for highway safety.)

I've been attending this conference with semi-regularity since the early 1990s, when I was one of some twenty people talking about bikes and pedestrians. Although our contingent has swelled to a whopping one hundred, out of twenty thousand or so, I still feel like a fish out of water.

William and I walk the audience through the delightfully wonky details of our study.[20]

"So now what?" the Cambridge bicycle coordinator wants to know. "Will blue markings be added to the Manual so that other cities can use it?"

"Well," I answer, "we've submitted our results and are waiting to hear back."

"If they had done their study under our auspices, then it would have been possible for us to consider it," adds Richard Mouer, chair of the National Bicycle Technical Committee, the federal government's de facto agent of bikeway markings and signs.

---

20 Birk, Mia, *Portland's Blue Bike Lanes: Improved Safety through Enhanced Visibility*, Portland Office of Transportation, July 1999. Hunter, W.W.; Harkey, D.L.; Stewart, J.R.; Birk, M.L., *Evaluation of Blue Bike-Lane Treatment in Portland, Oregon,* Transportation Research Board, Record No. 1705, 2000.

"Great," I think. "We tried to get permission, and the feds said no, and now, the lack of permission means we're going nowhere fast."

Later, Richard catches up with me sipping a neat tequila in the hotel bar and resumes our friendly discourse. "Look," he chuckles. "Submit your next project as an experiment, will you?"

I invite him to join me, and I admire the pictures of his new baby.

"Richard, look," I sigh. "Time's a wasting. Colored pavement is a proven bikeway safety technique. Since when does every single thing have to go through you guys anyway? Consider this: If we only rely on federal studies, we would not even have bike lanes. No studies were done back then. And look at the bike lane marking. First, it was the words "Bike Lane," then "Bike Only." Then there was a move to replace words with symbols, so we started using a bicycle accompanied by the HOV-lane diamond.[21] Then, folks decided that the bicycle should be replaced by a bicyclist to reflect that it's a person using the lane, and someone else decided the bicyclist should wear a helmet. Somewhere along the way, a wrong-way-riding bicyclist who mistook the diamond for a two-way arrow got injured, so then we replaced the diamond with a one-way directional arrow. No studies on that, but it made sense and helped reduce wrong-way riding."

"Times have changed. We've got a process," states Richard, kindly but firmly. In other words, if you want your kooky ideas to go beyond Portland, you need to play the game my way.

"And it's not just our committee, you know. We have to convince the higher-level committees. And if you think we're tough to get through, you have no idea...." He finishes his soda and takes off.

I look around that hotel lobby packed to the gills with folks still building auto-oriented transportation systems for a world that is changing before their eyes. I sip tequila and think about the layers and layers we will have to sway toward the validity of colored bikeways. If we do continue to push the envelope, what are we risking? Will we get sued? Ostracized? Tarred and feathered? Will federal funding be cut off? How will I know if we don't try?

I finish my tequila and walk down from the hotel on Connecticut Avenue into Rock Creek Park, pedaling grounds of my D.C. years. It seems I have a choice. Put my energy into moving us forward at the local level or waste it trying to convince the slowly fading old guard.

A nanosecond later, I've made my decision.

---

21 HOV = high occupancy vehicle

CHAPTER 12

Walk on Water

Once upon a time, river commerce ruled the day in Portland, Oregon. As time wore on, the Willamette became an industrial toxic stew, keeping boats afloat but devastating all its living creatures and degrading its majesty. Portland's dark history of shanghaiing workers may have faltered in part because the slaves were able to simply walk right across the thick sludge to freedom.

Jumping on the river-destruction bandwagon was the Federal Highway Administration, which invested $26 billion in 41,000 miles (65,980 km) of federal highways, a surface area equivalent to that of West Virginia. The concrete used would build six sidewalks to the moon. One of those highways, I-5, was plopped right next to the Willamette in the heart of downtown, in one stupendous example of short-sighted use of prime riverfront property.

The project's governor-appointed highway developer, Glenn Jackson, must have driven over from his rural Eastern Oregon home and stood on the Willamette's east side, thinking something like: "We've got to move 50,000 oil-leaking, fume-belching, dangerously fast-moving metal boxes as fast as possible through Portland every day. Might as well slap this sucker next to this here open-air toilet. No one'll mind."

It took no time at all for city officials to realize what a lemon they were stuck with.[22] City council spent the next two decades debating whether to move, bury, or make peace with the beast, reversing itself time and again depending on the officeholders of the day. Finally, in the early 1990s, Mayor Vera Katz and Commissioners Earl Blumenauer, Mike Lindberg, and Gretchen Kafoury declared they would see the downtown portion of I-5 in hell but, in the meantime, Portlanders and visitors alike would get to experience the Willamette's eastbank by foot or bike despite the freeway's looming presence.

"Hang out there if you want to, you miserable monster. We'll be over here ignoring you while we recapture the precious riverfront you stole

---

22 Kirchmeier, Mark, "The I-5 Story: $4 Billion And 10 Years Produced A Lot More Than Just Another Road," *Oregonian*, April 9, 1989.

from us." Thus began the reclamation of the Willamette River and the quest for the Eastbank Esplanade, a crucial connection in our bikeway system.

While I'm scurrying around reclaiming space from our roadways, Portland Parks Bureau landscape architect George Hudson is leading the charge to build paths off-street. Oddly, we barely know each other. Our paths cross only when our paths cross literally; i.e., where the trail intersects a road.

George is a small, intense man of Japanese heritage. Ferociously dedicated to his talented and high-achieving wife and daughters, and gracefully existing on but five hours sleep, his contributions to this point have included more than 20 miles (32 km) of prominent, popular off-street paths along abandoned and active railways.[23] With more than thirty local, state and federal agencies involved, the complexity of the Eastbank Esplanade makes my challenges to put in bike lanes and European safety techniques seem, in comparison, Mickey Mouse simple.

I run into George one day as I'm biking home along a narrow temporary asphalt path between the Hawthorne and Morrison bridges. One day soon, if George has his way, this path will be replaced by an elegant, concrete, art-adorned esplanade. George is standing in quiet contemplation, watching a dragon boat crew row in unison across the still water.

"Yo, George, what's going on?" I ask.

"Oh, hey, Mia," he responds. "I'm trying to figure out what to do about the pikeminnow."

"The whatminnow?"

"The pikeminnow. You know the floating section?" Where the freeway gobbles the riverbank, George and team plan to float the path on 150-foot-tall spires pounded deep into the river's bed. In the heart of downtown Portland, for 1,200 feet (366 m) you will walk or bike on water, in perfect harmony with the river's tidal level or flow. It will be the longest floating path of its kind in the United States.

Work hand-in-hand across bureaucratic boundaries to create complementary off- and on-street bikeways.

---

[23] George's accomplishments include the Springwater Corridor, Springwater on the Willamette, Peninsula Crossing Trail, numerous parks, and the Johnson Boat Landing path in Milwaukie, Oregon. He joined me at Alta Planning + Design in 2001.

"The U.S. Fish and Wildlife Service says the northern pikeminnow[24] are going to gather below the floating walkway and prey upon the steelhead smolt." George and his younger daughter Arianna love to fish on the weekends.

"The what?"

"You know, baby steelhead? They're endangered."

Yikes! So far, George has had to analyze impacts to the beavers, ducks, geese, herons, and salmon, all of which concern the United States EPA. The Lower Willamette steelhead is another level of headache. The feds want the City of Portland to pay damages for fish that might get harmed. Only problem is that the nasty pikeminnow have never once been spotted in the Willamette. And George isn't willing to pony up cash for nonexistent bully fish.

Like the price of eggs, the cost of each potentially harmed smolt goes up at each meeting. In the minds of the federal fish protection squad, hordes of these vicious beasts are gathering, flashing their gang signs, and preparing to invade the floating walkway, where they will gobble the smolt in a feast of Titanic proportions. You did not want to run into these bad boys in a dark alley, no sirree.

"Must seem like a cash cow to them," I chuckle.

"Yeah, by their estimate, we're supposed to pay tens of thousands for the potential fish damage." As a result, George is pushing the walkway farther into the deep water, where the demons of the dark will theoretically be less likely to gather. This too will be mighty costly. He idly strokes his black mustache, pondering.

He's also got another problem: He's missing a critical permit, which grants permission to build the path on state property sandwiched between the freeway and the eroding riverbank. So limited is the space, George's team develops new bioengineering techniques to build up and preserve the riverbank. They plant close to 44,000 native trees and shrubs, wrapped and layered in burlap sacks.

The state transportation department bureaucrat won't sign the permit until George gets permission from the Army Corps of Engineers. The very tight construction window, timed to be sensitive to fish migration, is fast approaching. Construction crews are ready to begin.

Finally, he gets the Corps permit. Like an assassin receiving his final instructions, Hudson jumps in the car and heads to the state capitol.

---

24 The northern pikeminnow can actually eat fish larger than itself and digest a fish as quickly as it can swallow it.

Vera Katz Eastbank Esplanade floating walkway

George paces the hall, clutching both the Corps paperwork and unsigned permission slip. George can see his target through the glass meeting room window. An hour goes by, then two. Not once does the dude acknowledge George's presence.

Finally, the door opens, and Mr. Permit-Holder-Upper marches out, full speed, not stopping to register George, who pounces Wile E. Coyote–style.

He comes up holding empty air.

"Hah," thinks George. "My marathon training comes in handy once again."

He tails him down the hall, turns the corner, and sees emptiness. Had the bureaucrat put on his invisibility cloak or beamed himself to another planet?

George spies the men's room door. Without hesitation, he slips in. His target is doing his business at the urinal. George stations himself inside the door and patiently waits until the dude finishes, zips up, and washes his hands. Then he heads toward the door, where he encounters George, who grimly announces "Gotcha," and hands him the permits and a pen.

Birthed in sewage and sludge, the Eastbank Esplanade is blessed for creation in another waste treatment zone.

⊛ ⊛ ⊛ ⊛ ⊛

From the day the mile-and-a-half (2.4 km) esplanade opens, bicyclists ride and joggers and plodders stride. The path's graceful curves, budding vegetation, art,[25] interpretive panels,[26] and luminous views do exactly what city council intended: They distract you from the freeway.[27]

The same *Oregonian* editorial board that decried the blue bike lanes is not impressed.

It's just a noisy new pencil-thin park along the freeway. At $419 a linear inch, Portland can still boast having the costliest bike and jogging path in America, if not the world.

Then, on September 22, 2001, more than a thousand candle-holding mourners turn the 2.5-mile (4 km) loop into a circle of post–9/11 solidarity, faith, and, most of all, community. By December that year, *Oregonian* columnist Jonathan Nicholas declares the Eastbank the city's best investment of 2001.

Civic curmudgeons delighted in pointing out that our Eastbank Esplanade cost $419 per inch ... a measure of cost-effectiveness they rarely employ when ranking the Trail Blazers. The waterfront walkway turned out to be enormously popular anyway, not least because it served as opening salvo in the resurgent campaign to detonate the eastside freeway.

And again in July 2002, the *Oregonian* eats its words.

The Eastbank Esplanade, now in its second summer as the eastside's window to the Willamette, has already become part of Portland's lore of livability in tourist guidebooks and in the minds of Portlanders. And no wonder: early-morning joggers will sometimes see a great blue heron perched on a log that rises from the river near the Morrison Bridge, with the downtown skyline as a backdrop. Parents hold their children, rapt in fascination, a few feet from freight trains as they

---

25 A local artist group, RIGGA, created four stunning pieces. *The Echo Gate* sculpture "echoes" the pier buildings and shanghai tunnels of Portland's past. *The Ghost Ship* grand lantern pays homage to the many ships that come through Portland and the ones that have gone down in crossing the Columbia River Bar. *The Stackstalk* is a hybrid beacon—part masthead, part wheat stem, part smokestack—that suspends a Japanese glass fishing float in the sky. *The Alluvial Wall* echoes the natural shape of the river before Portland was Portland.

26 Designed by Portland landscape architect firm Mayer/Reed.

27 The lead consultant was the San Francisco-based landscape architecture firm of Hargreaves Associates.

stand on the Steel Bridge's lower-level walkway. Bicyclists, walkers, hand-holders, runners, wheelchair users, dog walkers, photographers, skateboarders, and anglers find a peaceful, if noisy, refuge from the city on the 1.5 mile strand of once-forlorn riverbank.[28]

George's floating walkway is the show-stopping centerpiece. If you stop for a second and put your hand on a spire, you can feel the river moving beneath you. ⚷

Now that the path is open for business, the impending pikeminnow plague is imminent. "You've stalled long enough," say the feds. "Pay up."

Still, George, aka Captain Ahab, pikeminnow hunter, isn't ready to give in.

"Now, just you hold on a minute," he tells the feds. "Let me see if these little beasties really want to hang out under my masterpiece."

He sweeps under the walkway with nets...no minnow. He puts a bounty on their little fanged heads...no minnow. He tries to seduce them with sexy, flashy muscled fish dudes and dudettes...no minnow. He plays music to them, buys them their favorite foods...no luck. Finally, he sends a crackerjack team of scientists with waterproof cattle prods to shock the critters. For weeks and weeks they lay in wait for the whole gang to float up in group gore.

A sheriff once told me, "Mia, the bad guys are like cockroaches. Shine a light on 'em, they scatter." The pikeminnow, similarly, must have taken one look at the Vera Katz Eastbank Esplanade and fled in disgust, thoroughly and utterly dazzled by the emanating happy vibe.

⚷ **Iconic, highly visible, albeit expensive off-road urban bikeways are worth the investment.**

---

28 Oliver, Gordon, "Eastside Window To River, The Year-Old, $30.5 Million Eastbank Esplanade, Becomes A Landmark For Residents And Visitors," *Oregonian*, July 23, 2002.

CHAPTER 13

Bridge the Gap

"Saaay, Barnard, how's it going? Anything new to report?" It's 1996, and I've stopped by the cubicle-land corner of Rob Barnard and Ron Kleinschmidt. I stop by every few days. I am a pain in the tush. I don't mean to be, I just don't know any better. During my wheel-and-pony show days, I had heard loud and clear that our bridges are residents' top priority. So I'm bugging everyone who has anything to do with them, and Rob and Ron are working on the Steel Bridge, on which pedestrians and cyclists share a substandard sidewalk. (Substandard is a polite way of saying "it sucks.")

Only the most skilled riders brave the three-foot-wide (1 m wide) cattle chute on the top deck of the Steel Bridge.

Their charge is to hang a bike/walk path off the Steel Bridge's lower deck, thereby connecting George's Eastbank Esplanade to downtown. It'll be like taking a bridge from your Thomas the Tank Engine train set and carefully fastening an extra piece on one side. Only problem: It's not our train set. The lower deck is owned by the Union Pacific Railway (UPRR), a large and powerful railway company headquartered in Omaha. About a train an hour crawls over this bridge to points north and south.

Top priority: Upgrade bridges and pinch points.

This sign is both a joke and an insult.

From my perspective as a young, inexperienced bicycle coordinator, the pace of progress on this project seems unbearably slow. Patience has never been my strong suit.

Barnard looks up in annoyance. "Mia, as I explained to you last week, and the week before, and the week before that, it's moving along." I'm not sure why I think bugging him is going to help. He hunches over his paper-piled desk, red hair beaming a warning I am not getting.

"Come on, there's got to be news. Has the Union Pacific gotten back to you?"

Spurred by department head Vic Rhodes, Portland is attempting to do something no one has done before: cantilever a public bikeway off a privately owned railroad bridge. And I somehow think this is a task involving a series of quick phone calls. My naïveté is shocking.[29]

"No, they haven't. And when they do, I promise you won't be the first to know. Look, I've got work to do. If I give you a piece of candy will you promise to stay away for a while?" He waves me away with a tight grin and a severe but friendly glare.

---

[29] The complexity of trying to place a trail on an active, privately owned railroad bridge is mind-boggling. I know this now, because for close to four years, I led, lived, and breathed the U.S. Department of Transportation's *Rails-with-Trails: Lessons Learned* study (FTA-MA-26-0052-04-1, August 2002), available online. Rails-with-trails (RWT) are located on or adjacent to active rail lines, as opposed to rails-to-trails that replace an abandoned rail line. Examples include the Schuylkill River Trail on Norfolk Southern Railroad Company property in Pennsylvania; Tony Knowles Coastal Rail Trail on Alaska Railroad Corporation land in Anchorage, Alaska; and Seattle Waterfront/Elliott Bay Trail on City of Seattle right-of-way adjacent to frequent Burlington Northern Santa Fe Railway passenger and freight trains. Chapter 27 has more rail-with-trail stories and information.

For months that stretch into years, Vic, Ron, and Rob try to court the railroad to no avail. No way are they going to allow a trail on their bridge. To do so will be to invite thousands onto their property. Already, indigents, drunks, and others up to no good walk across it all the time. What if a train derails? What if someone wanders from the trail onto the tracks? What if a passenger throws something at a person on the trail? The railroad will be held liable, or, at best, incur significant legal fees to be held harmless.

In our camp is Union Pacific's Tom Ogi, an ex-Portlander with a soft spot for his hometown. But it's not enough; he's getting nowhere fast. The door is closed. In the meantime, we add 100, then 200 miles (321 km) of bikeways to Portland's roads. George adds off-road segments. The Eastbank Esplanade opens, and thousands of cyclists daily reach the edge of the Steel Bridge and offer silent wishes for a safe way to get to the other side.

Then, tragedy strikes.

On a day like any other, a sailboat skipper calls the lift operator to raise the bridge. He radios to Omaha for permission, then pushes the button. Like usual, the span's joint-holding hinges separate. The midspan slowly starts to rise. No one takes notice, not even the man who is lying on the tracks, passed out, an empty bottle of vodka still touching his fingers. With no cameras to alert the lift operator, he is crushed as the lower deck telescopes into the upper deck.

Not long after, tragedy strikes again. Amtrak passengers watch in horror as they slowly—no more than 5 mph (8 km/h)—pass by a couple hanging by their necks from the rafters.

Done with the ongoing specter of humanity abusing their property, the Union Pacific declares that from now on, the bridge will be kept in the raised position and lowered once an hour for a train. Ron Kleinschmidt, on the verge of retirement, throws up his hands in frustration, and then turns the project over to Karen Rabiner.

Brainy and tenacious, Karen is one of but two female civil engineers in Portland's transportation department. Encouraged by Vic Rhodes, she and compatriot Teresa Boyle delve deep into the project's details, research Japanese negotiating techniques, and talk to the smartest people they know about forging win-win solutions. Homework complete, they hop onto a plane bound for Omaha.

Karen and Teresa walk in the room radiating confidence. Karen spots Tom Ogi's briefcase that suggests a Portland State University alumni connection and smiles. A new era of collaborative problem-solving is about to begin.

Understand though, that this project is fraught with complexity. A win-win solution will—must—offer benefits not just for the city, but for Union Pacific. To date, the bridge is kept in the raised position and lowered once an hour for a train. With the trail, it will have to be kept in the lower position and raised, far more frequently, at maritime request. Once again, the Union Pacific will be open to the kind of unpleasant activity that led to the current situation. Karen, though, is prepared: the city will pay for cameras, gates, monitoring, and the added cost of raising and lowering the lower deck. In other words, in exchange for the UP allowing the new trail, the city will ensure that never again will a human being be crushed.

This is the turning point. The doors of negotiation crack open.

A couple of years go by, during which time Karen and Teresa listen carefully and offer solid solutions to everything thrown at them. Technical obstacles. Security concerns. Operational issues. Construction challenges. Time and again, Tom takes their ideas up the long chain of bureaucratic command, until only one line of resistance remains, and it's a doozy: the lawyers. The city must assume all liability responsibility, no matter what happens. If a train derails and smashes into the trail, a passenger chucks a baseball at a cyclist's head, maintenance workers accidently leave equipment or a rail tie on the trail, or anyone at all—including railroad employees—gets injured for any reason, it'll be on the city's dime, not the railway's. This level of indemnification will be unprecedented in the United States. To date, railroads always bear some level of responsibility in the case of negligent, reckless, or wanton behavior on their part. Nope, say the lawyers. To this point, humans are not legally able to walk on or adjacent to the tracks. You want to invite humans to have a picnic on our private property, then you pay for it when they stub their toe, get attacked by bees, or trip and fall.

Of course, the city's legal team has to ponder this one. What are the odds of a derailment? How much of a risk is truly posed? Another year goes by as the lawyers weigh the risks against the benefits. Karen and company explain: The trains go awfully slow, thousands of daily cyclists and pedestrians will liven up the area, and security cameras will carefully monitor both the trail and tracks. Yeah, we get all that, say the attorneys, but check out this reality: Something will happen, eventually. No way to avoid it. The solution: insurance. The cost: $50,000 a year.

Karen goes to city council, hat in hand. What choice do they have? After all they've gone through, how can they let a measly $50,000 stop the project?

Agreements are inked. Construction documents are drawn up. It's time to build.

Like a heart transplant, the stakes are extremely high. When the donor is on the verge of death, his or her heart must be extracted, transported, and transplanted within hours. The operation itself must be flawless, or the recipient dies. In the case of the Steel Bridge, the allotted construction period granted by the Coast Guard is precisely forty-eight hours, during which no river traffic will be able to pass. Two days. One—and only one— way-too-brief window of opportunity.

Every single piece has to be built off-site and barged downriver. The Riverwalk will be attached to the south side of the bridge. Exactly the same amount of counterweight has to be attached to the north side or the bridge will be out of whack. Everything—the concrete sections, gates, railing—has to be weighed down to the microgram. Not only does the lower deck have to be perfectly in balance, the upper deck has to be tweaked to compensate for the added weight below.

There simply can be no errors whatsoever. Succeed, and millions of residents and visitors of current and future generations will be able to loop the river by foot or bike. Fail, and we'll be stuck with the lemon of today's too-narrow, inaccessible upper-deck sidewalk.

When Keren Holtz was killed on Marine Drive in 1997, her parents faced that kind of pressure. Told she was on life support, they had but a few hours to decide whether to donate their daughter's organs. Her heart, lungs, liver, and kidneys went to six terribly ill people, each operation per- fectly executed. Karen Rabiner, Teresa Boyle, and Rob Barnard are like the surgeons rushing to move Keren's organs to the bodies of the living. Hovering over them are the patient's parents, the Union Pacific's Tom Ogi, his colleagues, and, of course, a legion of lawyers.

No sleep is permitted. The first few hours zoom by in a minute.

The contractor's got this big cage filled with counterweights that he's going to attach to the north side. He weighs and re-weighs every bolt, but keeps coming up short some minuscule amount. He can't be off at all or the bridge will be off-kilter. Millions of dollars and nearly a decade's work are on the line. The contractor starts walking up the railroad tracks picking up pieces of old railroad ties, and weighs one. It's a bit too heavy, so he hacks off a bit and tries again. Trial and error, hours and hours of weighing and tweaking, gets him to the point where he's ready to push the button to lift the bridge.

Thousands of pedestrians and cyclists a day enjoy the Steel Bridge Riverwalk.

The countdown clock reads forty-four hours, four hours ahead of schedule, and not nearly long enough to fix the bridge if it jams.

The construction team, high as kites on adrenaline and caffeine, gathers. They cross their fingers, close their eyes in silent prayer, and hold their breath. Barnard gives the signal.

The lift rises slowly in one perfect, fluid motion. The cheers are so loud they can be heard all the way in Omaha.

SECTION III

The Devil's in the Details

Have you ever watched an airport tarmac? Planes are landing and taking off; luggage carts and maintenance vehicles, coming and going. Air traffic controllers guide planes to a safe landing, gate attendants check people in, crews clear the planes, and sophisticated computer systems manage passenger bookings. The airport—both inside and out—hums with life, and the vast majority of us arrive in one piece, mostly on time, reasonably content.

Imagine that the airport director decides that now, some people—a lot, actually—are going to fly in and out by hang glider. Why hang gliders? Because they're non-polluting, good exercise, relatively low-cost, and super-fun. Air traffic control now has to land these unfamiliar nonmotorized contraptions amid the jet planes. The tarmac's old striping doesn't work; space must be carved out for the gliders' ground movement. Maintenance vehicles and luggage carts have to service these flyers. Union rules and training and computer programs have to be revamped. Layers upon layers of systems must be tweaked.

All the humans involved are told: get with the program. But on a visceral level, they don't understand. They've all been transported by an airplane, but almost none have ever experienced the joy of gliding on the wind's currents. Now they have to learn a whole new system because a few visionaries—or troublemakers, depending on how you look at it—want to change things?

A community transportation system is a similarly complex, multi-layered organism of vehicles, systems, computers, and trained, round-the-clock workers. So when we announce that now, bicycles are a part of this complex mix, it's a safe bet that we'll find trouble just around the corner.

CHAPTER 14

Broken Glass

A typical schizophrenic Portland spring day, 1994: The sun is shining, temperature in the fifties, ominous storm clouds looming to the east. Showers or possibly hail are coming, and soon. Riding through a dense neighborhood of townhouses and apartments, I can see a rainbow in front of me, the lovely lingering mark of a storm just passed.

My mind wanders as I inhale the aroma of the exploding pink cherry blossoms. I've got a public meeting tonight...hopefully it will go all right. What should I wear? Maybe that cute black-and-white spaghetti-strap dress I got at the consignment store last week? Kind of chilly though...perhaps with tights...

Suddenly, I'm down. I get up off the blacktop and brush myself off. My front wheel is lodged in a trench. Three feet long and a few inches deep, it spans the entire right side of the road. I see no warning cones, plates, flashing lights, or signs.

"Gosh," I think, "I work for the Office of Transportation. It's my job to look after the public." I double back to my downtown cubicle to do my civic duty.

First, I try the main city information line. "Hi. I'm Mia Birk, City of Portland Bicycle Coordinator. I would like to report a hazard on Northwest Davis between Twenty-Fourth and Twenty-Third."

"Hmm, that's a tough one," observes the operator. "Why don't you try the maintenance bureau?"

Alrighty, I'll do that.

"Hi. I'm Mia Birk, City of Portland Bicycle Coordinator. I would like to report a hazard in the road on Northwest Davis in between Twenty-Fourth and Twenty-Third."

"Let me get this straight," says Violet, in a Cyndi Lauper "Girls Just Wanna Have Fun"–voice. "You're riding a bicycle? And your problem is?"

"My bike got caught in a trench. It's clearly a hazard that needs to be fixed."

"What do you mean by trench?"

"It's like a big pothole."

"Hmm.... Well, I don't know what to tell you."

"I was hoping you can tell me you can get it fixed, because it's dangerous and people are going to fall in it, just like I did."

"You could try calling Street Services. Let me give you that number."

"I'm confused. I thought I was talking to Street Services."

"Oh, no no no." She giggles merrily like Glinda the Good Witch. Apparently this is a common misunderstanding. "We're the Maintenance Bureau, not Street Services."

"I'm confused. What's the difference? Aren't you responsible for the upkeep of our roads?"

"Yes," she explains. "But someone cut the so-called trench, and therefore it's not a maintenance issue." What is this, Terry Gilliam's *Brazil*? Or Lily Tomlin's giddy *Laugh-In* phone operator? ("We don't care. We don't have to. We're the phone company.")

"Serenity now," I chant, before trying again. "Can you just tell me who can get the problem fixed?"

"Good question! Well, whoever cut the trench had to have a permit, didn't they? We don't issue permits. Street Services does."

For four hours, I talk to similarly polite and unhelpful people. Someone in Street Services finally concludes that there must be utility work going on, which, apparently, is beyond their jurisdiction.

Back at the site, I find a fallen sign; the phone number directs me to Northwest Natural Gas. On a cell phone, I speak to a gas company representative, Mary, who claims it must be a subcontractor, or possibly a subcontractor to the subcontractor. Sorry, nothing they can do, but I can contact the sub-subcontractor if I can figure out who it is.

As Mary wishes me good luck, a motorist approaches at a decent clip and gets jammed in the thing. He calls 911. Twenty minutes later, a crew arrives with barricades, warning signs, and metal plates. (Of course, metal plates are jarring and slippery, but better than a hole in the ground.)

For hours, I've been getting the runaround. Mr. BMW gets instant results. I stand to the side watching them cover the trench. Another storm hits, this one a mix of rain and fury. The drops slap me in the face, stinging with their callous indifference.

Bicycling is all about the small details. My D.C. years had taught me what shards of glass can do to a tire. Then, I patched tubes weekly. Here in Portland, not a day goes by without a cyclist bearing the brunt of the woeful state of things: tire-shredding broken bottles, wheel-grabbing drainage grates, jarring potholes, face-whipping branches.

We can put in bike lanes on every freakin' street in the city, but if they're full of obstacles, they're useless.

"Not our problem," sings merry Glinda.

I raise my face to the sky, eyes closed, rain pummeling my skin.

"I'll get you, my pretty, and your little dog too," I cackle. Sorry, Glinda. I'm going to make it your problem.

I strap a box of donuts to my rack and forge my way through the industrial area surrounding the city maintenance yard. The building is a concrete slab, a planet away from our downtown office towers. The backside is a little boy's fantasy: an enormous truck yard packed with front loaders, back loaders, front-and-back loaders, concrete mixers, asphalt spreaders, bucket trucks, tow trucks, cranes, forklifts, and street sweepers. They zoom around, trimming sign-blocking branches, replacing vandalized and stolen street-name signs, refreshing faded lane lines, laying out fresh crosswalk markings, pouring concrete sidewalks, and rebuilding cracked streets.

If it weren't for signal electricians monitoring and adjusting signal timing, we would all crash into each other. I think about the never-ending stream of maintenance issues at my one hundred-year-old house, and shudder at the complexity and volume of maintenance needs for our expanding, aging, transportation system.

Although it's past midnight, the yard is humming. No break for these workers. When the weather is at its grimmest, when the rest of us hunker down in our homes or offices, they are out in the elements, working even harder to keep us safe.

Figuring that gaining a better understanding of the maintenance side of things would be wise, I'm heading out with one of the night sweepers, Jim. I smile and hand him a latte, then climb up a stepladder into the cab of a Zamboni on steroids.

We head toward downtown and turn onto the Burnside Bridge. Just about every day, someone complains about glass in these bike lanes. Jim flips a switch that activates the giant circular brushes. It feels like a dentist is polishing the ground under our feet. He shifts the truck to the right so we can sweep against the curb. When we reach the other side, we get out and walk back up.

Tiny shards of glass twinkle in the night sky. The bike lane is still a mess.

"Would you look at that," Jim exclaims. He climbs back in, cracks his knuckles and starts pushing buttons and flipping switches, murmuring to himself. Ten minutes later, we make a U-turn in the middle of the bridge. (Kids, do not try this at home.) Another pass, and voilá, the bike lane is clean.

"So, Jim," I ask. "What would it take for you to sweep this puppy more frequently?"

"How often?"

"How about every night?"

"See, it's not hard to fix," explains Fred Burckhardt in a fatherly way reminiscent of *Happy Days's* Tom Bosley. We're out at Southeast Twenty-Eighth, where a few days earlier a bike messenger named Nicoli crashed, then found his way to my cubicle, bloody and spitting mad, simultaneously crying and apologizing. I located a few Band-Aids and promised to see what I could do. The gap between the slats of a drainage grate had caught his wheel, chucking him over his handlebars.

Fred pulls out a stack of two-foot-long metal slats and welding equipment. "I just lay these on top of the old ones, you know, like a tic-tac-toe board? 'Course, they don't make 'em like this anymore."

"How many of these old grates are out here?"

"Dunno. Hundreds, I imagine."

"What would it take to get you to fix all of them?"

I park myself in the mad scientist lab of John Bustraan, a graying signal engineer about my size. "How come the signal at Ladd and Division won't turn green for me?"

"You're not tripping the loop." He smiles faintly, eyes on a bank of monitors showing traffic in various locations around the city.

"OK, John, I'll bite. Is this something I can do without ingesting anything illegal?"

Now he looks at me. Not amused. He ushers me out the door. "About half the signals are activated. Meaning, you have to push a button or drive over a loop detector, which is a magnetic coil of wire buried under the pavement."

We jam my bike in the back of his van between traffic signals, lenses, spools of heavy-gauge wire, tools, control boxes, and switches. He continues the Signals 101 lecture. "When you trip the loop, it sends a message to the signal control box."

"Oh, I get it. A bicycle is too light?"

"No, it's the metal in a vehicle that trips the magnetic loop, not the weight. If the bike is made of metal, it's detectable. Let's go experiment."

We mark the signal-tripping sweet spot, but still, few cyclists understand it. When I see a cyclist standing on the side waiting for the green that is not going to come, I demonstrate what to do. Without fail, they are grateful. Knowledge is power.

The problem was that I was staying to the right, and therefore missing the loop completely.

"Perfect," I think. "The law says bicyclists have to stay to the right, but if I do, I can't make the light turn green." Even after I place my bike on the loop, the signal doesn't trip.

Carefully, he increases the signal sensitivity, but not to 11, where it might pick up the cars in adjacent or opposing lanes. I bike up, wait in the sweet spot, and the light turns green.

"Cool, John! Thanks! Can you do this again?"

"Where?" he asks.

"Everywhere."

$100,000. For some reason, I fixate on this number. I need money, that's for sure, because the maintenance guys are willing to play ball if I show them the moolah. $100,000: nice and round, impressive enough to command respect, small enough to be a drop in the bucket.

"$100,000," I suggest to Doug, Lewis, Roger, and Jeff at the Lucky Lab. "Roughly 1/1000th of our maintenance budget. With that, we can tweak hundreds of grates and signals, sweep a thousand street miles, fill in every aggravating pothole or trench that's ever eaten our freakin' tires. Is it too much to ask?"

"Dream on, baby," says Lewis. He hands me a beer, pats me on the back sympathetically, and goes back to flinging darts at the wall.

"$100,000. Please?" I hound Rob, beg his boss, Goran, and spin elaborate fantasies of hacking into the computer system, like Richard Pryor in *Superman III*, to redirect just a fraction of every penny to bikeway maintenance.

$100,000. The number obsesses me, haunts my every waking moment.

"Will you marry me?" asks my boyfriend, after a grueling six-hour ride to Bear Camp Summit near the Oregon Coast.

"$100,000," I reply.[30]

I can't wait anymore. Summer is approaching. Cyclists are packing away their raingear and heading to the Bike Gallery for tune-ups. I am on the phone constantly, fielding complaints, or riding around town, cataloging problems. Surreptitiously, I create, copy, and deliver five hundred copies of a complaint card to local bike shops. Similarly, Fred Burckhardt decides he's

---

30 Actually, I said yes, then crashed and broke my collarbone.

not going to have anymore Nicolis on his watch. Before I can say "criss-cross applesauce," he fixes all the offending drainage grates. Good man.

We set up a new automated hotline and I spend hours each day sweet-talking my new pals into sweeping streets, patching holes, trimming trees. More often than not, they head out within days, even hours, and fix the problem.

Every pothole filled and pile of broken glass swept to oblivion fills me with satisfaction.

"Kate just crashed! On a pothole!" I recognize the voice of my friend Kurt on the hotline. His wife has wiped out on a steep incline coming down from the Oregon Zoo. By the time I visit the site, the hole has been filled.

Kurt sends a note of gratitude to city council.

Rob walks into my cubicle and slams an inch-thick, spiral-bound report on my desk, sending my papers flying.

I look up, bemused. "Hello to you too, buddy. What did I do this time?"

He flips to page 27. There, buried deep in a long list of project names and numbers, it reads, "Bikeway Spot Improvement Program, $100,000."

After a year of tracking sweeping requests, I sit down with Dick God-frey, Jim's boss. Dick ponders the map of trouble spots I lay in front of him. He pats his blond swoop of hair. For just a second, I see him as Dallas Cowboys coach Jimmy Johnson.

He traces a finger on a big fat red line across the Burnside Bridge, where problems are reported almost daily.

"Actually," he observes, "we go over Burnside almost every night, since we sweep downtown streets six out of seven. I guess we can just sweep her while we're going over or out."

"Helloooo...How come no one told me this before?" I ask, indignant.

Dick chuckles, then uncaps a yellow marker and starts rerouting the sweeping trucks to hit the bike lanes more regularly. 🔑

"Now Dick," I suggest, after giving him a maple bar and a two-minute respite. "Can we talk about those nasty metal plates?"[31]

🔑 **Institutionalize care of bikeways into daily maintenance practices.**

---

[31] Later, we change the construction code to require a smooth asphalt lip and nonslick surface.

CHAPTER 15

All Aboard!

More than a million residents and visitors annually experience Portland's inner industrial area and eastside farmland and suburbs as they pedal or walk the Springwater Corridor.

On a warm spring day, I am pedaling along one of George's masterpieces, the Springwater Corridor, a 16-mile (25 km) abandoned rail line-turned-trail from inner east Portland to the town of Boring. (Yes, this does make David Letterman's Top 10 Most Embarrassing Town Names list.)

"Would you look at that!" My companion, transit agency (TriMet) general manager Tom Walsh, wolf-whistles at Mount Hood shimmering majestically in the distance. This ride isn't a chance operation. I have an ulterior motive: get Tom to agree to improve TriMet's bicycle-unfriendly policies and practices.

At a charity auction for an environmental group a few weeks earlier, I purchased an afternoon with Tom for fifty bucks. It sure seemed a small price to pay for a one-on-one audience with the guy leading the mass transit revolution. If I can just get him to see that we're on the same team. Truly, we should be best pals.

A few weeks earlier, TriMet staff had invited me to celebrate their new low-floor train cars' bicycle provisions. We drank sparkling cider and ate cookies and oohed and aahed at the new cars. No longer would a person in a wheelchair have to wait for a lift to unfold. No longer would cyclists have to haul their bikes up the stairs. The cars are spacious and filled with natural light. Nifty new bicycle stickers proclaimed a dawning new era.

Rick Gearhart, TriMet's burly, teddy-bear staffer, demonstrated. He walked a bike onto the train, turned its handlebars toward the left, shimmied it 180 degrees, and leaned it up against the wall separating the seats from the standing area. Alert woman that I am, I observed a teeny problem: The bike was blocking access to the aisle. Everyone else chatted and smiled. I gazed into my sparkling cider, which now looked less like champagne and more like spiked punch, and wondered, what are we celebrating?

"Excuse me," I interjected. "I hate to be a party pooper, but I'm confused. Cyclists are allowed to inconvenience other passengers? What about that area there?" I pointed to a big empty space in the middle of the car.

Disabilities consultant Bob Pike wheeled to the area and explained, "This is the wheelchair area."

"I get that, Bob," I responded. "But when it's not in use, why can't bicyclists stand there with their bikes? Other passengers are allowed to sit or stand there in this area. When a disabled person comes, the bicyclist will move out of the way, same as everyone else."

"Well, what if the bicyclist won't move out of the way? Then what?"

It felt like someone had just told a joke and I was the clueless one who didn't get the punch line. Why were bicyclists being treated like a special class of bozos? Why would a person, by virtue of his or her use of a bicycle, be any more or less discourteous to a disabled person than anyone else?

Transit–bike integration is a basic component of any and all great bicycling cities, extending the reach of both transit and bicycling. When we get a flat, need help up a steep hill, or want to bail out in miserable weather, trains and buses are our ally. Every Japanese and European transit system welcomes bicyclists with excellent bike parking, hooks inside cars, even extra bicycle-specific space. Even the transit systems in Washington, D.C., and the San Francisco Bay Area welcome bicyclists.[32] 0—x

---

0—x   Fully integrate bicycling with your transit system.

---

[32] For more information, see *Integration of Bicycles and Transit: A Synthesis of Transit Practice*, Transit Cooperative Research Program (TCRP) Synthesis 62, Transportation Research Board, 2005 and *Caltrans Pedestrian and Bicycle Facilities Technical Reference Guide: A Technical Reference and Technology Transfer Synthesis*, California Department of Transportation, 2005.

TriMet recently added racks on the fronts of buses and allows nominal bicycle access to light-rail. However, most of the stations lack sufficient bike parking. Bicyclists are allowed to board only during nonpeak hours, and are welcome only after visiting a licensed training center, watching a video, paying a small fee, and obtaining a permit. And this appeared to be the best they could come up with for their new transit cars.

It was time to bump it up a notch.

Tom and I pedal along, chatting about the evolution of the Springwater Corridor. He reminds me of Ron Howard with his jeans and freckled, reddish complexion. We stop at a traffic signal at a busy five-lane highway.

"Check this out. Pedestrians push this button, but cyclists activate the signal by cycling over this spot." I point to one of John Bustraan's loop detector diamonds etched in the trail.

"And if you're on horseback, you push that button up there." It's up six feet (almost 2 m) high on the pole, the first equestrian-height signal in the country.

"Let me tell you, it was a bear to get this approved." We walk our bikes across one leg of traffic to the landscaped median island that breaks up the lengthy crossing distance.

"We asked the highway department for permission to put in a signal," I explain. "First response: no. Not enough bike/walk traffic. Can't justify disrupting motorists."[33] It was a classic catch-22: no trail exists, ergo zero bike/walk traffic.

We start pedaling again, until we are slowed by a gaggle of little kids. Tom calls out "on your left," causing about half the kids to veer toward the left. He tries again. "Other left!"

I ding my bell until they make enough space for us to zip by. One kid gets confused and loses control. I pick him up, brush him off, and hand him to his grandma.

"Yeah, Tom, little kids don't know right from left. Anyway, Rob and Doug showed the highway guys that the Burke–Gilman Trail in Seattle has really high usage, which we'll achieve, but only if we make it possible to cross. But even those numbers weren't high enough to "warrant"

---

33 At the time, the *Manual on Uniform Traffic Control Devices* stated that the threshold to "warrant" a traffic signal was 190 cyclists or pedestrians in one hour. Whether at a school, along a trail, to reach a park, or in a business district, this number was virtually impossible to meet. In other words, to "warrant" disrupting motor vehicle traffic, you need to see a ton of cyclists and pedestrians, which, of course, you don't because it's so unpleasant to cross. The 2009 Manual takes a step in the right direction by valuing delay to the pedestrian or cyclist over volume.

disrupting auto traffic per the Manual's standards. So then Rob Burchfield—you know him, right?" Tom nods.

"Rob came up with a brilliant idea: He declared the Springwater Corridor a local road."

"I don't get it."

"See, it's easier to get approval for a signal to help motorists cross a major road than a signal to help pedestrians or cyclists. So Rob decided that the Springwater Corridor is really a road, albeit one for nonmotorized traffic only. After some major armwrestling, he prevailed."

Tom shakes his head. "I had no idea. I wish traffic engineers could all be as enlightened as Rob." I nod and take a deep breath. The moment has come.

"Tom, in that same vein, I've got a bone to pick with you." My tone is warm, but firm.

"I just saw how TriMet is planning to accommodate bicyclists on the new light-rail line. Frankly, it's not good enough. You're doing such an amazing job expanding transit in this region. Finding ways to integrate bicycling with transit is a win-win solution for both modes."

"Mia, you know as well as I do that we have liability concerns about bicyclists using transit. And the trains are already crowded."

Certainly, concerns about space are legitimate. A bicycle is typically six feet (almost 2 m) long. A number of us had suggested bike-hanging hooks, but had been rejected.

We continue pedaling. It's a flat grade, and Tom seems relaxed and barely winded. We pass an area recently upgraded with native plants by a Boy Scout troop, and a farmhouse where the owner, who once sued the city to prevent the trail, provides a watering station for horses and dogs.

"Tom, the new low-floor cars have plenty of room. It's time to evolve. A person with a bicycle is simply a passenger."

We sit on a bench by a pond of singing frogs. I down some water and nuts, then launch into a story.

For a long time, the City of Montreal excluded bicyclists from its subway system. One day, the late, great bicycle advocate Tooker Gomberg gathered a few friends. One pushed her adorable twin boys in a five-foot-long baby stroller. Another brought his cello. It's about six feet (almost 2 m) tall. The third guy carried a load of rebar, six feet long.

One by one, they each got on, no problem. Finally, Tooker tried to walk on with his bicycle. He was denied access.

With Tooker was a friend from the local newspaper. An immediate public outcry followed the story, and the transit agency soon reversed the bicycle-exclusion policy.

Tom looks down at his hands, pondering. "You make a good point. Do me a favor, put it in writing. I'll see what I can do."

Put it in writing, eh? I know this trick—use it all the time when a cranky citizen calls to yell at me. Just yesterday a cyclist gave me an earful about people who park their cars the wrong way on his street. Apparently someone pulling out from the curb almost hit him, and he wanted me to get the police to enforce wrong-way parking. I explained that I don't personally have the authority to force the police to do anything, nor was I able to bump this concern to the top of my priority list. But if he wished, he could write a letter. He hurled nastiness on me and hung up. It looks like Tom is giving me the same brush-off.

Later, TriMet adds bike-hanging hooks to each transit car and better bike parking at stations. As of 2010, about 4 percent of transit passengers access trains by bike.

We bike back to Portland, chatting about life and politics, all the while my brain racing. You bet I'll write you a letter, you bet.

In the months prior, I had forged a coalition of government officials working to better bicycling conditions beyond the city limits. Truth be told, for quite a while, it was just me and a county official, shooting the breeze over beers and darts at the Lucky Lab every month, but eventually it grew to include a bunch of like-minded transportation dorks.[34]

---

34 The Portland region is comprised of twenty-seven cities, three counties, Metro (the regional government), the Oregon Department of Transportation, and TriMet.

In a collective mind-meld of regional unity, we send a letter to Tom respectfully submitting that people with bicycles are no less polite than any other transit user. How about a test? Let's see what happens if we allow bicyclists on trains at all hours and in all parts of the cars.

After three months, the results are in: Cyclists are cool. TriMet eliminates all restrictions. This time, the champagne tastes as sweet as honey.

Forget bonding on the golf course, and to heck with the three-martini lunch. The new paradigm for deal-making is a 10-mile (16 km) bike ride on a path of our dreams. **O—ㅛ**

O—ㅛ   **Build relationships with local leaders and take them on rides to see the good and bad and to envision future possibilities.**

CHAPTER 16

The Straw That Broke
the Camel's Back

Deeper and deeper we go into the reform of our transportation system. Claiming small amounts of roadway space, adapting European safety techniques to our American streets, keeping bike lanes glass-free, eliminating unnecessary transit restrictions...we're making progress, that's for sure. The people behind the scenes are evolving too, with the eyes of traffic engineers, maintenance personnel, and transportation leaders opening wider each day. **⊙━ㅜ**

But we're missing something fundamental: There's almost nowhere to park, not at our schools, light-rail stations, or office buildings. At apartments, you better haul your bike inside. Better yet, drive. Don't even think about going out for a meal by bike, or stopping at the bakery or grocery store. You're not welcome if you're not in a car.

We're trying our best to remedy this with a smidgen of funding gleaned from renting bicycle lockers (metal boxes, located mostly in garages). This funding allows us to install a hundred or so bike racks a year on the sidewalks in front of businesses. Helpful, to be sure, but it's not doing a thing for workers, students, or other folks who need a higher level of security since their bikes will be left for longer periods of time. At this pace, I'll be lucky if we're done before my kids' great-great-great-grandkids get to college.

The bicycle friendly cities of Japan and Europe welcome thousands of bikes at transit stations and in central cities. Of course they do, 'cuz it's a great deal: you can store some ten to twenty bicycles in each and every auto parking space. Structured auto-parking costs $20,000 per space. A decent bike rack for eight to twelve bikes costs less than a thousand bucks. I'm no mathematician, but it sure adds up in my mind.

⊙━ㅜ **Retrain officials throughout every facet of government to understand the needs of people on bikes.**

Bike parking is a tiny line item for any new or reconstructing building. It's not hard to do, nor expensive, but it does require a solid set of standards so that the right rack is located in the right place. Every dollar counts, though, and building owners count every dime.

⊗ ⊗ ⊗ ⊗ ⊗

"When is this silliness going to stop?" asks Susan McLeod, representing the Building Owners and Managers Association (BOMA). "What's next? Are you going to require us to put in ski racks or toy chests, too?"

The woeful state of bike parking

She taps her bright red fake fingernails on the table in exasperation and adds, "We have hundreds of biker parking spaces in our garages." Her bleached, starched hair stands three inches (almost 8 cm) high at its peak and cascades like a fountain to her ruffled Victorian shirt collar.

I've told her several times that we prefer to use "cyclist" or "bicyclist," because "biker" is the term normally used for motorcycle riders. Her whining pronunciation—drawing out the i, emphasizing the k—makes the word sound derogatory.

"Only fourteen *bikers* used them all week. We'll be happy to put in more *biker* parking, as soon as these racks fill up."

I sigh. "Susan, please, look at these pictures. How can a cyclist even find this rack on the third floor behind the dumpster? Look at this one. See that broken wheel and frame? It's because the rack is so crummy thieves cannibalized the bike. And this one: cyclists need to lift their bikes over parked cars to reach it. This other one is so close to the wall you can't park at all."

No wonder the demand is so low. Besides the crummy quality and location, the quantity she claims is nowhere close to reality. Wave-shaped racks purported to fit eight bikes can actually only accommodate three.

"I agree with Susan," chimes Carl Hansen, representing our public school system. Carl is a ruddy, stocky fellow, and a generally nice man—when he isn't fighting me.

He insists, "Kids don't bike to school. Not allowed! Not OK!"

"Is that your official school district policy?" I want to know.

"I'm the facilities manager! It's my job!! If I put in bike racks, kids'll destroy 'em!"

Susan nods in support.

I plead my case. "Carl, Susan, look. Of course people aren't leaving their nice bikes locked to a crummy rack they can't even find. If you want people to bike to your buildings, you've got to encourage them with a decent place to park."

Carl and Susan are unmoved.

If not locked, bikes tend to disappear, fast. Colin Frost leaned his bike up against the window of a convenience store and dashed in for a soda. Two minutes later, it was gone. Running late, Shannon hastily locked her front wheel to a pole in front of her office. Six hours later, she found her wheel, still locked to the pole, the rest of her mount long gone. Lawyer Mark Ginsburg had his high-end racing bike lifted from his car's hatchback. A Lycra-clad thief walked into a museum show on the history of bicycling in Oregon, hoisted a $2,000 super-light iridescent Klein onto his shoulder and walked out like he owned it. The guard didn't even notice.

The bike of a newspaper reporter was stolen by clever middle-of-the-night thieves, who removed the bolts securing the bike rack to the sidewalk. The victim was so incensed that he wrote an article insisting the city remove all bike racks until we could "guarantee" security. (Follow his logic, and we also need to remove all on-street car parking until the time in our fantastic future when we can guarantee cars will never be vandalized

Crummy bike parking is not our friend.

or stolen.) Sad fact: Leaving your bike locked to an unmonitored pole, rack, or tree outside all night long will "guarantee" theft. My maintenance bureau buddies responded, though, by welding the bolts to the racks and switching to a combination of nonsimilar bolts, forcing thieves to carry many tools. It seems to have worked; I don't believe any bikes have been stolen in quite that manner since.

It took a thief approximately thirty seconds to break my Kryptonite lock, in broad daylight, with so-called security officers nearby. Thankfully, bike locks have gotten more theft-resistant since then.

Bike theft is a part of life, and there's no way to guarantee security. But we do know a lot about how to minimize the damage.

In this era, the early 1990s, building owners are coming to grips with the cost of new earthquake-protection requirements. A simple tenant remodel can trigger an entire building to be reinforced from the ground up, costing tens, even hundreds of thousands of dollars. Adding to that, the new Americans with Disabilities Act mandates buildings and public spaces provide equal access for all. This means larger bathrooms, wider hallways, bigger elevators, and ramps at no more than 5 percent grade. Again, additional costs can add five or six figures to a tight budget.

Then, as part of an effort to make walking more pleasant, the city developed new requirements for landscaping and sidewalks in parking lots. A project worth more than $10,000 in remodeling, internal or external, triggers this. Even a bathroom remodel can easily cost $10,000. Just asking for a change in occupancy, going from an office to a restaurant, for example, means you're on the hook for parking lot landscaping.

Then I come along and tell building owners that the city wants them to pay for parking for bicycles, which they equate with children's toys. It's the straw that breaks the camel's back. They aren't going to take this one lying down.

We meet monthly: Susan, Carl, bike advocates, folks from other business groups, and I, plowing through issue after issue. Most aren't that big a deal. You need a certain amount of space for each bike, and the rack can't be too close to the wall, for example. You need to be able to secure the frame and a wheel, not just the wheel. (Old-style "wheelbender" racks damage bikes and invite theft.) Near the front door is the preferred location, for short-term bike parking. If it were all this easy, we probably wouldn't have gotten into the battles we did.

Think about a place you love to walk, some little street where you like to window-shop, stop in for ice cream, or take a break on a bench. These storefronts are usually right next to the sidewalk, not located behind a sea of parking. Should the bike parking be crammed onto the sidewalk? If not, where should it go?[35]

If staff or residents can bring their bikes into the building and store them in their offices or apartments, does that qualify as long-term bike parking? How would the city regulate that?[36]

Susan insists that the requirements should be based solely on demand. In other words, businesses would only have to upgrade if their racks, no matter how shoddy, isolated, or inadequate, overflow with bikes. We push back: Demand is low *because* of rack quality and placement.

But we work through it all, rather collegially, or so I think, and by spring 1996, we've forged a series of compromises. I head to Europe for my research fellowship, confident that we're in good shape.

Am I delusional? Naïve (again)? Thoroughly out of touch?

One thing for sure: I am wrong.

Two months later, I return refreshed, exuberant, and totally inspired by all I've seen in eighteen bicycle friendly cities. Thousands of bike racks at train stations, sophisticated bike parking garages, racks on every sidewalk...the complaints of local building owners over the cost and hassle of racks seem ridiculously petty. I am ready to rock and roll.

I stop by Rob's office.

"We ran into a little problem while you were gone," he says in a dour voice I know from experience to mean serious trouble. His cheekbones protrude over his gaunt grimace. "The planning commission was a little concerned about how they would execute and enforce the code."

"What do you mean?" I'm getting big-time nervous.

"Well...see, it's kinda complicated down in the permit center. They weren't sure who would check the plans for bike parking. They might even have to hire more staff. You know how strapped for money they are." He's making no sense, and doesn't look at me.

"Rob, what are you saying?!" My voice has lost all its holiday serenity.

"Well...the planning director decided it would be best to make the code, you know...voluntary. That way we could post guidelines and let businesses check their own plans, and then..."

---

35 A decade later, the city began trading off on-street auto parking spaces for bike racks.

36 It really can't, so we require building owners to provide bike parking in their garage, courtyard, parking lot, or plaza.

I cut him off. "Voluntary?? Meaning: not required. Meaning: not a code at all. How is voluntary enforceable? Nobody's voluntarily putting in bike parking now. Why would they do that? AAARGH."

The information sinks in like a pulled muscle that begins to torture you the day after a tough tennis match or long ride. You wake up sore, and discover that walking, even just moving, hurts. Years of work down the drain. There's no way to sugarcoat it. No matter how you dress it up, no matter how much lipstick you put on it, it is still a nasty, unenforceable, useless pig of a sham of a farce of a "code."

"I am so sorry," I inform the advocates in a series of phone calls. "The bike parking code has been shifted to a 'voluntary' set of guidelines."

Architect Rick Browning is so angry he drops out of the process. "Mia, I've been working on this, on my own time, for more than five years. Frankly, I've got better things to do than go in circles." Who can blame him?

The planning commission is an appointed body that reviews and recommends changes to city code and policy. In front of each of the volunteer commissioners—people from the business, planning, and architecture worlds—is a huge binder packed with hundreds of pages related to whatever they're being asked to consider. It's the very first time most of them have ever heard of bike parking.

Chairwoman Joan Scott opens the meeting with a tap of the gavel from the table in front and approval of last week's minutes. Turning to the agenda, she whines, "We seem to be doing an awful lot for these *bikers* already. What does this have to do with transportation?"

"We stand by to encourage our members to add more *biker* parking if needed," testifies Susan, in perfect rhythm to the tapping of her fingernails. "Anyway, we do not need additional *biker* parking at this time." She passes out copies of their so-called survey.

"Bike parking is expensive and hard to maintain," states school district rep Carl. He contends, "It's simply not in our mission."

"Rob," I growl from the peanut gallery. "You better hold me back or I'm going to rip out his throat." I am not invited to respond.

The planning commission approves the voluntary "code" by near-unanimous consent.

Clockwise from upper left: two-tiered indoor bike parking, on-street bike corrals, racks in garages and on sidewalks. These all meet cyclists' needs.

I start to need some counseling, badly. Sleep only comes in angry fits. In a beautiful camping spot by the foot of Mount Adams, I toss and turn for hours, pulsing with fury, reliving Susan's clicking fingernails. My mind churns, and then hits upon a new outlet for my anger: the planning bureau.

Come Monday, I barrel into the office of planning director David Knowles and demand, "How could you betray us like that?"

He looks up, sharp-eyed, black crest of hawk-hair standing up in bewilderment. "Huh? Who are you? Oh, right, you're the bike person. Here's the deal. We don't have the capacity to check the bike parking plans for every building permit. You want to get us more funding, be my guest."

"Capacity, schamacity. Apparently, I have more faith in your staff than you do." I am totally out of line. "You didn't even let them find a solution for this not-at-all insurmountable problem! You destroyed years of hard work. Look at these gray hairs! I'm only twenty-eight years old! Just look at them!"

For this tirade, I earn a trip to city councilman Charlie Hales' office. It's my first meeting with him. I expect the worst. Charlie's passions lie in developing streetcar lines, new urban development projects, and an aerial tram. Bicycle transportation is low on his list, as far as I know. I'm not sure he's ever been on a bike.

I miss Earl.

We must have sounded like a couple of fighting kids: me ranting, David defending.

Charlie listens calmly. A no-nonsense guy, he leans forward and smacks the table. "Let me get this straight. The school district has $120 million in bond money and they're fighting bike parking?"

As if putting an exclamation point on the absurdity of the opposition, he orders, "Double whatever you've proposed."

Lifeline thrown, I start to smile. Why did I assume that his background in development necessitated a contrary stance?

Charlie continues, "I'll call Jack. I guarantee he won't give you any more trouble." Apparently he has a history with Jack, the school district superintendent.

"Now," Charlie points a finger at David and me. "You two: work it out. Come back to me with a package I can support."

His push is exactly what we need. After that, the dominoes fall quickly. David works out a cost-effective solution to their issues. A number of downtown business owners pledge to install racks "voluntarily" to prove the merits of the concept. We cut deals with the other groups and quickly pull together a winning—although not perfect—package. A month later, the city council overrides the planning commission and adopts a code with teeth.[37] ⭕━🔑

Certainly, it's not everything we wanted, but it's a baby step—the very hardest step to take—in the right direction.

⭕━🔑 **Integrate requirements and incentives for bike parking, showers, and lockers into building codes.**

---

[37] For more information about bicycle parking, see *Bicycle Parking Guidelines*, published by the Association of Pedestrian and Bicycle Professionals (www.apbp.org), 2010.

CHAPTER 17

Be the Bike

"You're not going to believe this," comments Jeff Smith from his side of our shared cubicle wall.

"Believe what?"

"There's no bike parking shown on these plans at all."

One of Jeff's responsibilities is reviewing building plans to determine compliance with the hard-fought code. This isn't just any building's blueprints he's got rolled out on his desk, though. It's our beloved, historic city hall, a four-story neo-Renaissance structure undergoing a $29 million interior seismic and safety upgrade. Somehow, the renovation team neglected to include a single bike rack in the building redesign, despite the new code requirements, despite the Bike Master Plan, despite the clear city commitment to bicycle transportation. Someone apparently forgot to get the message over to the Bureau of General Services.

Jeff and I head downstairs to take a look at the adjacent building. Two sides are built right up to the sidewalks. The east entrance is through a double colonnade supporting the upper two floors of the central wing that encloses the council chamber. The portico is surrounded by a half-block's worth of stone courtyard. The west features a rectangular porte cochere, a driveway outlined by red granite columns, and six car-parking spaces.

We stand in the empty courtyard scratching our heads.

"Frank says there's no room," explains Jeff. "Also that bike parking is ugly and doesn't mesh with the historic character of city hall."

What, is he trying to push my buttons? Bike parking, ugly? No room? Not historic? What could be more historic for a building built in 1895, right smack in the heyday of the League of American Wheelmen? Portland's own history of that era is rich with bicycle enthusiasts.

I take the elevator to the sixth floor and locate Frank's office, which has an actual door, indicating a relatively high level of authority. With no compunction, I stick my head in. "Hi, Frank. Really nice to see you. How're the kids?"

The photo on his desk reveals three smiling kids and wife in white shirts, encircling him in front of a fireplace. His size and build smack of a former high school linebacker gone soft.

"Super, Mia. What can I do for you?"

"I'm confused. For the last few years, I've been tearing my hair out to adopt this new building code that requires bike racks. So it seems there's been an oversight in your city hall plans."

I hand him a marked-up blueprint indicating a number of options for bike rack placement.

He nervously pats his crew cut. "Yes, well, we need to preserve that space for events."

"Oh I see, events...How many of those do we have, anyway, like two a year? Alrighty then, how about over here? Let's see, since city hall was built in the pre-automobile era, and since city policy says to reduce driving and increase bicycling, and I know for a fact that Mayor Katz hardly ever drives and at least two Commissioners bike on a semiregular basis, why don't we put a bike rack right smack in one of those car spaces? Whaddya think? Love it?"

He pushes his glasses back up his nose and shoos me out of his office.

I feel like a hypocrite. It reminds me of my days traveling around Asia proselytizing about transportation energy-efficiency while we Americans are the most gas-guzzling hogs on the planet. Here we are forcing private buildings by hook or by crook to put in bike parking, and the city—my own employer—won't put in a single bike rack?

It turns out that it's not enough to adopt a bicycle plan, building code, or maintenance practices. We've got to retrain all the humans involved, both inside and outside the government. Otherwise, all we've got is words on paper. From the very second a building owner or developer decides to invest money, bike parking needs to be part of the deal. Architects need to know what the requirements are. Booklets detailing rack types and placement are not doing the trick.

Will the employee in charge of reviewing the permit applications know to check for bike parking? Will he or she know good from bad? Will the placement of the bike rack on the third floor of the parking garage behind the dumpsters be flagged as a problem? What if the plans show decent-enough bike parking but the building inspector couldn't care less if the racks actually go in?

With deep chagrin, I realize that city hall is merely a harbinger. The hard-fought code rewrite was only baby-step one. The real work—reprogramming

Bike racks can indeed be beautiful. Cyclists can chain their bikes to leaves of steel inspired by plants growing along a bike trail in Austin, Texas; a fish in Beaverton, Oregon; and a dollar sign on New York City's Wall Street.

everyone involved in every step of building planning, design, construction, and remodeling—is yet to come.

⚙⚙⚙⚙⚙

"Friends, we are gathered today to discuss the science and art of bike parking."

I've donned a short flouncy brown skirt and cropped pinstriped suit jacket to reinforce the message that this is both a serious training and an opportunity to have some fun at this first-ever bike parking class.

Thanks to the American Institute of Architects, which agreed to bestow continuing education credits upon participants, we've got about sixty attendees: young architects, advocates, planners, even an engineer or two. The science part is simple enough: A series of slides to accompany the booklet, a list of acceptable racks and manufacturers, and code specifics (one space per every 3,000 square feet (914 sq m) of office space, two spaces per elementary school classroom, etc.).

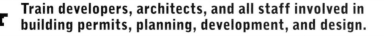

Train developers, architects, and all staff involved in building permits, planning, development, and design.

Eventually, the powers that be commissioned these covered racks. I'm not sure they're terribly historic-looking, but it works for me—and for the city council, pictured above.

It's time for our challenge: design bike parking that meets both the letter and spirit of the code. The subject of our little creative assignment: city hall.

In less than an hour, we've got a dozen ideas. We can make the bike racks look like a series of horse-hitching posts, or a structure that mimics city hall. We can blend them into the landscaping, tuck them under the portico, and emulate the Doric columns, rusticated stone facing, or segmental flat stone arches.

We can send the message that bikes matter, that the new code has teeth, and that we're on the right track. Because bike parking speaks to all that is good about sustainable communities. Or, we—folks like Frank—can continue to fight against the changing tide, until we sink.

The choice—no matter who we are or how we get around, whether we play a role behind the scenes or simply travel through the system in our daily lives—is ours: Be part of the problem or part of the solution.

Plant Seeds and a Garden Will Grow

Once you build it, people will come. This, we know.

But if we build it and then encourage people to use it in ways that are meaningful to their lives, they will come in flocks, droves, maybe even stampedes.

This, we learn.

CHAPTER 18

Slugfest

On your mark. Get set. Go! It's the 1996 bike–bus–car race...and the contestants are off! Revving the engine of a red Mazda Miata in the parking lot of Perry's Restaurant on Northeast Fremont is locally renowned drag queen/cabaret entertainer Darcelle, dressed to the nines in a green sequined full-length gown and jacket. Her neck and ears glitter like chandeliers.

"They're my 'summer' diamonds," she announces. "Some'r diamonds, some'r not." Her blond wig is big enough to get her welcomed in Texas, where the saying goes, "the bigger the hair, the closer to God."

Last year, revered race car driver Monte Shelton, widely hailed as the fastest man in the Northwest, cheated. When not racing his beloved Porsches, he owns a Jaguar dealership downtown. He could have shown up that morning with an XKE or a Speedster. Instead he chose a rather more stately conveyance—a glorious 1922 Moon.

This magnificent vehicle—almost the size of a bus—could scarcely move more quickly than a bicycle. But Shelton did not win all those racing trophies by failing to think ahead. And so it came to pass that, as the three combatants jostled their way through neighborhoods streets, across the Willamette River, and into the heart of downtown, Shelton appeared, well, calm. Part of the challenge, of course, was that Shelton was required to park the car, properly, legally, then proceed to the finish line. And what a fortunate coincidence...just as he reaches the final stretch, why, here comes a car pulling away from the parking meter that just happened to be closest to the finish line. Into the vacant space slid the Moon. Onlookers interviewed at the scene swore the car was a Jaguar and that the driver—who had been parked there reading the newspaper for more than an hour—bore a striking resemblance to one of Mr. Shelton's employees.

Shelton, incidentally, is a cyclist who happens to own one of the city's finest collections of vintage two-wheelers.

This year, we've told Darcelle that she has to find her own parking space, just like any commuter would have to. Cheaters will be publicly flogged. She gets the message, evidently, because peeking out from her gown are white Nike running shoes to aid in sprinting from wherever she finds parking to the finish line.

"What do you think?" she asks. "Do they make the outfit?"

Bounding up the stairs of the #33 bus is the amiable, silver-haired regional government councilor Ed Washington, in a stylish gray business suit, matching gray-and-gold patterned tie, and round shades. He is all smiles, but serious about showing that transit is competitive time-wise for the 2.5-mile (4 km) trip to the downtown finish line.

Last but certainly not least, we have State Representative Chris Beck dressed like a college student on a date in baggy khaki pants, blue button-down shirt, and wide black tie with red and yellow diagonal stripes. His tools for the day—the white Styrofoam inner portion of an aged helmet and an old blue Schwinn with a rusty chain and borderline flat tires—give a hint as to how frequently he bicycles. He too is all smiles as he wraps a Velcro strap around his right ankle to keep his pant leg from getting ripped by a chain ring.

Darcelle floors it for about a minute, then hits the first red light. She turns south and then west onto busy Northeast Broadway. Ed's bus slowly travels along a parallel street, while Chris, accompanied by Bicycle Program colleague Roger Geller, heads down to Northeast Knott, a tree-lined residential street, and makes excellent time thanks to a spacious, virtually empty parking lane. In the 1980s, the city had tried—and failed—to garner enough support for reallocating the lightly used on-street parking to bike lanes, since most houses along Northeast Knott have generous driveways and garages. The negative public uproar so rattled the city's politicians that almost all bikeway development was halted until I was hired to give the bikeway program an energy infusion. Stopped at a traffic signal, Roger restrains Chris from running the red light—a no-no in this race and in general for our staff, who all try to model law-abiding bicycling behavior.

It's 7:45 a.m., in the thick of the morning rush. Darcelle and Ed inch along in their respective motorized mounts, while Chris and Roger bypass the line of stalled cars and buses. It looks like Chris is going to pull off a stunning victory.

Meanwhile, downtown at the finish line in Pioneer Square, once the site of a parking garage, now known as Portland's living room, groups of cyclists arrive. Volunteers and city staff hand out bananas and donuts to the hungry Lycra-clad troupers. By 8 a.m., we're a rainbow crowd of 150 enthusiastically carbo-loading yellow, green, and purple rain jackets. Karen Frost, the fit, youthful, forty-something telecom company executive turned Bicycle Transportation Alliance executive director, welcomes the crowd from the podium.

Chris and Roger reach the last stretch before the river, bypassing traffic in the new Northeast Broadway bike lane. They start to climb the gentle hill up the Broadway Bridge sidewalk when out of the blue, Chris' dry chain snaps, less than a mile from the finish line. He hops off and stares in dismay at the hanging pieces. It's a helluva monkey wrench. It seems a tragic end to his historic attempt to demonstrate the superiority of bicycling in a short-distance urban time trial.

Left to right: Chris, Ed, and Darcelle

Salvation comes in mere seconds. "Chris, here, take my bike," says Roger, and hands him his red Cannondale. He's always been a clever one, that Roger, smarter than your average bear. Chris doesn't hesitate. He throws his leg over the saddle and blasts forward into downtown. Darcelle, in the meantime, has passed him up, and is circling Pioneer Square looking for a parking spot, which she finds but a block away. She grabs her commuter accoutrements—a pair of sparkly high heels, purse, and lunch bag—and elegantly jogs to the finish line without tripping on her gown. Too late! Chris has already made it in and is savoring his victory with a bagel and coffee. Ed's bus delivers him to the celebration a few minutes after that. Not long after, Roger, the unsung hero of the day, having pulled off the broken link and reunited the chain, quietly pedals into the square.

It's big fun, celebrating the hearty souls who ride to work no matter what the weather or infrastructure conditions. But after several years of organizing, advertising, printing, rounding up bagels and bananas, and driving—yes, driving—on Bike Commute Day in a van full of posters, boxes of maps and brochures, tables, chairs, microphones, canopies, and prizes, I begin to wonder.

Is this helping get more people out riding? Is my time best spent running events like this, or working on bikeway projects? We have almost no bikeways, and few people bicycling. Chicken or egg...focus on getting more people out riding in the absence of bikeways, or focus on developing bikeways to encourage more people to ride. In the absence of bikeways, some people will bike. But if we get a bikeway system developed, it will be far easier to sell the public on bicycling as a serious means of transportation.

I bring the dilemma to Karen Frost. The BTA has a tiny donated one-room office, a space typical of nonprofit groups on a shoestring: cramped, chaotic, and brimming with messianic enthusiasm, stacks of bike maps, and bikes parked every which way. I perch on a corner of her desk and stuff fundraising letters into envelopes as we talk.

"So, Karen, here's a question: Would the BTA take over Bike Commute Day so I can focus on the Bicycle Master Plan and development of bikeways? Here's the deal: We'll provide funding and support for a couple of years to get you going." She flashes me a generous smile and agrees to take the proposal to her board.

Karen then decides to turn it into a month-long Bike Commute Challenge, whereby businesses and organizations will log their bicycling miles in the spirit of competition.[38] ⊙━⚿

Turn a bagels-and-bananas lovefest into an all-out slugfest for recognition and fabulous prizes? Why not? It's the American way.

⊙━⚿   **Encouragement key #1: Celebrate bike commuters with contests and fun events.**

---

[38]   See bikecommutechallenge.com for more information.

CHAPTER 19

Cubicle Charm

After the BTA takes over Bike Commute Day, I focus my energy on the Bicycle Master Plan and implementing bikeways. Then I hear that the Oregon Department of Transportation is organizing a team for the Bike Commute Challenge. I'm not about to let a bunch of state highway engineers show up us cool city folk. We need our own burly bureaucratic biking team.

For weeks, I walk the aisles of orange cubicles, charming, cajoling, and corralling dozens of colleagues into riding to work.

"Hi, Robin!" I stick my head into the workspace of spunky, delightfully freckled, red-headed Robin Gunn, originally from Savannah, Georgia.

"Oh, hi, Mia. You know, honey, I just don't feel comfortable riding a bike," Robin drawls in a Southern accent so sweet I can almost smell jasmine.

"No problem." I am not so easily daunted. "We have seven guided rides leaving from different parts of the city. Tell you what: I'll have someone pick you up."

"Aw, that's alright. Ah'm just not really sure bicycling is for me. Go on now..." She is a snappy dresser, and is concerned, and I accept the legitimacy of her dilemma, but I've got the dress part down. High heels, skirts, make-up, hair: no problem.

"Tell ya what, Robin. I'll come over with Rich this weekend and we'll do a practice ride." I stand in her cubicle, grinning like the Cheshire cat, who won't disappear no matter how long you wait.

"Oh, alright." Exasperated, she gives in.

She and Rich Cassidy, a compact man in his thirties, handsome and ridiculously fit, are good friends. As we pedal to Robin's, he tells me that he just started riding a year ago.

"I used to work out at the gym," he explains. "It was from hanging around the likes of you that it started to sink in that bicycling to work would be a good idea." We pedal east up a quiet neighborhood bicycle boulevard, Southeast Salmon, slowing down a bit on a half-mile of gentle hill.

"At first, I would only bike on Fridays, and only early in the morning, before rush hour, because I was nervous, really nervous about traffic. Then I added Mondays and Wednesdays, but still only early in the morning." This worked well for his schedule anyway, because he could leave work early to pick up his daughter Andrea. After six months, Rich was hooked.

"The best part is I don't have to run like a gerbil on the treadmill anymore."

Rich and I pump up Robin's tires, stash her purse and briefcase in a pannier, and escort her the short mile and a half (just over 2 km) into downtown. Despite the support and easy ride, she is still nervous as heck. In this, she is in good company with millions of women for whom safety fears are paramount. For moms in particular, these fears lead to a vicious catch-22: Because of all the motorized traffic around schools, we're afraid to let our kids bike or walk, so we drive them, contribute to the problem, and perpetuate the cycle.

The more we're improving Portland's bikeway network, the more women like Robin gain comfort. When we reach the time that more women than men cycle on a daily basis, as in the Netherlands, we'll be able to declare victory.[39]

⊛⊛⊛⊛⊛

A few cubicles over, Truc Nguyen, a slight, twenty-ish financial analyst of Vietnamese heritage, seems interested but has a few issues.

"I don't have a lock."

"No problem, Truc! At least you have a bike!" I've rounded up several loaners for the bike-less.

"And I don't have a helmet." Easy one...we've got helmets to give away.

He isn't sure of the best route, but doesn't want to join an escorted ride. I make him a personalized map. He is concerned about coming in sweaty. I show him the showers down on the third floor.

On Bike Commute Day, he is a grinning, happy camper. He had left himself an hour for the three-mile (5 km) relatively flat ride, but it took only twenty minutes. Like most people, he underestimated how long it

---

[39] In the U.S., men's cycling trips surpass women's by at least two to one. In the Netherlands, where 27 percent of all trips are made by bike, 55 percent of all riders are women. In Germany twelve percent of all trips are on bikes, 49 percent of which are made by women. "Women are considered an 'indicator species' for bike-friendly cities for several reasons. First, studies across disciplines as disparate as criminology and child rearing have shown that women are more averse to risk than men. In the cycling arena, that risk aversion translates into increased demand for safe bike infrastructure as a prerequisite for riding. Women also do most of the child care and household shopping, which means these bike routes need to be organized around practical urban destinations to make a difference." Baker, Linda, "How to Get More Bicyclists on the Road," *Scientific American*, October 2009.

takes him to drive and park, and overestimated how long it would take to bike. Delighted by this whispered-on-the-wind revelation, he becomes a daily bike commuter. For the record, 10 mph (16 km/h) is a no-sweat, easy-to-achieve pace.

Despite my considerable energy and persistent Saint Bernard–puppy slobbery charm, I can't motivate all my colleagues to become like Truc. Many live more than a few miles away. Many more aren't ready to consider it. Mark Cherniack, mentor and friend from my energy conservation days, joins me for a margarita one night and consoles, "Mia, it's hard enough trying to get people to purchase and screw in an energy-efficient light bulb. You're trying to get them to change their behavior. That's way, way harder."

Point well taken. Truth be told, though, I have a critical edge. Compact fluorescent lightbulbs save you a few bucks over time and allow you to feel eco-friendly during the twenty seconds you're actually screwing them in, but they don't improve your health, reduce your stress, allow you to bypass traffic, connect you with your community, and put a smile on your face. Let's face it—sorry Mark, just being honest here—double-paned windows, solar panels, and bottom-loading freezers are excellent energy savers but aren't in any way going to get your heart pumping or tone your legs.

On a typical spring day, I might get pelted by hail, then regaled by a double rainbow. Spring in Portland is stunning in its beauty,

Portland's excellent bikeway signs display not only mileage, but estimated time to reach key destinations. You'll be bicycling along and see a sign like this and make a mental note, "Good, I'll be there in 10 minutes." When you arrive in six minutes, you feel strong and speedy, like Truc did that day.

 **Encouragement key #2: Invest in one-on-one mentoring to overcome resistance and mental barriers.**

 Tie your bikeway network together with signage.

week after week offering new and tantalizing eye candy: swirls of cherry blossoms, breathtaking lines of white ornamental pear trees, pink magnolia explosions, and a dazzling array of yellow, green, pink, white, and purple camellias, dogwoods, and rhododendrons. You just don't get the same level of flowery intoxication sitting in a car.

I wave constantly at my neighbors and at strangers who stop for me at stop signs. Often, they wave me through although they have the right-of-way. For many years, I would assert my presumed equality by motioning, "No, you go ahead, really." But then I realized that when someone offers me kindness, it's my responsibility to graciously receive. Besides, when you're on a bike, momentum is your friend, and I think the motorists waving me through must understand that. Perhaps they themselves bike from time to time. I always smile and wave in gratitude. And since this happens numerous times a day, I'm always smiling and waving, waving and smiling, happy, happy, happy as I pedal along, until I arrive at work or a meeting or home feeling pleasantly hungry, energetic, even buzzed. **O—r**

Yes, Grasshopper, these pleasures can be yours too...but only if you try it. How to impart upon the masses that bicycling, particularly on the network of bikeways we're speedily creating, is pleasurable and fun, something delightful to do, not a chore, not a hassle, not scary, not a pain in the ass? (True, sometimes bicycling does cause pain in the rear and other body parts, but it's the good kind, the kind that means you're alive and using your body for all it's worth.)

If I can walk the halls and pedal my wheel-and-pony show and simply through talking to folks break down enough barriers to rally 5, 10 or 20 percent of folks to at least give it a try, what would happen if I could multiply myself? Or, since cloning is not an option as of yet, how can I spread the fun further and faster?

Clearly, I can't do it alone.

O—r   **Be courteous, obey the law, and smile and wave at any motorist who shows you the slightest shred of courtesy.**

CHAPTER 20

Enjoy the Ride

One afternoon, a lunchtime ride finds Rob and me in a heated debate. The topic du jour: How to get more people to experience the joy of bicycling.

"What about the Neighbor Rides?" I ask. "How come only twenty or thirty people show up?" These weekly, short-distance, low-sweat, escorted rides are fairly well publicized.

"Hmmm," Rob furrows his brow in concentration as we climb through a gorgeous hillside neighborhood. "It's just not big enough or sexy enough. I mean, what's so special about riding your bike on city streets shared with cars? You can do that any day of the week."

I nod in agreement. After they've done it once, participants rarely return. Still, it's a good program, a helping hand in getting newbies on the road.[40]

We turn onto a road section so steep we have to stand to pump, even in the lowest gear, to avoid toppling over backward. Weeping willows and powerful, ancient Douglas firs rustle in the light breeze.

"What about Cycle Oregon? Why is it so successful?" Rob ponders. The wildly popular annual ride is in its tenth or eleventh year.

"Several reasons, I think. First, they pick awesome, drop-dead-gorgeous, low-traffic routes. Some of the roads are closed to cars or have police escorts." I had ridden most of Cycle Oregon's 500 miles (804 km) in 1994, before I crashed and broke my collarbone.[41]

I take a sip of water, then add, "It's well supported. Decent and plentiful food, music at the rest stops, and in camp, incredible volunteers. And, it's just so fun. You're hanging out with two thousand happy people who have nothing to do but ride all day. Plus, you know you're supporting a good cause." Cycle Oregon's proceeds are plowed into projects that benefit rural Oregon and promote bicycling and bicycle safety. Of course, it helps that its founder is newspaper columnist Jonathan Nicholas, who promotes the ride with unapologetic mania. He describes a ride so sensational, scenery

---

40   The current incarnation of Neighbor Ride is called Portland by Cycle.
41   I've also gone on Cycle Oregon's Weekend Rides starting in 2007, when I became a board member.

so spectacular, that you're ready to mortgage your home so as not to miss out on the experience. No wonder Cycle Oregon sells out every year. No wonder communities clamor to have Cycle Oregon grace their town with its vibrant cavalcade of happy cyclists.

"OK," said Rob, "so there's our answer." We'll plan a humongous, super-fun blast of a ride that will get tens of thousands to try bicycling. It should be on a unique, car-free course, one that you don't get to experience every day, and support a worthy nonprofit activity.

We reach the top of our climb and stop for a moment to marvel at the majestic mountains within view. Rob scribbles notes on a little pad he pulls from his jersey pocket. We head downhill, buzzing with the adrenaline of possibility. Fifteen bone-chilling minutes later, we rejoin civilization.

Rick Bauman sits in a brain-deadening meeting in an office tower pondering his future. Tall and lean with a pale, freckled Midwest complexion, thinning hair, and crooked smile, he has just lost a race for state legislature and is trying to figure out his next act.

The bike tours he leads in Vietnam, South Africa, and Morocco are interesting, but not enough to keep his hyperactive brain fully engaged. Gazing out the window on the many Willamette River bridges below, he starts doodling a series of loops and figure eights. He looks down at his drawing, then back to the two auto-only freeway bridges. He closes his eyes and imagines the views. Mount Hood, bare of snow but for a white cap and glacier ribbons that are slowly disappearing as the planet warms. Flat-top Mount St. Helens, roundish Mount Rainier, and perfectly peaked Mount Adams. Bald eagles floating above their nests on the unmined, forested riparian portion of Ross Island, home to at least fifty species of birds including ospreys, eagles and herons.

Rick opens his eyes. He knows, with 100 percent certainty: If we can get cyclists and pedestrians up on those freeway bridges, it will be awesome.

Rob and I try to interest a local event promoter in organizing our big car-free event. We research various marathons and events like the Turkey Trot in Dallas, which my family does en masse on blocked-off downtown streets each Thanksgiving. The Tour de l'Île offers a 32-mile (51 km) course on once-a-year car-free streets in Montreal, and New York's Five Boro Bike

Tour winds through Manhattan, Brooklyn, Queens, Staten Island, and the Bronx. We know we're onto something, just not sure how to get there.

Rick Bauman in the meantime is in Montreal, then New York, checking out the action. With a Cycle Oregon seed grant in hand, he comes to Rob with the idea of the Bridge Pedal. Not just two, but all ten bridges will be closed, if he has his way. His idea is ambitious, audacious, unrealistic, brilliant. Exactly what we had in mind, only bigger, bolder, better.

I offer to pay for printing and help organize volunteers as Rick embarks upon the tortuous process of procuring permits to commandeer ten river spans for one long, lovely morning. One of Rob's traffic engineers, Doug Thompson, helps with traffic closures and routing. Within short order, Rick's got permission to use eight of the bridges. This alone is an impressive feat by any standard. Two remain: the freeway bridges.

For months, he goes around in circles with state transportation staff, whose administrative rules state that a freeway can only be closed for maintenance or an emergency. A bike event? No way. The weeks fly by faster than a speeding bullet.

"Help!" he begs anyone who will listen. In his mind, the ride is worthless without those two bridges. You can bike on all the others any day you want. Adding insult to injury, spring 1996 is one of the rainiest on record. Rick has financed tens of thousands in fees and food, rider numbers, booths, and bands. Credit card bills are piling up, staff are demanding payment, and rain keeps falling.

"Hey Rick. Heard you're having trouble with those permits. I think I can help." Not a minute too late, to the rescue rides Eric Fishman, a communications expert with deep ties in government. His mission: Procure the permits.

The charismatic Eric[42] is handsome and spiffy in a mafioso kind of way. He glides into yet another meeting and gently suggests that cooperation is in the state's best interest.

"Look, rules are rules. I can't change them," replies the state engineer.

Something in his tone stops Eric from giving up. He replays the statement in his mind: "Rules are rules. I can't change them. *I* can't change them. *He* can't change them. Is he giving me a hint?"

---

[42] Our children go to school together. Since he's taken over our school foundation, I've gotten to see firsthand what a terrific organizer he is. Not for nothing has he built his company, Metropolitan Group, into a nationwide strategic communications powerhouse.

After the meeting, he takes him aside. "Bruce, if you can't change the rules, who can?"

"The Oregon Transportation Commission," Bruce replies, then walks away.

"Progress?" asks Rick, calling Eric from the basement of his house, where he's sitting among piles of T-shirts and registration forms.

"Patience, my friend," replies Eric. "Patience and faith."

In my attempts to create bikeable conditions, I tackle people head-on. With words and studies, I try to convince them, regardless of their history or origin of the superiority of my argument. I talk and talk and think that if I just try hard enough, they'll see how wonderful bicycling is for our community. They too will get on board, and we'll all be one happy family. It's no wonder Earl Blumenauer calls me pathologically optimistic.

I could learn a lot from Eric Fishman, a lifelong Portlander schooled in politics who sees every person as a decision-maker with a history. Step #1 in changing people's minds: connect with them on a personal level. He researches each of the appointed transportation commissioners individually. It turns out that several are fellow Willamette University alumni.

Using the alumni connection as a calling card, he tries to conjure in each a positive association with bicycling. It turns out that several have ridden or are planning to ride Cycle Oregon. Eric slyly takes them down memory lane to that gorgeous highway in Eastern Oregon and that amazing bridge at the coast, facilities the state allowed to be temporarily transformed into cyclist nirvana. The sacrifice of a few hours of motorist convenience pales, seemingly, in comparison. Then, he pulls out the Oregon Bicycle and Pedestrian Plan, which clearly locks the state government into promoting bicycling.

By the time he testifies before the transportation commission, just weeks before the event, the highway department's opposition is but a faded memory. They give Bauman a one-year revocable permit.

The Bridge Pedal is on.

For weeks, every single day has started damp and progressed to deluge before retreating to dismal darkness. The day of the event, permit in hand, barricades in place, media ready to report on the sad failure of Rick's dream, the skies part. The people of Portland wake up, caffeinate,

The superb view from the Marquam Bridge

stretch, and look out the window to see a glimmering yellow orb inviting, beckoning, even insisting that they come see what the pied piper has in store for them. Six thousand follow the music of sunshine to the start line on the river's edge. Rick's team, expecting a whimper of a crowd, finds itself stuffing cash into grocery bags.

It's BikeFest all over again. An enormous latent demand for car-free experiences unleashed, wildly surpassing the organizers' expectations.

It's not perfect. Crowded in parts, slick in others. Carpet intended to add traction to slippery metal honeycomb bridge-decks wiggles and detaches. A few people crash on railroad tracks; a few get lost.

But the vast majority loves it. The views from the two bridges are so stunning, they inspire a thousand family photos and two proposals of marriage. Smarty-pants Rick sets up a table for folks to write out thank-you notes to the highway department. Given their normal correspondence load of complaints, the unexpected, unprecedented surge of love mail prompts

Send thank-you notes to public officials who support bicycling!

The cyclist-filled Fremont Bridge

a permanent revision to the rules. The Bridge Pedal becomes enshrined as an annual approved event.

At the top of the Fremont Bridge, a woman touches me on the arm. It's Paula, the woman I met at one of my early wheel-and-pony shows.

"This is the woman who got you free bike helmets," she says to her son and grandkids.

The kids, who look to be about four and six, shyly say thanks. Her son shakes my hand.

She hands me knitted ear warmers into which you slip your helmet straps. "What do you think?" she asks. "Will they be a big seller? We're doing a fund-raiser for bike helmets."

⊕⊛⊛⊛⊕

The week after Bridge Pedal, my corner of cubicle land is flooded with information requests from people who hauled their bikes out of the garage, took in the view, and breathed in the potential.

"Now what?" they want to know.

We're more than happy to oblige.

Encouragement key #3: Hold big, mega-fun, car-free community events.

CHAPTER 21

Touching Souls

I am not a happy camper the day I meet Brian Lacy. I had set out for work in these cute, flowy blue capris that I had bought at a trendy store I would normally never go to, because I buy most of my clothes at consignment stores. But I had given my stepdaughter Sierra a gift certificate for Hanukkah, and, miracle of miracles, she had given me one—for the same store—in return. This led to the obvious concept of us going on a shopping date. The last time we had tried such a thing, just before I married her dad, she was a sullen mass of teenage angst and barely said two words. This time, we chatted and laughed and I ended up buying these blousy pants for well beyond the gift-certificate value.

Two blocks from work, I felt an odd pulling-tugging-ripping sensation below my right knee. The fabric of my right pant leg had blown toward the front wheel, where it somehow twisted itself in circles around the brake pad. Trapped, I had to rip a hole to release myself.

I walk into my cubicle in a dark, grumpy fog. Sitting on my chair is a cute young man with wavy brown hair, in cycling shorts and a colorful batik button-down shirt. His eyes peek from behind small oval glasses and train on the big grease-marked hole in my spendy new pants.

"Don't even ask," I warn. "What can I do for you?"

"I left the Bike Gallery in 1992 and was wrenching for City Bikes out on the sidewalk," he explains. "Kids would show up out of nowhere and help true wheels and tweak brake cables." They loved getting their hands dirty, and it seemed to empower them. A shy kid would start talking while cleaning a headset to perfection. An obviously neglected kid would repack ball bearings and stand up a little straighter. 0━⊤

Brian hands me a flyer for his new organization, the Community Cycling Center (CCC). He's got a few thousand dollars from Cycle Oregon and his old boss, Jay Graves. Having Jay on board means a lot. His six Bike Gallery stores make him one of the United States' largest bike

---

0━⊤ **See the bicycle as a tool for empowerment and social change, not just sport or transportation.**

dealers, but it is his personal vision, dedication, generosity, and relentless optimism that have won him a shelf full of awards. Intrinsically, he understands that creating more opportunities for people to bicycle, whether for transportation, recreation, or racing, is good for our world, and of course, for his bottom line. But his generosity goes beyond a profit motive; were it not for all the money Jay has donated to bicycling causes, he could have long ago retired to a small tropical island.

Thanks to bike dealers like Jay Graves, bicycling is increasingly a mainstream form of transportation.

A slender blond with a bucktooth, never-ending smile, Jay can disassemble a bike's bottom bracket and put it back together in less than ninety seconds, blindfolded. He'll make younger men cry uncle in a bike rodeo. At his fiftieth birthday party, he won in beer pong, downed several shots of tequila, got the dancing going, and showed no signs of slowing down long after the rest of us were curled up under the table.

I think there's not a single cyclist or cycling activity in Oregon that is more than two degrees of separation from Jay Graves. Come to think of it, everyone who buys a bike from a retail establishment anywhere in the United States is connected to Jay thanks to his leadership of the National Bike Dealers Association, and that means we're all connected to each other.

❋ ❋ ❋ ❋ ❋

Brian's plan is to take donations of used bikes, then fix them up through a combination of volunteer labor, labor-swap, and fee-for-service bike repair. They'll donate the refurbished bikes to low-income kids. Through after-school riding clubs, they'll teach safety. Neighborhood youth will have a safe place to hang out, learn skills, earn a bike, and connect with community members.

Stunning in freshness and clarity, Brian's fresh, warm breeze of ideological brilliance dissipates my dark mood in a flash. In my vision, the bicycle is a tool for transportation, health, fitness, and clean air. In his, it's a simple and smart tool for community connection, youth empowerment, and societal change.

⚬━⚸ Foster community groups to recycle/reuse bikes for the good of underprivileged youth.

I look at my leg and laugh. I know better than to wear such ridiculous pants. Then, I look at him and smile, my heart soaring.

We've got bikeway infrastructure and big rides. Another piece of the puzzle—grass-roots commitment—clicks into place.

I reach out my hand. "Count me in."

It's love at first sight, not just for me, but for everyone who hears about the Community Cycling Center. We love it in direct proportion to our level of involvement. The more we give, the more we receive.[43]

Brian brings in local business owner Stan Jackson to balance his energetic romanticism. Later, they are joined by Ira Grishaver, a soft-spoken, ponytailed idealist. Day and night, people drop off used bikes and volunteers wrench damaged wheels off rusty frames, polish gear wheels, grease chains until they glow, and shoot the breeze. The Community Cycling Center quickly becomes the focal point of a neighborhood economic renaissance.

Then two peace-loving hippies named Tom and Joe decide to paint a bunch of bikes yellow, and from its quiet community corner, the CCC is unwittingly and unfortunately launched into the national limelight.

The idea: Round up old bikes, paint them yellow, leave them around town. The good people of Portland will see one, run an errand, and leave it somewhere else for the next person to use. The media loves the quirky concept and slots it with various feel-good stories that save us from a daily slide into the pit of despair. You've got your new baby elephant at the zoo, the alligator that turned up in little Johnny's bathtub and the woman who rode naked on her horse in the holiday parade. Grand Poobah of the freak show is the Yellow Bikes Program, picked up not just by all the local outlets, but by *The Today Show,* the *New York Times,* and National Public Radio. Joe and Tom become instant celebrities.

As if this is an official government program, my office is deluged with information requests. Free bikes are indistinguishable from bike lanes in the media's mind. They're all part of our kooky bike plot.

---

43 For more information, see www.communitycyclingcenter.org. The website for the International Bicycle Fund—www.ibike.org—lists many such community bicycle programs, found all over the world, under "encouragement."

Today, Paris, Montreal, and numerous other cities have successfully taken the bike sharing concept much further into the modern era with sophisticated, well-managed systems. I'm involved in programs in Melbourne, the D.C. area, and Boston (as of this writing) through Alta Bicycle Share, Inc., of which I'm a co-owner.

The media attention is, frankly, the best thing Yellow Bikes has going for it. The reality is 180 degrees from the hype. From day one, the bikes fall into disrepair, disappear, are vandalized, or thrown into the river. This is exactly what had happened with similar bike-sharing programs in Europe, even those with significant investment. Copenhagen, for example, invested more than a million dollars in shared-bike kiosks. The bikes are god-awful heavy, and no components can be used on any other bikes. Getting a bike is similar to the way you get a luggage cart at many airports. Each bike is attached to a horizontal bar by a chain and a handlebar-mounted coin box that releases the bike when fed a twenty-kroner coin (worth about five dollars). Return the bike, you get your coin back. Good concept, but the chains break easily and many bikes never make it back.

Tom and Joe have no system in place to round up, repair and replenish the bikes. I take one out for a spin to see what the hype is all about. With barely functioning brakes and a wobbly, borderline flat tire, the short ride leaves me both skeptical and concerned.

Lacking management, organization, and funding, Joe and Tom turn to Brian, who is abruptly anointed king of Yellow Bikes. He wins the Robert

Rodale Environmental Achievement Award and flies to D.C. to accept, bringing along with him a yellow bike for President Clinton.

But along with the attention comes headaches. Hundreds of volunteers are eager to help but need to be trained, organized, and managed. Well-meaning residents leave a zillion bikes on the sidewalk in front of the small shop. I arrange for the county government to donate a storage warehouse, but now Brian needs trucks to transport the bikes back and forth. The company that initially donated the yellow paint closes up shop. Stretched, stressed, stunned, and struggling, Brian begins to wonder if he's fulfilling his original mission. He and Stan start to fight.

By the time I arrange a meeting in 1995 with Commissioner Blumenauer, the Yellow Bikes Program is on fumes.

"Welcome, gentlemen." Earl shakes hands around the little conference-room table, smiles his crooked smile, and raises his eyebrows in positive reinforcement. "We've heard so much about Yellow Bikes. Tell me what we can do to help."

Joe, an aspiring Green Party politician in a tie-dyed T-shirt, starts. "Commissioner, we believe that a contribution of $55,000 will provide the funding we need."

"Tell me more about what the funding will be used for," queries Earl.

Brian jumps in. "Actually, we really need help setting up a bike repair and volunteer management system..."

"Like you would know what we need," Tom snaps at Brian. Earl and I stare in disbelief as the men continue to argue as if we're not in the room.

Earl squints at me a "What the hell?" look. I shuffle my papers in embarrassment. Earl puts both hands firmly on the table and pushes himself into a standing position. "Thank you, gentlemen, for coming in. When you've figured out how we can help you, you let me know." Meeting adjourned.

While the Yellow Bike Program, a worthy idea whose time had not yet come, quietly fades away, the Community Cycling Center is too precious to let go. It stumbles, soul-searches, and evolves. Brian moves on, followed by Stan and Ira. New leaders come and go, but one event holds constant through thick and thin: the Holiday Bike Drive.

One chilly December morning, I bike to Legacy Emanuel Hospital, where a long line of economically distressed kids, parents, foster parents and volunteer Big Brothers/Sisters patiently wait in line. I stoop down to greet a six-year-old girl who is hiding behind her mom. Maria is a second-generation American, her parents from Mexico.

"Hi, sweetheart! Welcome! Are you ready to get a bicycle?"

Extreme levels of happiness envelop all who participate in the Holiday Bike Drive.

The bicycle is both a tool for empowerment and a vehicle for change.

Maria slowly peeks her head out and nods; brown eyes, wide.

"Great!" I reach out my hand. "First things first! It's bike helmet time! Let's see, I think we'll need a medium for you."

I lead Maria to the helmet area, where she picks out a purple one. She allows a nervous smile as a volunteer gently places it on her head, snaps the strap under her chin, and makes a few adjustments so it fits snugly but not too tight.

The next station is the best: a long line of refurbished bikes.

"Go ahead, sweetheart, pick out a bike." She looks at me, her confusion palpable. Just walk right up and take a bike? When has she ever in her life gotten to just walk up and take something for her very own self? She dashes behind her mother's skirts again, and we move slowly up and down the aisles as a group.

"How about this one? It'll match your helmet."

She nods ever so slightly toward the sparkly purple beauty and reaches out to fondle the handlebar streamers. We wheel it to the tune-up station, where mechanics remove the training wheels, pump the tires, raise the seat, and grease the chain. Last stop: the practice course, where her shyness evaporates in a heartbeat.

I kneel down and shake her hand good-bye.

"Gracias," she whispers, unprompted.

"No, thank-you," I whisper back, beaming, choked up, and utterly grateful for the opportunity to touch a young spirit, who will carry forward her newfound freedom into her community, family, and future.

CHAPTER 22

Let the Rain Come Down

"Hey, Mia, I've got an idea. Call me." Uh-oh. It's Earl Blumenauer, his beautiful brain teeming with ideas, as usual. But my plate is oh-so-full already... Perhaps I can just delete it, and no one will be the wiser? Nah. I need him, admire him, and appreciate everything he's doing. Plus, he's technically my boss.

"Hi, Earl, got your message. What's up?"

"I am really tired of people whining about how hard it is to bike in the rain," he starts. "Come on, it's not like you melt or anything. It's just water. Like a mister, cooling you down. What do you think raingear is for? So, listen, I want you to pick the worst day of the year and organize a biking event. We'll invite local bike shops to show off their raingear and show people that it's really not that bad biking in the rain. It'll be fun."

"Riiiight. Got it. Talk to you later, Earl." This does not sound like my kind of fun. Frankly, so far I find the winters of my new home to be rather dismal.

Sorry if this sounds like whining. I'm not saying I want to go back to Texas. Really! That's because a) it's too darn hot in Texas, and b) rain in Portland means snow in the mountains due east, and I adore cross-country skiing.

Like the Eskimo vocabulary that purportedly includes a hundred variations on "snow," a highly nuanced set of descriptors capture our 36 inches (91 cm) of annual moisture: rain, hail, wet snow, drizzle, sprinkles, spittle, showers, mist, deluge, rainstorm, downpour, inundation, monsoon, torrent, cloudburst, light rain, heavy rain. When we're wet, we are soaked, sodden, sopping, damp, dripping, drenched.

Then there's the gray: overcast, cloudy, partly cloudy, partly sunny, gloomy, dreary. The dim-light situation gives us our own psychological diagnosis—seasonal affective disorder—whereby sun-deprived people fall into a pit of depression best remedied by a winter-break escape to Mazatlán. But then comes summer, when we bask in the gloriousness of eighty degrees. Under blue skies, surrounded by the lush results of the winter torture, we radiate relief and stream outdoors, refuse to stay indoors, sleep under the stars, kick all the kids out into the bright light, and lock up the TV room. Just about every afternoon, I happily oblige the neighbors who stop by wondering when I'm gonna fire up the blender for some strong Texas margaritas (made properly with top-shelf tequila, triple sec, and Rose's lime juice, not that corn-syrup margarita-mix crap) because there's no time like the present, and it's always happy hour somewhere.

During the summer, few voluntarily leave the Northwest. The swell season is our reward for winter's attempt to drag us down, whereas this same period in Dallas fries your brains and skin. "Oh, I just ride early in the morning and wait 'til it cools down a bit in the evening," a Texan friend of mine says. "Or look, if it's too hot, just take a few days off. We get nine months of mostly decent sunny weather before you can fry an egg on the sidewalk."

I could stop riding in the winter, sit on the bus, and longingly watch cyclists zoom by as we crawl along at a snail's pace, stopping every few blocks for passengers. Or I could drive and find my stress level rising as I sit in traffic, circle the block looking for parking, and watch the cyclists pass me by. But lack of exercise and fresh air makes me crankier than water and dark skies.

When I first moved out to Oregon, I wore rain booties, a rain jacket and pants, and Gore-Tex ski over-mitts. Then I switched from the booties to lined waterproof rubber boots, and changed into nicer shoes at the office. Nowadays, I just wear solidly stylish boots courtesy of La Canadienne or Timberland, and never change shoes.

On top, one word: layers. Essentials: rain pants and a light Showers Pass jacket with a hood that fits under the helmet. More rain-riding essentials: a plastic bag to cover your seat, plus fenders. You've got to have fenders! Otherwise you get a skunk stripe up your backside. This, my friends, is not a good look.

"What on earth are you complaining about?" ask cold-climate dwellers. Put on your studded bike tires and ultra-cold mittens and enjoy, say the good cyclists of Anchorage.

In Stockholm and Oslo, snowplows tend to the bike paths just as they would any road. I'm not saying you should head out in a blizzard, or throw common sense out the window like I did the day I stupidly plunged into an ice-covered Rock Creek Park, underdressed and ill-prepared. Perhaps the trouble I got in was a reflection of my Texas youth. I thought, "Yeehaw! Rock Creek Park is going to be stunning blanketed in white!" I bundled up, yanked on wool socks and hiking boots and my warmest gloves, wrapped a scarf around my face, and took off with childish abandon. I had no trouble on the powdery snow in our neighborhood, but under the trees in the park was a sheet of solid ice. I gave it my best shot, creeping along, struggling to stay up, until the unmistakable sensation of back wheel scraping ice penetrated my thick skull.

I pried off the tire and tube, laced a spare tube back into the tire, wrestled it back onto the wheel, pumped, and got back into a slow, steady rhythm. By this point I was pretty cold, especially my hands, which had been necessarily glove-free for many hard-working minutes.

Not two minutes later, the bike slid out from under me: The back tire was flat again. I had forgotten one of the cardinal rules of flat-fixing: run your fingers around the inside of the tire to rid it of the thorn, shard of glass, or tack that caused the flat in the first place. This time, spare tube ruined, I yanked out the culprit—a mean-looking wood splinter—and got to work with the patch kit. Patch glue has to dry completely before the patch will adhere properly, but it wanted to freeze, not dry. Six patches went to waste before one submitted to my desperate Lamaze blowing. By then, forty miserable minutes later, my fingers and toes were numb. My normal daily partnership with Mother Nature had morphed into a battle. In real danger of frostbite, I needed to get off the trail and moving, pronto.

Conceding defeat, I tried walking toward the parallel road, only an eighth of a mile away, but my treadless boots added insult to injury. I ended up crawling most of the way, dragging my bike behind me. My officemates didn't laugh when I walked in, two hours later, shivering and humbled. My toes ached for years to remind me of my idiocy.

I told this story to an Alaskan friend, who scoffed, "You've got to treat the weather with respect. If you head into the mountains in winter by car, you dress properly, put on your snow tires or chains, and bring along an emergency kit. Traveling by bicycle must be treated the same—even more so."

Near as I can figure, no matter where you live, you get some kind of weather torture. In D.C., the summer humidity was so cloying it was like riding through thick, hot mud, my tires slowly disintegrating into the bog below. Northerners battle snow, ice, and bitter cold; Californians, wildfires and smog; Heartlanders, wind; Southwesterners, extreme heat (and I'm not even the least bit fooled by their rationalization that it's a dry heat).

Whatever the weather, we amazing humans somehow go about our lives. So the question becomes: Given that there is no avoidance of the sky's daily mood and not a blessed thing we can do to control it, why do we let the weather keep us from moving our bodies by bike? Do we let the weather control our choice of transportation, or do we open our faces to the sky and let the pure rainwater nourish our souls?

What Earl wants to know is: Can we find a way to make peace with whatever—hail, snow, oobleck,[44] or rain—falls from the sky?

While I agree with Earl that we should encourage people to suck it up and embrace the bounty of our Oregon sky in sun-colored jackets, this activity doesn't rise to the top of my priority list. I had just successfully off-loaded Bike Commute Day and I am trying to stay focused on bikeway planning and design.

For a few weeks I keep my head down and stay out of Earl's way.

He catches me in the hall, "So, Mia, how's that rain ride coming along?" I do a little distract-and-dodge dance away from his piercing gaze.

He calls again. "Mia, I'm serious. Make it so." Crud. It's the third request. He must be serious. Time to give in. I call the National Weather Service and determine that the best (worst) day is January 29th. Sharon Fekety agrees to round up ride leaders. Jay Graves agrees to donate a rain jacket from the Bike Gallery. We issue a press release. I pull all this together in a few days, and frankly, it's pretty lame. I'm not a great event planner.

The big day dawns cloudy and cool. It's possibly the only time I've ever done a rain dance, begging the skies to burst. I set off under light wind, fully dressed to thwart all nature. The closer I get to downtown, the lighter the clouds get, until rays of sunshine warm all forty of us pathetic diehards as we show two or three reporters the valiance of rain-riding. Oh yeah, we show 'em all right.[45]

Why not ride in the rain, snow, or heat? Salmon swim upstream. Why shouldn't we?

⊶　Don't let weather challenges dissuade you from creating bicycle-friendly infrastructure.

---

44 Very sticky greenish goo, as described in Dr. Seuss's *Bartholomew and the Oobleck.*

45 In the spring of 2001, Good Sport Promotion's Porter Childs, a shy, dark-haired New Englander, is stuck inside surrounded by sports equipment and bemoaning the clear skies. After six straight rainy weekends, a sunny 70 degrees seduces every living creature outside. The month before, a big charity ride of his had been rained out. He becomes determined to find a weatherproof event. Born soon after is the second incarnation of Earl's defiant "bring-it-on" vision. As of this writing, more than 3,000 people participate annually in the Worst Day of the Year Ride. The weather gods seem amused by this, for they always hold their wrath for another day.

CHAPTER 23

Zen and the Art of Bicycle Maintenance

Growing up, I didn't learn how to use any of the tools hung in neat rows on Dad's Peg-Boards in our garage. While my brothers learned how to change the car's oil, saw boards, and drill holes, I, like the rest of my girlfriends, learned sewing and cooking.

I'm glad I made that A-line skirt in high school; my rudimentary sewing skills have saved me money and preserved beloved clothes. I understand that we are hard-wired, to a certain extent, to our DNA. And I know that the reason that my Dad focused his handyman training on brother Bruce was not born of sexism or favoritism. Dad would ask, "I need some help. Which one of you lazy bums wants to get off the couch?"

"Sorry, Dad," the rest of us would plead, our eyes never leaving *Gilligan's Island*. "They just figured out how to make a radio out of a coconut! We have to see what happens next!" Bruce would flash his dimples at us and follow Dad to the garage to work on the latest sprinkler-head casualty of the gas-powered lawnmower.

On a conscious level, I didn't know that I was afraid of touching tools. I do know this: When Jan VanderTuin of the Center for Appropriate Transport (CAT)[46] in Eugene, Oregon, patiently teaches me how to disassemble, tune, and rebuild my bike, I feel like I've been handed the keys to a knowledge that has always been waiting for me, just on the other side of a secret door.

I've just moved to Oregon when I meet Jan through his former business partner George Bliss, who in my D.C. life impressed me with his eloquent depiction of the critical mass of cyclists in China. In front of a roomful of suits at the World Bank, Bliss, who developed a line of pedal-powered dump-truck tricycles in New York, unabashedly insisted that bicycle transportation had a role to play in our modern world.

---

[46] hpm.catoregon.org/

My connection to Bliss gains me an introduction to Jan, and I am pleased as punch when a tall, skinny, gray-haired, soulful-eyed Bliss look-alike picks me up at the Eugene train station on a double recumbent tandem. (Guys, a little hint here: tandems in all forms are very romantic.) We pedal over to his warehouse. I follow him around like a hungry kid in a candy shop, as he shows off where they refurbish donated bikes, run a repair shop, and teach kids bicycle safety. CAT, the inspiration for Brian Lacy's Community Cycling Center, also publishes a monthly paper, operates a cargo-hauling bicycle-messenger service, and builds and sells bike racks and recumbent, folding, and cargo bikes.

Within an hour, we've got my bike up on a stand. It's a relief to know that when my brakes feel squishy I can twiddle those little knobs by the handlebars. When the brake cables get too stretched for the twiddling to help, it's not that hard to tighten or replace the cables. Before long, I've learned to take off, replace, clean, and lube the chain, adjust the gears, and replace cogs.

Behind the now-open door of self-help is a whole host of daily home repair opportunities. "What the heck are you doing?" my friend Catherine Ciarlo demands when she finds me in the upstairs bathroom with a wrench in hand, surrounded by toilet parts.

"Um, it needed a new dealy-bopper," I explain, pointing to the stopper part. "The guy at the hardware store told me to replace the whole thing."

She's the director of the Bicycle Transportation Alliance, solid on the women-bikes-empowerment concept. Yet she admonishes, "Mia, you're eight months pregnant. Enough with this Missy Fix-it–phase, all right?"

Even if nowadays I take my bike to the Bike Gallery for major tune-ups, I still like putting my bike on the stand, giving the frame a good rubdown, and polishing my chain with a toothbrush and fresh oil.

Firecracker ex-Texan Janis McDonald is on a mission to help women overcome their fears about bicycle transportation. A big-hearted woman whose resemblance to Janis Joplin seems more than coincidental, she has the big-boned strength of Serena Williams. After a grueling, scorching 90-mile (145 km) ride one August, the rest of us laid on our backs begging for someone to pour beer down our throats. Janis set off for another 10 or 15 miles (24 km) of fun.

One late fall evening, a frigid east wind blows hard from the Columbia Gorge. I click on various blinkie lights, pull on wool tights under my skirt, wrap a scarf around my face, and pedal hard over to Seven Corners Cyclery for Janis's Women on Bikes repair class. About twenty

The more women are comfortable riding for daily transportation, the healthier our communities.

middle-aged women are standing with their bikes in a chilly warehouse-like room among rows of new bikes.

"Come on in!" she invites, and hands me a cup of hot chocolate. Her first simple lesson: Put one hand on the back downtube and one on the front fork, lift, and flip.

Janis encourages, "Ladies, don't be afraid!" A palpable sigh of relief raises the room temperature a couple of degrees as each woman successfully balances her bike on its handlebars and seat.

"Now, we're going to take the front wheel off and repair a flat tire. Locate the valve stem..." And so on, until every one of them vanquishes her monster under the bed. Knowledge is power.

The following week, I lead them on a ride through the neighborhood and down the Springwater Corridor, every one of them smiling despite the wicked east wind. It's one more step in our quest to get more women out on a bike. ⛓

Teach a man to fish and he'll have food for his family. Teach a woman to fix her bike, and she'll understand that nothing is outside her potential.

⛓ Encouragement key #4: Focus on women!

CHAPTER 24

Metal Cowgirls

Of course, neither Janis nor I can claim to be the first woman in history to discover the power of bicycle transportation. This honor goes to women such as Elizabeth Cady Stanton and Susan B. Anthony, leaders of the movement to gain the right to vote, to be considered something other than property of their husbands, to gain access to jobs, to be granted equal pay and benefits, and to control their own bodies. It's easy to forget how repressed women were at the beginning of the twentieth century, and how hard they had to fight for basic freedoms we take for granted, such as the right to wear pants.

"Why, pray tell me, hasn't a woman as much right to dress to suit herself as a man?" Anthony asked a reporter in 1895. "The stand she is taking in the matter of dress is no small indication that she has realized that she has an equal right with a man to control her own movements."

"Men found that flying coattails were ungainly and that baggy trousers were in the way [when cycling], so they changed their dress to suit themselves and we didn't interfere," Stanton told a journalist in 1895. "They have taken in every reef and sail and appear in skin-tight garments. We did not bother our heads about their cycling clothes, and why should they meddle with what we want to wear? We ask nothing more of them than did the devils in Scripture—'Let us alone.'"

A woman with a bicycle no longer had to depend on a man for transportation—she was free to come and go at will. She experienced a new kind of physical power made possible by the bicycle. Between 1891 and 1896, it is estimated that the number of female cyclists grew between 100 and 400 times, with 1.3 to 3.2 million female cyclists in the United States, Great Britain, France, and Germany by the end of that period.[47]

Reported the *Boston Daily Globe* in 1895, "All sorts and conditions of women have enrolled themselves among [cycling's] devotees. The timid woman has cast away her fear, the stickler for proprieties has overcome her scruples, and the conservative has become a radical advocate of the

---

47 Zheutlin, Peter, *Annie Londonderry's Extraordinary Ride*, Citadel Press, 2007.

163

merits of the wheel—it looks as though the whole feminine world, which does nothing by halves and is ever ready to follow a popular fashion, had gone wheel mad."

In 1896, Susan B. Anthony said, "Bicycling has done more to emancipate women than anything else in the world."

In 1898, she elaborated,

The moment she takes her seat [a woman] knows she can't get into harm while she is on her bicycle and away she goes, the picture of free, untrammeled womanhood. The bicycle also teaches practical dress reform, gives woman fresh air and exercise, and helps to make them equal with men in work and pleasure; and anything that does that has my good word. What is better yet, the bicycle preaches the necessity for woman suffrage. When bicyclists want a bit of special legislation, such as side-paths and laws to protect them or to compel railroads to check bicycles as baggage, the women are likely to be made to see that their petitions would be more respected by the lawmakers if they had votes, and the men that they are losing a source of strength because so many riders of the machine are women. From such small practical lessons a seed is sown that may ripen into the demand for full suffrage, by which alone women can ever make and control their own conditions in society and state.

⚙️⚙️⚙️⚙️⚙️

It's an interesting paradox that the clothing revolution associated with the bicycle afforded women a quantum leap in basic freedom. Today, the clothing associated with bicycling holds many women back. Take, for example, Vivian, a blond, blue-eyed beauty who happens to be the fashion editor for the *Oregonian*, and the wife of Cycle Oregon founder Jonathan Nicholas. Despite her familial connection to cycling, Vivian is decidedly uninterested. Her objection stems first and foremost from the common misunderstanding that bicycling requires jamming one's legs into thigh-pinching butt-pad shorts.

"Mia," she explains with a touch of disdain, "you are not going to convince me that Lycra shorts are fashionable." We're at a somewhat swanky reception, and I'm sporting a flouncy, knee-length, linen black skirt and lacy pink chemise under a black and white silk-wool cropped V-neck sweater with tiny pearl buttons. Caressing my feet are knee-high black suede boots. And yes, I did ride my bike to the event. 🗝️

🗝️ **Put away the Lycra for short trips and embrace cycle chic.**

Inspiration, in spades, comes from the fit, stylish women of Copenhagen, who propel one-two-three kids in front-mounted kid-carrying bikes. From the men too: tailored suits masking muscled legs, briefcases strapped to a rack. Bicycling and fashion indeed can be best friends. For all your fashion biking tips, see: www.copenhagencyclechic.com and numerous related cycle fashion websites.

"Heck no! I'm not even going to try!" In my world, fashion is about showing up at a meeting by bike, looking fabulous, without having to change a single thing. "Vivian, I'm with you: padded Lycra shorts are not our friend. Not sexy. Not sassy. We look like we're having a maxi-pad disaster."[48]

She looks me up and down, intrigued, but unconvinced. For close to twenty years, her husband has been setting off for long rides, thighs crammed into tight shorts, chest inflamed in loud logos.

For the next ten minutes, I do my best to convince her that cycling fashion has nothing to do with speed-demon apparel. Sweat is not the objective, although the by-product is still a fit physique. First the bike: I prefer a utilitarian beauty with a step-through frame, fenders, rack, kickstands, skirt-guard, and lights. Solid, upright, comfortable, and stable—this is one fashionable bicycling look. Of course, hundreds of varieties of bikes—from speedy to sturdy and everything in between—means there's a sweet two-wheeler to match every personality.

---

48 Don't get me wrong. I too like padded shorts for fitness rides of longer than, say, two hours. I also like skirts with back pockets, which I put into double duty for tennis.

The absolute pinnacle of fashion: Jay and Alison Graves at their wedding

Then the clothes: your skirts shouldn't be too short, long, tight, or flowy. Use a pants strap if your bike lacks a chain guard. Try light, breathable layers on top, paired with solid heels of just about any height. Finally, don't forget to pair your outfit with delightful, delicious accessories. From pink-flowered waterproof Ortlieb panniers to a front-mounted Toto basket into which you fling your briefcase or purse, there's certainly a way to carry your stuff.

Not long after our initial conversation, Vivian sends a photographer to my office; she's decided to feature cycle-chic fashion in the newspaper. The article profiles a number of stylish daily cyclists, including fifty-two-year-old architect Rick Potestio, who travels by bike in his spiffy Italian suit. He explains, "The last thing you want to do is show up at a construction site in Lycra. I'd get laughed off the job site."

THE COPENHAGEN CYCLE CHIC MANIFESTO

I choose to cycle chic and, at every opportunity, I will choose Style over Speed.

I embrace my responsibility to contribute visually to a more aesthetically pleasing urban landscape.

I am aware that my mere presence in said urban landscape will inspire others without me being labeled as a "bicycle activist."

I will ride with grace, elegance, and dignity.

I will choose a bicycle that reflects my personality and style.

I will, however, regard my bicycle as transport and as a mere supplement to my own personal style. Allowing my bike to upstage me is unacceptable.

I will endeavor to ensure that the total value of my clothes always exceeds that of my bicycle.

I will accessorize in accordance with the standards of a bicycle culture and acquire, where possible, a chain guard, kickstand, skirtguard, fenders, bell and basket.

I will respect the traffic laws.

I will refrain from wearing and owning any form of 'cycle wear.' The only exception being a bicycle helmet—if I choose to exercise my freedom of personal choice and wear one.

Notes retro-hip planner Jessica Roberts, decked out in a vintage 1950s housewife dress that matches her cute old Raleigh, brown and cream, with a wicker basket, "My bike is my main form of transportation. It's not OK if I dress like a schlub." Plus, she adds, "I chose my haircut to go with my helmet."

Chiming in with her own cycle-chic routine is my friend Catherine. "When I work downtown, I wear what I am going to wear. I have little kids and meetings and schedule things closely, so it's not practical to change into a completely different outfit. So yeah, I wear high heels when I bike."

The article explodes nationwide. Suddenly, daily cycle fashion is being celebrated everywhere from the *New York Times* to dozens of blogs. A few weeks later, I run into Vivian again. This time, though, she's on an Amsterdam Electra.

"Vivian, look at you! You're riding!" She looks adorable in a short brown skirt, leggings, and tartan scarf.

"Our conversation helped me understand that bicycling isn't just about going fast and working up a sweat," she explains, tilting her head toward her husband, with a wink of collusion. "Plus, you said that you ride in whatever you're wearing. I never realized before how much the notion of having to change clothes bugged me."

Right on, girl!

Once women like Vivian feel safe and confident, overcome seasonal objections, handle bike maintenance, and look mighty fine, we find ourselves seriously out of excuses. (A woman out of excuses is a woman of action.) Then, propelled by toned legs, we show up everywhere, confidently, as we are: cyclists, metal cowgirls, women.

CHAPTER 25

Bike to the Future

Jeff Smith sets off for work on a cool fall day. Just a couple blocks from his house is Lincoln Street, Portland's best bicycle boulevard. Once a major traffic thoroughfare, now concrete curbs divert most of the cars to parallel arterials. Formerly suspicious, worried, or downright angry neighbors freaked out about impacts to access, safety, and property values now wholeheartedly embrace the changes. Day and night, the air is filled with whooshing tires, jingling bells, and chattering folks dressed in work or casual clothes, on an enormous variety of speedy and utilitarian bikes, sporting a briefcase clipped to a bike rack or dangling grocery bags from their handlebars.

Next to him is six-year-old Flannery, excited to get to her first-grade art class. Dad and daughter pedal along quietly, Flannery's mind creating a new Picasso, Jeff's working through a list of bikeway maintenance requests for the new Bikeway Spot Improvement Program. Flannery's little legs pedal three strokes for every one of Jeff's.

Five minutes later, they arrive at school. Flannery hugs her dad goodbye and disappears into a gaggle of giggling girls. Jeff looks around for a bike rack. Seeing none, he locks her bike to the fence.

Jeff spends a happy day riding around southeast Portland, measuring streets to see if bike lanes can fit. He ends his fieldwork back at Richmond Elementary just as the bell rings. Flannery hands him a sheaf of colorful drawings. So realistic are her renderings, he wonders whether a career as an artist might be more than a childhood fantasy.

There, on Flannery's bike, is a scolding note stating that bicycling to school is not allowed.

Jeff walks back in and confronts the principal. "Why on earth would you prohibit children from bicycling to school?"

She looks up from her stacks of papers sighing in annoyance. New math standards, budget cuts, a disgruntled parent, a teacher requesting leave...now this?

"Oh, it's not my policy, it's the PTA." Back to her papers.

❁❁❁❁❁

Jeff calls the PTA chair at home that night.

"No, it's not our policy," she explains. "It's the school district's."

Next day, Jeff is on the phone in the cubicle next to mine.

"Why does your policy say kids can't ride to school?" he's asking someone at the school district.

The reply: "We don't have an official policy about bicycling. You should talk to the principal at your school."

Jeff slams down the phone in aggravation. He's getting the runaround. He doesn't like it, any more than I did the day I spent hours on the phone in a fruitless quest for relief from a wheel-eating trench.

Does the school district discourage bicycling, or is policy set on a school-by-school basis, and if so, by who? Why wouldn't they—the principal, PTA, and school district—want kids to bike to school? Richmond Elementary is located in a quiet residential neighborhood and is easily accessed by foot or bike. What about schools in less bike-friendly neighborhoods? Does the district, principal, or anyone else really get to decide how kids get to school? Why would they care? Shouldn't they care?

I sit in the office of the principal of Buckman Elementary, an eighty-year-old school in a middle-class neighborhood on a two-lane street. Nothing a few crossing guards can't handle. Almost no one bikes or walks here, though, and I'm trying to figure out why.[49]

"Tell me about Buckman," I suggest. Principal Ray is average-sized, neither particularly fit nor overweight, with a ruddy complexion destined to be burnt at the beach.

"We're an arts magnet school, drawing kids from all over the district. Got about five hundred kids, kindergarten through fifth grade."

I think for a second. "Doesn't that mean that some kids live pretty far away?"

"Well, yes," he says proudly. The notion that kids live miles from school, have few friends in their neighborhood, and have to be driven to school isn't his problem. Enrollment is on track, his funding and position secure.

Every morning and afternoon, the school is completely encircled by slow-moving and idling metal boxes jockeying for position. No wonder so few kids walk or bike from the surrounding neighborhood. It sure doesn't feel safe,

---

[49] This grant-funded research is intended to probe why more kids aren't bicycling to school. Through focus groups, we probe the attitudes and fears of parents, students, teachers, and administrators. Through physical assessments, we look for challenges and opportunities in the physical environment: the presence and/or condition of sidewalks and crossings, bikeway facilities, parking and loading zones, travel patterns, and major barriers and impediments. Later, these issues are coalesced under the national Safe Routes to School movement.

given all the car traffic. It's a vicious circle: Parents feel it's too unsafe to let their kids walk or bike because of all the parents driving their kids to school.

For decades, urban flight depleted Portland's school population and budget. A touted solution to recapturing middle-class families: Offer choices. Portland, like many school districts across the nation, opened up special magnet programs in Spanish, Japanese, Chinese, science, arts, and environmental education. In academic and budgetary terms, you can call the choice concept a success. But from a transportation and community perspective, it's a problem. Add into the equation private schools and the Bush II–era Federal No Child Left Behind legislation, which allows kids in underperforming schools to transfer to a higher-performing school, and we've got an outright disaster. On any given street, three out of five kids are driven to a nonneighborhood school. The downside: declining community cohesion, loss of local investment in neighborhood schools, increasing traffic throughout cities and around schools, loss of independence, and a horrific rise in obesity and related diseases. Large, complex, abstract issues that make my head spin and heart ache.

One step at a time, I tell myself, one baby step at a time.

Like Richmond, Buckman has no bike racks. Ray tells me, "I am not willing to take responsibility for kids getting hit on their bikes or bikes getting stolen."

"Why would you be responsible?" I query. "Are you responsible for kids who are injured in a car crash or who are not strapped into a car seat?"

He leans back in his swivel chair and points to a relatively small sea of asphalt, more like a pond really, only enough for twenty cars. "You see that parking lot? Teachers and parents are constantly asking when they can use it. No one asks for bike parking."

He pauses, anticipating my next move, like a poker player. "I will not spend school resources on bike parking."

Alrighty then, I see your twenty, and raise you fifty more. "We can give you free racks." I whip out a picture of blue staple-shaped bike racks.

He examines his cards carefully, keeping his expression neutral. "I won't accept them. It would imply we are endorsing bicycle riding."

My eyes come to rest on a family photo. A girl and boy, maybe eight and ten years old, and a golden retriever.

"Do your kids bike?" I ask.

"Oh, heck no." He shakes his head. "It's not safe."

I tell him about Winterthur, Switzerland, where every child learns bicycle safety: rules of the road, hand signals, operational skills, balance, and troubleshooting. Not surprisingly, drivers, who all learn what it feels like to bicycle, are super-tolerant and cautious around cyclists.

"Sounds like a good idea," he posits.

Flannery at the new bike rack at Richmond Elementary

"So, Ray," I suggest and throw down a winner. "How'd you like to be the first to try it?"

During graduate school in Washington, D.C., we held a school-sponsored happy hour on Fridays. Always fun, always interesting, but something nagged at me: the waste. More than a hundred students obliviously chucked their beer bottles in the trash each week.

One evening I hauled in a trash can and taped to its side a homemade "Bottles—Recycle Here" sign.

I separated the colors myself (disgusting job) and drove them over to the recycling center. After a few weeks of this, I rounded up three bins, and proclaimed myself "recycle cop."

"Children, children," I would tease, "the green beer bottles go in the bin labeled GREEN GLASS HERE. No, not in the brown bottle bin. Come on, work with me, people, work with me."

When the stale beer fumes started to trigger my asthma and affect my grades, I screwed up the courage to ask the administration if they could absorb this nasty task into their janitorial service. While they're at it, how about reusable mugs in the coffee shop? No problem, said the powers that be, and thanks for asking. Within short order, recycling became a part of the school's code of conduct.

Over at Richmond, Jeff and a buddy form a "committee." After many entertaining Lucky Lab meetings involving microbrews and darts, they write a "report" recommending that Richmond School both allow and encourage bicycling. We install bike racks free of charge. Immediately, dozens of children start bicycling on a regular basis. Jeff's daughter Flannery cruises through her youth a fit, daily cyclist, a harbinger of good things to come. ⚷

Behavioral change takes time. It has taken close to a generation to teach people to place their bottles, cans, paper, and plastic in recycling bins. It will take a generation or more to integrate bicycling and walking into daily life, but only if we get rolling.

⚷ **Encouragement key #5: Invest in comprehensive Safe Routes to School programs. Start now!**

SECTION V

Spreading the Love

1999

Is it true that all good things must come to an end? For six years, we've been going like hell. More than 160 miles (257 km) of new bikeways allow and encourage two Bridge Pedal's worth of residents to travel safely and healthily to their jobs every day. Thousands of new bike parking spaces advertise the city's newfound commitment. We're making inroads in schools. No longer is the "no one bicycles" argument in play, because everywhere you go, bicyclists abound.

But the winds are blowing in another direction. Commissioner Earl's long gone. Charlie too. Our team—me, Roger, Jeff, Barbara, a few others— has been shifted out from under my buddy Rob. Bikes aren't on the top of today's leaders' priority lists. The end comes quickly and without much fanfare, disguised in a memo. The bicycle, pedestrian, and traffic-calming programs are eliminated, the individuals shifted into other groups.

Should I be devastated? How can I be? I'm in love...with olive-skinned, blue-eyed baby Skyler Josiah, who has forever changed my perspective. I want to be with him, with all my heart and soul.

It's time to move on.

CHAPTER 26

Cockroaches

I wait outside the airport terminal at Houston's Hobby International Airport. Charlie Gandy,[50] the wisecracking founder of the Texas Bicycle Coalition, pulls up in a bright-green hippie-RV. The AC blows hot air. It is precisely 114 degrees plus humidity. It's so hot you can fry an egg on the car seat. Charlie isn't hot, he's happy; his ten-year-old daughter is with him, and he's impervious to the inhumane conditions. That's what parental love does for ya.

Charlie's RV won't clear the underground garage of the government office tower, so he wanders the streets of downtown Houston making only right turns, due to some kind of steering wheel problem, until he finds us a nice parking place at a gas station about a mile away.

"Oh yeah, the Gandy man can," he cackles like Charlie Sheen in *Two and a Half Men*.

We jump out of the RV into air so thick you can cut it with a knife. I haul out my rolling suitcase stuffed with a laptop computer, PowerPoint projector, extension cord, technical memos, duct tape, push pins, maps, and backup CDs, plus hard-copy back-ups. Like most consultants, I have learned through trial and extreme error that it is best to assume everything will go wrong.

Not long after the City of Portland downsized the Bicycle Program, I got a call from Michael Jones of Alta Planning + Design, a two-person California firm dedicated to bicycle, pedestrian, and trail planning, design and implementation. Casual in dress but ferocious in business acumen, Michael had been frustrated with his two previous employers, both mainstream planning/engineering firms that failed to take bicycling and walking seriously. Standing at the top of a ski lift at the Alta resort in Utah, he saw another path. Shortly after, he took his portfolio and clients and founded his own firm. He offered me a part-time job out of my house, perfect for a new mom. I took a deep breath and plunged headfirst into my new career: consulting.

---

50 As of this writing, Charlie is the mobility coordinator in Long Beach, California.

At the City of Portland, Roger takes charge of implementing the Bicycle Master Plan. The pace slows, given the diminished political importance of bicycle transportation, but the seeds planted a half decade ago continue to take root, sprout, and spread. Bike use, safety, air quality, health, and prosperity are all on the rise in Portland.

And I'm out in the wide, wild world, juggling contracts and childcare, administration and analysis, and spreading the bicycle transportation gospel far and wide. Folks want to hear it; that's for sure. Build it, and they will come. The devil's in the details. Plant seeds, and a garden will grow. Persistence pays off. Make it work for women and children, and it works for everyone. Portland's lessons seem universal.

Or are they? Can I apply what I've learned to other places? I'm about to find out, starting with a little gig in my childhood home, the Lone Star State.

⚙⚙⚙⚙⚙

Charlie and I walk at a snail's pace to a meeting. This is the life of a consultant: meetings with government officials, public meetings, field-work, analysis, writing, more meetings. Still, far fewer than the six or more a day I had as a city employee.

Charlie and his daughter hold hands and chat up a storm, lost in a divorced-dad–daughter love bubble, while I trudge along, dragging my suitcase, each step an effort. Heat-conducting glass, asphalt, and steel are the only materials in sight; hasn't Houston heard the news that trees are a good thing? I'm sweating so badly I look like I'm in a *Girls Gone Wild* wet T-shirt contest (sort of... I'm actually not built that way). Motorists project pity—or is it disgust?—from their protected air-conditioned metal boxes. We must be escaped patients from a mental asylum. Why else would we be walking in downtown Houston in this heat? I'm remembering why I left Texas.

Inside, the AC is set—per Texas law, I believe—at fifty degrees. Of course, I left my jacket to melt in the RV. "Can I get you a coke?" asks Houston Bike Coordinator Mignette Dorsey. (In Texan, "coke" translates to soft drink, pop, or cold refreshment of any kind.)

"Can I have hot tea?"

The room is silent. I sense an emotion akin to horror.

"You mean iced tea?" she gently rebukes and hands me a tall glass of ice with a splash of brown liquid thrown in for good measure. More evidence of why I left Texas.

I graciously reach for the glass.

"Remember," I tell myself. "What doesn't kill you makes you stronger."

❋❋❋❋❋

Our client, the City of Pasadena, is a working-class suburb south of Houston built around the oil refinery industry. Like much of America, its roads were built without sidewalks or bike lanes, leaving almost no place for residents to walk or bike. I'm 2,000 miles (3,219 km) from Oregon, but the situation is the same.

It turns out that the shelf of each bayou makes for a perfect trail.

That's the bad news. The good news is that, like many Southern towns, stormwater is controlled by a system of concrete canals (aka bayous) paved by the Army Corps of Engineers during the 1930s public-works era.

Charlie and I put on thigh-high waders and hack through brush. We ford across streams and slither under roadway overpasses.

After a 6:00 a.m. start, and meetings interspersed with fieldwork and stops to cool Charlie's radiator, we head over to the local tourist attraction: Mickey Gilley's, famed honky-tonk bar from the Debra Winger/John Travolta flick *Urban Cowboy*. After two or six margaritas, we call it a night. Charlie drops me at the Motel 6 then heads out to discreetly park his fluorescent tank somewhere close by.

I distract the 18-year-old concierge from her Mexican soap opera to get my room key. "Elevator no funciona," she informs me. I haul my suitcase up the stairs and wind my way around the balconies until I find my door. Inside, I am greeted by a four-inch-long (10 cm) flying water bug (aka cockroach). A half second later, I'm pounding on the desk.

"Hello! I need help!"

Apparently, this is a crucial moment in the drama—Maria has caught Emilio having an affair with her best friend! "Un momento," she calls out from the back room.

"Now, please! Es muy importante! Es un mucho grando cucaracha in my room!" I hold my fingers a foot wide to clarify the severity of the situation.

Unfortunately, all other rooms are full—there's a sales convention going on—so the only defense is a good offense. Together, we tentatively open

Me with Skyler, who, tragically, starts out hating bicycling (especially the helmet) but later in life evolves into quite the avid rider

the door. We're soul sisters now, united in a killing mission. We find the monster lounging on the curtain. The concierge takes aim with a flyswatter. The beast laughs and flies around the room in a show of strength, laughing, "Hah, you think you can kill me with that puny plastic waffle?"

We retreat to the bathroom to regroup. She starts babbling in Spanish and disappears. I sit on the toilet and take deep breaths. My other reasons—heat, humidity, and excessive use of ice—for abandoning Texas pale in comparison to this one: the preponderance of nasty, flying, biting, stinging, allergy-inducing creatures. The concierge returns with a can of Raid. Now we're talking! A half hour later, we emerge victorious, having drowned the monster. (Y'all from the South know what I'm talking about. Raid is like ice cream to a roach. The only way to kill it is to drown it.) The concierge is never seen again. Drowning bugs to appease a crazy American woman is apparently not in her job description.

I lie on my bed, heart pounding in response to the possibly dangerous inhaled combo of Raid and albuterol (asthma med). What am I doing here, battling a prehistoric flying beast? I miss Skyler, my two-year-old, who I left in Dallas with my folks. It's only one night away, but still, I miss him.

How can I possibly help this godforsaken place? I long for the stable bureaucrat's life.

"Listen to how ridiculous you sound," I argue with myself. "You had public meetings almost nightly back then. This is a huge opportunity to make a difference! Stop whining! Pull yourself together!"

I call my Mom to check in. "How's Skyler doing?"

"Good. You sure were right about him being a puzzle whiz! He put together a brand-new hundred-piece puzzle like it was nothing."

"Yep, that's my boy. Thanks, Mom!"

If he's fine, then I will be too. Mr. Dead Bug is just a symbol of a bygone era, sent to scare me into retreating from my mission by dredging up childhood terrors. Not gonna work, no sirree.

I drift off to sleep picturing Skyler putting together his Thomas the Tank Engine puzzle, finding all the edge pieces first, building the frame, and then carefully turning each piece until it fits just right.

"My doctor said I need to get out and walk more." An elderly resident at a public meeting wants to know if our project will help her. Pasadena's one "trail"—a sidewalk around the perimeter of Strawberry Park—is thronged every night. Unfortunately, it's nowhere near her house. She reminds me of Paula and a hundred others from my wheel-and-pony days. Like so many elderly suburban residents, she is trapped in a place where walking is simply not an option.

The head of the chamber of commerce is next. He's a big man, not even remotely on the hefty-but-fit side. He jokes, "Now look, y'all. I've got my SUV idling outside. I just came for the free donuts." General hilarity ensues.

"Seriously, y'all, this is what I'm hearing: Businesses say they can't attract workers to come live here if we don't provide parks, exercise, and safe places for their kids to ride. Bottom line: Businesses need fit and healthy employees, not couch potatoes."

"Hooligans! Last month, one of them had the nerve to wave at me. He did! He was staring! I was sooo scared. And then..." *Dramatic pause.* "They went down to the boat dock to hang out. We had to put up a gate to keep them out!"

This comes from a severe-looking June Cleaver, in a higher-income area of town near NASA where we're recommending a trail. Of course, she totally supports the concept of trails, just not here. We're at the final stage of our project: a city council hearing to approve the plan. In this woman, I see shades of Ken Wilhelm, supportive of bike lanes anywhere but on his street; crying Julie, fearful of change; and Chad the restaurant owner, opposed to all government activity except that which benefits him personally.

Heard it all before, back in Portland. Trails will bring crime, lower property values, facilitate bad behavior, erode privacy, reduce safety, and bring on the ten plagues. Whether in the urban Northwest or suburban deep South, the concept of a trail seems to trigger primal fears; once touched, these fears take on a life of their own, far beyond the boundaries of rational or logical thinking. Battling bugs in a fleabag hotel room is nothing compared to the fight for the hearts and minds of residents mired in fear of change.

 Face the naysayers with solid research and facts.

From the podium, the city project manager gently notes, "Well, good for you then. Looks like you already solved the problem."

Glaring, not even flustered, the NIMBY[51] woman harrumphs, tosses her sprayed-to-perfection brown bob, and switches her argument. "I spoke to a wildlife expert about this. The trail will harm the deer, rabbits, and the rest of the wildlife we have worked so hard to nurture in our lovely community." She chokes up a bit, her shoulders heaving in emotion.

She begs, "Tissue, please? Can someone please get me a tissue?"

A city staffer whispers in my left ear, "Last week, she was in here asking permission to shoot the deer for eating her tomato plants."

She concludes her testimony with a petition and threat of a lawsuit.

A guy sitting on my other side shakes his head in disgust. "Gawd, I can't stand that woman."

"Do you live in the area?" I ask.

"Sure I do."

"Really? Would you please testify?"

"Heck no! She and her friends are crazy. Just know that most of us support the trail."

Up to the microphone steps a Canadian Mountie in both size and temperament. Standing very straight, with the full weight of the authority vested in him, Sheriff Johnson declares, "Folks, listen. The bad guys are like cockroaches." He too pauses for dramatic flair, then fixates each of the city councilors with an intense Earl-like gaze.

"Cockroaches! Shine a light on 'em. They scatter."[52]

I start giggling. A light! Of course! Try to smash roaches head-on, they shrug it off. Poisoning them takes a long time and, in my case, backfires because the fumes provoke wheezing. Shine a light on 'em, they scatter. Good to know.

The lesson is deeper still: Shine a positive light not just on the bad guys to make them scatter, but on the good that our work does. As Pasadena's leaders and residents move forward to adopt this plan, then build and enjoy the envisioned trails, they will vanquish outdated attitudes and take steps toward a brighter future. And every light I shine into residents' hearts and minds makes the sacrifices—time away from my son, the misery of seedy hotels and inhospitable climates, intense competition, and responsibility—worthwhile.

---

51 NIMBY = not in my backyard.
52 This declaration leads us to develop a program called Trail Safe, which is based on the proven concept that when you bring good folks into nice areas, bad guys go away. In our context, that means opening up dark places, adding lighting, cleaning out trash and debris, applying a high level of aesthetic design, and engaging residents in keeping eyes on the trail.

CHAPTER 27

Biggest Bang for the Buck

I'm not that much of a water babe, but when I smell, hear, or see the ocean, I am drawn like a moth to a flame. I want to walk the shore slowly, feeling both its vastness and my own comparative insignificance. My daughter, Sasha, on the other hand, born three and a half years after Skyler, must get wet, immediately. There's no stopping her from rolling in and inhaling prodigious quantities of sand.

From the looks of this wide, flat, scenic swath of rail line parallel to the ocean in San Diego, California, she and I are not the only ocean-drawn moths. Up and down the rail line is evidence of people crossing the tracks

Rails-with-trails (RWT) are located on or adjacent to active rail lines, like this one in New Jersey, as opposed to rails-to-trails that replace an abandoned rail line.

from their neighborhoods to the beach. A beaten path winds along the rails too, and so I can understand why planners from the six neighboring cities envisioned a trail not unlike Portland's Springwater Corridor.

To the railroad company, however, this idea is about as popular as New Coke, the Ford Edsel, or the Guns n' Roses comeback attempt, akin to the Union Pacific Railway's initial reaction to the Steel Bridge Riverwalk: Buzz off.

So incensed are the railroad officials, they lobby for a national ban on trails collocated on active rail lines, aka, rails-with-trails. This in turn incenses the well-respected Rails-to-Trails Conservancy, which recently published a study demonstrating the success of such trails. To the rescue comes my boss-turned-business partner Michael Jones, who successfully argues that a better approach than an outright ban is dialogue, research, and analysis.

My assignment, should I choose to accept it: determine if such trails are safe and, if so, develop guidelines that could affect rail corridors throughout the nation.

My background in both international and localized diplomacy could come in real handy. Negotiating between tough, take-no-prisoners railroad officials and wide-eyed, optimistic trail advocates will not be unlike trying to reach peace accords in the Middle East. My public meeting experience will be mightily tested.

I'm too naïve and sleep-deprived to recognize that it's a project so fraught with pitfalls it could break Alta.

"Sure, sounds good," I tell Michael.

His marching orders: answer the question as to the safety and wisdom of putting trails adjacent to moving trains. "We are not advocating for an outcome," he says. "Leave no stone unturned, and keep asking questions." With that, he's off to other projects, and I am off to learn some really good lessons, for both myself and anyone dealing with railroads.

"I was coming up to a trestle when I saw the guy lying on the tracks. There was no way I was going to be able to stop in time. I blew the horn, and he got up slowly, as if he didn't have a care in the world, turned, and faced me. Time stopped. He looked me right in the eye and held out his arms like Jesus on the cross. There was no way I could stop. No way."

The wiry man in blue jeans and a maroon ballcap is lost for a moment in his own sorrow. Part of me silently begs him stop talking; I don't want to hear the rest. He regains his composure, just long enough to transfer his anger to me.

This photo provoked tremendous emotion amongst train conductors.

"That photo you showed, with the kids on the tracks..." He stabs his finger at my chest. "And the way you described trains as 'romantic' in our culture...Don't you dare call kids on the tracks 'romantic!'"

In my rails-with-trails wheel-and-pony show is a photo of two small children playing on the tracks adjacent to the Railroad Trail in Michigan. Perhaps they were placing pennies on the tracks. Perhaps they were just hanging out. Either way, to this man, to the railroad officials at this conference, those kids are far from nostalgic Norman Rockwell Americana. To him, that picture is a slap in the face, a PTSD trigger of the moment when a stranger forced him to end a human life. I'm giving this presentation at a conference sponsored by Operation Lifesaver, a nonprofit organization set up by train operators and their families to encourage people to stay off railroad tracks. This is because just about every train operator at some point will kill someone. The most common deaths are drunks or suicides, impatient motorists who try to go around lowered gates and stall out, or daredevils who trip as they race or dash in front of the train. The train operator almost never has enough time to stop. He and his loved ones become emotional casualties along with the family of the deceased. Operation Lifesaver allows these victims to channel their sorrow into safety activities targeted at kids, drivers, and pedestrians.

"Look." He shakes his head and raises his eyebrows, looking around to engage his comrades in explaining to me the realities of train operation. "I run the train along the east San Francisco Bay. It's often foggy. At least once a week, I come around a blind curve and some idiot is too close to the tracks or crossing the tracks. You're telling me you want to invite thousands of people to get in my way every day?"

"No, sir," I respond somberly, "I'm studying if and when a trail next to an active rail line makes sense. And I'm trying to figure out if providing a trail in a location like yours actually will make things better, not worse."

Undercrossing on the well-designed Tony Knowles Coastal Rail Trail in Anchorage, Alaska

In Alberta, Canada, tracks run on the edge of a residential neighborhood. Every morning and afternoon, children stream across the tracks to get to school. They dodge trash and junk, see graffiti, and try to avoid down-and-out folks using the bushes as their homes or toilets. Like many railroad corridors, this one is degraded, neglected, and far too extensive for effective daily policing. One day, a second grader is surrounded by menacing strangers who steal his backpack and send him home sobbing to his father, Constable Bill Landson. Bill isn't just any law enforcement officer, though. He's the Canadian Pacific Railway's hired hand.

Just like Sheriff Johnson down in Texas, Bill figures that the best way to get the crap out of the corridor is to clean it up. In short order, his company builds a trail, tunnels under the rails to build a safe crossing, plants flowers, and adds a picnic bench and lighting. Sure enough, the vandals vamoose, a trend mirrored in Western Australia, throughout Europe, and in dozens of American states.

"Yo," calls out a railroad lawyer from the audience, "We're still the deep-pocketed robber barons in most people's minds. It doesn't matter how drunk or disturbed, stupid or arrogant, inattentive or deliberate the victim is. People want cold hard cash."

184

Despite strong legal protections in every state, and even though fault almost always lies with the deceased, railroads often shell out a settlement because it is cheaper to settle than to risk losing a bigger payout at the hands of a non-sympathetic jury.

"I don't care how strong those protections are," the attorney flatly states. "We're going to get sued, and it's going to be costly to defend. Welcome to America. The more money you've got, the more you have to pay." Can't argue with that one.

But I've done my homework. The only known incident of a trail user getting hurt by a train is in Alaska, when a boy walking along the Tony Knowles Coastal Rail Trail crawled under a chain-link fence and attempted to jump onto a moving train, with tragic results. The railroad was not held responsible. Given hundreds of miles of trails in existence, this one incident speaks to an excellent safety record.

After the presentation, the San Francisco train conductor hands me his card. "How can I help?" he asks. "How can we all help?"

The net result of our study is this: properly designed rails-with-trails reduce trespassing, vandalism, and nuisance crimes. Often, as with the Steel Bridge Riverwalk, they can be win-win solutions for both the railroad and trail agency.

Down in San Diego, these facts do little to advance the Coastal Rail Trail. To the contrary, railroad officials dig their heels in further. Not one of the hundred-plus American, Canadian, European, or Australian trails we've studied is relevant, in their minds. They commission a video showing a twenty-pound girl-like, round-bottom blow-up mannequin weighted down by sand (think "Weebles wobble, but they don't fall down") next to the train. As the train zooms by, the little "girl" gets knocked over by the force of the wind.[53] Her blood-red scarf flutters in the air and floats down the tracks. It's the most ridiculous piece of propaganda since the 1950s commercial showing a little girl cowering in her prairie shack, the totally screwed survivor of a nuclear attack.

Understand all sides of an issue. Look for win-win solutions.

---

[53] Two Federal Railroad Administration studies on the aerodynamic effects of high-speed trains concluded that beyond 4 feet (slightly more than 1m), the air pressure effects on bystanders of trains traveling as fast as 150 mph (241 km/h) are likely insignificant, and that a flat-nosed train traveling at 90 mph (144 km/h) should not produce such winds beyond a distance of 23 feet (7 m).

I seek counsel from George Hudson, pikeminnow stalker, permit procurer extraordinaire, who is now my business partner along with Michael. Surely we can outfox the railroad.

We set up our own wind velocity tests,[54] using not a weighted-down balloon but a real live adult and his actual seventy-pound, ten-year-old son. No goofy crash test dummies for our team of professionals. At 15 feet (4.6 m) away from the tracks with no barriers, the wind, debris and sound impacts are noticeable although not destabilizing, while at 30 feet (9 m) they're but a cool breeze at the beach.[55]

Take that! The rail board votes to endorse our recommendations and orders its staff to play nice. It looks like a victory, it smells like a victory, but it is not to be. Through some magical bureaucratic mumbo-jumbo, the rules as written require the trail be located 50 feet (15 m) away from the rail centerline. It's a distance impossible to meet, a deal-breaker.

Even as we stall out on the Coastal Rail Trail, though, we open doors all across North America, from Victoria, B.C., to Austin, Texas, to Cambridge, Massachusetts, and beyond. The study pay-off is beyond huge.

And it occurs to me, finally, that I owe Portland engineer Rob Barnard an apology for my immature impatience with the miraculous Steel Bridge Riverwalk, the only trail ever cantilevered onto an active rail bridge. With seven thousand-plus bike/walk trips a day and a spotless safety record, it is proof perfection that persistence pays off.

---

[54] Birk, Mia, *Trails and High-Speed Rail: Are They Compatible?*, National Center for Bicycling and Walking, December 2003.

[55] We also shoot video holding a wind meter. At a distance of about 22 feet (6.7 m) from the track centerline, there are no substantial wind effects — even when a flat-nosed train passes at 90 mph (145 km/h).

CHAPTER 28

Learning the Ropes

Sometimes, my job boils down to preventing bad ideas from happening. It's not nearly as far-reaching as a national study of rails-with-trails or the Portland Bicycle Master Plan, but important, nonetheless. This I learn in a nearby town that is preparing to widen a six-mile-long (almost 10 km) roadway. They hire a large engineering firm, BBS,[56] which brings me onto the team at the county's request.

The half-hour bus ride from Portland lands me and my bike at a huge bus transfer station. Across the street is a new family subdivision. Catty-corner is a high-school complex; opposite that a vacant field/utility corridor behind which are hundreds of new homes. It's a two-lane rural road surrounded by exploding humanity. The disconnect screams for attention.

A half-hour ride reminiscent of my early days exploring the gritty bike-unfriendly areas of Portland, and I arrive at a meeting already underway. Six male engineers are examining plans to widen the intersection to a proper suburban size. One asks if I am making a delivery.

"Ah, no, I'm not a bike messenger. I'm on the consulting team." I introduce myself to the county officials and BBS staff and place my helmet on the chair next to me.

When it's my turn, I pass out a ten-page memo and explain that our projections show that hundreds of students and transit riders want to cross the street, but the current conditions are terribly uncomfortable.

"We need wide sidewalks and median refuges. I recommend we keep the crossing distance as short as possible, and limit the number and width of travel and turning lanes. Specific techniques include high-visibility crosswalk markings, bike lanes, and leading pedestrian intervals."[57]

You could hear a pin drop.

The county engineer, a Pakistani immigrant with an impeccable British accent, chuckles dryly, then raises his left eyebrow as if to say, "Who

---

56 Build Big Stuff. Not their real name.
57 Leading pedestrian intervals give pedestrians three to five seconds of green in advance of motor vehicle movements. This way, pedestrians are more visible to left-turning traffic because they're in the middle of the crosswalk.

invited this chick, and what exactly is she smoking?" He then launches into a discussion of the county's land-use and traffic models, which project increasing traffic due to unbridled suburban-style sprawl.

As he continues to hold court for his five nodding and smiling yes-men, I feel like a balloon deflating. I reach in my memory bank for my visits to Islamabad, Pakistan, and understand how his engineering training on a highway-transportation system financed by the World Bank and Asian Development Bank could lead him to be excited about blowing up this two-lane country road into a five- or seven-lane highway.

I examine my fingernails, make a grocery list, and wonder how I could have so misunderstood my role. "Hello, gentlemen...you're paying me for my 'input,' right? Can I get my check now?"

BBS's lead engineer, a square-faced sixty-five-year-old who had spent three decades at the Army Corps of Engineers converting wetlands to concrete, snaps the room to attention by slamming onto the table a handful of glossy brochures. "Here's what we're a gonna do," he announces. "We're gonna build us a spewey."

At least that's what I think he said. Donald's Southern accent makes it sound like he is a farmer's wife calling out for the pigs to come eat their slop. Leafing through the booklet, I learn that the "single point urban interchange" (SPUI) is one of the world's most efficient intersection treatments. For motor vehicles, that is.

Maybe you've been to the movies when, during the previews, they show that commercial for the concession stand, the one where space cars fly around, *Jetsons*-like, dodging popcorn? You wonder: in this new space

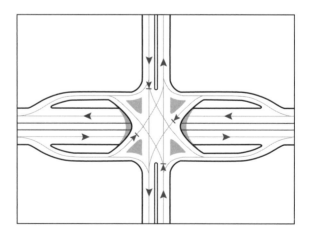

Example of the hostile "single point urban interchange"

world, where are the people? This is what the catalogue for the SPUI looks like. Flip through page after glossy page and you will see not one human, for the basic concept of the SPUI is that the most efficient signals only involve motor vehicles.

Introduce pedestrians or bicyclists into the equation and the SPUI becomes less of a miracle worker and more of an instrument of torture. We analyze the beast from a human standpoint and find nineteen to thirty-six points of conflict. It makes me want to spew. And if this is the future of American cities, we are in colossal trouble.

⊗⊛⊛⊛⊛

"You have to signalize the ramps," I tell Donald a few months later, as we go over the third or fourth of our memos. "Or pedestrians and cyclists won't get any gaps."

"Of course they don't get gaps!" he bellows. "That's the whole point of the SPUI!" Pedestrian and bicycle signal phases will degrade its efficiency, causing traffic to back up, cars to crash, and nations to crumble. Plus, it will piss off our client, big-time.

"Listen up, Donald," I explain. "Dress it up, put on a bow and lipstick, and the beast is still a beast." The SPUI may make sense, in some locations, but not, for criminy's sake, at the intersection of a high school and transit station in a residential neighborhood.

⊗⊛⊛⊛⊛

My role as reluctant naysayer proves effective; eventually the SPUI is beaten back to its cave in the mountains, leaving us with its slightly less hideous stepmonster cousin: numerous turning lanes, more than one hundred feet (30 m) to cross in each direction, and few pedestrian features.

For me, this is a decidedly unpleasant experience. We are paid some $60,000 for our work, at least $40,000 of which went to fighting the SPUI. I'd much rather be developing bike and pedestrian plans, recommending trails, and writing bike parking codes,[58] than fighting against an engineering nightmare.

O──⏋ Fight just as hard to avoid bad facilities as to create new bicycle-friendly ones.

---

[58] Not one of the dozens of bike parking codes we've written has suffered anywhere close to the level of rancor as Portland's did.

"Oh, well," counsels my dad via the phone from Texas. "You had a job to do, and you did it. Welcome to consulting."

It could have been worse. The SPUI could have been built. So there you have it, another lesson: Sometimes, avoiding a disaster is as much a victory as creating something new.

Hope in the Burbs

My next gig sounds promising: A trails plan in a fast-growing Southeastern suburb built around a hundred-year-old Wild West–themed town square. It's one of dozens of projects I've taken on of late, thanks to the addition of a legion of top-notch young smarties cultivated through graduate-level planning courses I teach at Portland State University. These planners, data whiz kids, cartographers, writers, designers, and dreamers, all walk the talk and infuse my every waking moment with positive energy. Together, we can do two, then five, then ten times the volume of projects and plans, touching exponentially more people and communities than I can on my own.

Our first stop is city hall, where chief planner Grady Sloan welcomes Allison Wildman and me into a small conference room whose windows overlook a big plaza and fountain. City hall doubles as a community and aquatic center, and it is crackling with life.

Sloan, a slender, mousy blond man, explains that residents are demanding parks and trails. Like so many suburbs, this town's country way of life is rapidly giving way to fast growth and relentless traffic.

Fact: If we build houses far from work places, groceries, parks, and schools, and provide no mass-transit service, bikeways, or walkways, the vast majority of us will drive. Obesity, stress, and pollution levels are higher in sprawling areas, which are less safe overall, factoring in both crime and traffic safety. Older suburbs often have no sidewalks. Schools are often located on major roads. Parents are expected to be chauffeurs. At a young age, kids become addicted to auto transportation. It's hard to break these habits later in life. Suburban residents are so acculturated to driving everywhere that they simply cannot imagine doing it any other way.

"Over here," Sloan points out a creek on an aerial photo, "we've had a serious problem with flooding." Dozens of houses had been built right up to the edges of quaint bubbling streams that in a storm quickly become roaring rivers. Homeowners learned this lesson when their houses took in water and started sliding.

Sloan continues, "We think there's a pretty good opportunity to put a trail along this power corridor." He traces a finger along a swath of green. "But I'm not sure how to cross this creek. And if we can't cross the creek, we'll have to route trail users onto the road." The seven-lane roadway looks to be a horrific compromise.

We note vacant fields to the north, unspoiled creeks, schools, community centers, a freight rail line, newer housing developments, and shopping areas. Plenty of opportunities, it seems, to develop the infrastructure that will allow people to integrate bicycling and walking into their daily lives, if not for every trip, at least for some. Tens of millions of people live in burbs like this one, and they aren't going anywhere anytime soon. **0——⊤**

Here, there, everywhere, no matter where I go, I find promising rail and utility corridors, big roads with excess space, neighborhood streets waiting to be calmed, narrow streets needing to be shared, and people desperate for places to walk or bike. From California to the Rockies, up and down the East Coast, at the beaches, on the plains, and in large cities, small towns, suburbs, exurbs, and the heartland of rural America, hope for a more healthy future is in full blossom, a veritable field of wildflowers as far as the eye can see. It's up to us to transform hope into reality.

Allison rolls up the maps and we set off to do our field work. With her cropped honey-brown hair, unapologetic muscled build, and solid sense of herself, Allison would be a superstar bicycling/climbing/Frisbee-playing Mia Hamm if the economics had permitted such a thing. Some people convey information through words; Allison speaks the language of movement and art. Her hand-drawn renderings get our projects to yes faster than a thousand public meetings. I'm lucky to have her along.

On the way to the vacant fields, we drive along rows of brand-new, two-car driveway snout-houses—two-story, one-story, each the same style and color, the exact $60,000 and $80,000 starter houses Sloan had described. "Developers are building this crap down here. Zero percent down! Zero percent financing! It's all gonna fall down in a few years." He was so negative I doubted he would last long in his job.

Not a single human is to be seen on the small, manicured lawns on streets lacking sidewalks. It's like the 60s protest song: "All the boxes, little boxes, little boxes made of ticky-tacky. And the people live in boxes, little boxes made of ticky-tacky." Allison and I look around for the cameras just in

---

0——⊤ In the burbs, focus on off-road paths and short trips in neighborhoods rather than the hard-to-affect work trip.

case we've stepped into *The Truman Show*, the movie in which Jim Carrey doesn't realize that his suburban life is being filmed as a reality-TV show.

Behind the ticky-tacky is the promising green corridor. A prefabricated bridge will solve the creek-crossing problem. Hope surges through me. Next, we head to a creek site marked on the map as an opportunity.

"Something's wrong," Allison wryly suggests, and the hope dissipates in a sunny, wispy whimper.

Backhoes and front-loaders are clearing the land right up to the creek's edge. Stakes and orange ribbons mark lot perimeters. Construction crews are digging sewer-line trenches. There will be no trail here, nor sidewalks. Opportunity lost. Worse, problem perpetuated: These houses too will flood and slide.

Back at the city, I inform Sloan that a construction crew appears to be building a subdivision on the supposedly vacant greenspace.

"Nope, don't think so," he argues. "Don't recall us issuing any permits."

It's a weird moment. "Ummm, well...I was just out there, and I'm not an expert in development or anything, but I did spend an awful lot of time with my son watching construction during his three-year-old truck-obsession phase. Those sure looked like bulldozers and diggers—not the technical term, I know." I hand him my evidence via digital camera. Apparently, the government is standing still in comparison to the Speedy Gonzalez–pace of development.

"Listen," I console, "I have some recommendations. First, we need to get the trail network adopted on your planning maps ASAP and require developers to build the trail as part of their subdivisions. You can apply for grants or finance the rest of it. And you need to require houses be set back from the creek edge by 20 feet (6 m). This will ensure that the next time a rainstorm comes, the houses aren't flooded."

Sloan looks bewildered. "We can't require developers to put in a trail or sidewalk."

"Why not?"

He frowns in irritation, "It's illegal."

"No, it's not." I promise to send him development-code language used in hundreds of cities. Don't they teach this stuff in planning school? Both local development standards and all roadway design guides can and should require complete streets with sidewalks, bike lanes, frequent and short pedestrian crossings, and landscaping along roads and in parking lots. It's 100 percent worth it, and way, way less costly and challenging than coming back to retrofit the streets later.

"It won't hold up in court," he insists.

"Of course it will."

I wish I could say that this is a *Field of Dreams* moment, that the town then builds it, and people come, ride, and walk, and no other schlockily built homes are consumed by the creek. But to tell you the truth, I don't know. I do know that we gave them the necessary tools—a concept network of bikeways, walkways, and trails along with design guidelines and code amendments—to prevent a cul-de-sac, drive-through future. What they do next is up to them.

CHAPTER 30

Sharrows

"Yikes, these streets are steep!" Mind you, I'm trying not to complain, but I am seven months pregnant with Sasha, and biking is a tad uncomfortable. I'm following the lead of Oliver Gajda, the guy charged with improving San Francisco's bicycling conditions.

We've already been out for a couple of hours and my back is starting to seize. And oh, do they have challenges. Really narrow roads steeper than a stairway to heaven, heavy demand for on-street parking, huge demand for bike lanes from a ferociously strident advocacy community, a challenging bureaucratic structure and a rocky political climate.

Young, earnest, square-jawed and relentlessly caffeinated Oliver seems oblivious to both the hills and my condition. Ten miles (16 km) later, I am cooked, french fried, and fricasseed, and insist on turning around. But not before I've come to understand that this is the perfect place to apply another of the European treatments, the shared-lane marking, aka *sharrow,* which indicates that motorists and cyclists are meant to harmoniously coexist even without a bike lane. ⚿

The problem: It's not in that darn Manual of Uniform Traffic Control Devices. My assignment is to apply the sharrow, study it, and gain acceptance from the body that tightly controls California's version of the Manual. I'm so tired of hearing about the Manual's limitations that it's becoming personified in my mind. Not just an evil cube, the Borg, determined to assimilate everything in its wake, but an evil control freak, Manuel, holding a pinkie to his mouth and cackling from far, far away, "I'll give you sharrows for ONE MILLION DOLLARS."

Oliver wants a replica of the Portland blue bike lane marking study and I want to succeed, not just for him, but for all the communities striving to become more bicycle friendly. But here, like in Portland close to a decade

---

⚿ **Use sharrows in slower speed conditions or to fill in short gaps, but preferably not as a substitute for bike lanes.**

---

ago, I am about to come face-to-face with the realities of trying to evolve bikeway design standards in an auto-oriented world.

I crawl along for an hour and a half in smoggy, hot Los Angeles air in a rented, canary yellow PT Cruiser. The front desk clerk at the California Department of Transportation waves me to an elevator bank that descends into the world of traffic standards.

The elevator leaves me in a cavernous, windowless basement, in the front of which sits, like a row of judges, a panel of traffic engineers, troopers, and AAA officials. I quietly roll my wheel-and-pony show along the rows of folded chairs and sit down next to a man with tanning-booth-orange skin and stiff, over-gelled hair. His pin-striped suit is well-worn and a bit too small for his oversized frame. My first thought is of sweet, lonely shower-curtain-ring salesman John Candy in *Planes, Trains, and Automobiles*; the second of desperate William H. Macy in *Fargo*.

Up at the front of the room, a rangy Willem Defoe—actually, important traffic official Eldon Nasher—announces that next on the agenda is Chris Kelly of Traffic Sign, Inc., here to discuss a proposed color change for school-zone signs.

"That's me," whispers the John Candy look-alike. I shift my knees to the aisle as he stands up and tightens the knot of his purple and gray diagonal striped tie. His scuffed, over-polished shoes look as if they have walked many miles.

Kelly explains that lime-colored school-zone signs are far more visible than yellow.

The panel wants to see his evidence. "Where have you studied this sign?" asks Nasher.

"Well," harrumphs Kelly, clearly taken aback by the question. "We've got one up in a school zone in Mendocino."

"Probably his kid's school," comments someone from behind me. "These guys are always trying to sell us some new product."

The panel takes a quick break while I set up my projector and laptop. Down in these depths, we've got no natural sunlight with which to contend.

I introduce myself as the former bike coordinator in Portland, turned principal at Alta Planning + Design. "Good morning, gentlemen! I'm here today to talk to you about shared-lane markings, aka sharrows. Now, you all know what a bike lane is, correct?" Heads nod.

"You probably also know that sometimes, cities can't or won't put in bike lanes. The law dictates that cyclists ride as far to the right as possible, but unfortunately that puts them, on many streets, real close to parked cars.

Clockwise, from top left: shared lane markings at the time in Gainesville, Florida; Denver, Colorado; Paris, France; London, England; and Copenhagen, Denmark

When a driver opens a car door, the cyclist is in real danger of being hit. The sharrow is a compromise, a big 'share the lane' marking that encourages cyclists to ride outside the 'door zone.'"

"What does it look like?" asks Nasher.

"Great question. I've looked all around the world and found no uniformity whatsoever. Check out this variability in color, size, style, and placement." I gleefully flash slides of sharrows from cities in the United States, Denmark, Australia, Switzerland and the Netherlands. They are big and small, white, green, or yellow, in the middle or to the side of the lane—in sum, a hodgepodge of ways to shout out to motorists, "Yo, share the lane!"

"Gentlemen, therein lies the rub. Which marking should we use? Now, I'm happy to experiment with all of them, but my clients in San Francisco say I have to stick to a budget." I can envision Oliver, a man of mixed Polish and Vietnamese heritage and stoical New England upbringing, wringing his hands in worry at the escalating cost of the study.

Nasher and cohorts direct me to come back with a specific recommendation on the marking. I pack up and drive back to the airport, noting both the consistency of traffic signs and utter lack of bikeways on L.A.'s streets.

Meeting two, I return to L.A. to report on our analysis of three of the most frequently used markings.[59] The standard bike-lane marking, sans line, seemed to confuse folks. They thought the arrow meant "go straight," like a prescriptive directional arrow. They pretty well understood the other two markings: the bike-in-house, aka Sergeant Cyclist, and bike-chevron (see photos on previous page).

We plan to videotape before-and-after motorists' and cyclists' behavior on ten streets,[60] analyze the data, and conduct surveys of motorists and cyclists.

"Take note of how this young woman is handling her study," Nasher warns the lime-sign salesmen Kelly, who has returned to peddle a new flashing stop sign he coincidentally installed in the same school zone as before.

"This is what we want to see, a thorough and thoughtful scientific approach."

I beam at the praise. Kelly intercepts me at the door and asks if I have time for coffee.

It turns out he's a well-meaning and starry-eyed inventor. I'm not sure if he truly believes that lime is more visible, or that illuminated stop signs will increase safety, but at the rate he's going, his ideas aren't going to bring home the bacon. The panel's reluctance to approve his products seems right-on to me, for he hasn't offered one shred of proof in his favor. Thank goodness someone is keeping folks like Kelly from selling lord knows how many orange, vibrating, or flashing signs.

And yet, I myself am hoping to convince this very same panel that sharrows are a good idea. Listening to Kelly rail in quiet desperation, I hope he has some other income-generating mechanism—say, an actual job—to support his wife and kids.

Our study methodology, in contrast, is scientifically valid. If the evidence shows the sharrow is a loser, I will encourage San Francisco to back away. But if it's a winner, I'll do my darnedest to advance the cause of creating more safe and comfortable conditions for cyclists.

---

59 Human factors analysis carried out by Professor Ron Van Houten, an expert in behavioral science from the University of Western Michigan, who analyzed the reactions of groups of cyclists and motorists to photo renderings of sharrow-marked streets.

60 Some of the streets are two lanes, some four. One is used primarily for recreation on the weekends, while most are used by bicycle commuters during the week.

Sharrow on a San Francisco street

About nine months later, Kelly pats the chair next to him. Does he attend every single meeting?

"How's Marie?" I ask.

"Good, good!" He whips out his wallet to show me the latest kid photos. Nasher invites me up.

"I'm pleased to tell you," I offer, "that the bike-chevron marking works the best, and quite well. Cyclists position themselves away from the door zone. Bonus: They stop riding against traffic. More good news: Motorists seem to drive more safely around cyclists, and both motorists and cyclists like the markings."

For me, for the City of San Francisco, for all the communities looking for a way to communicate a simple message in a complex world, these results spell success.[61] The panel votes to accept the study results, and Kelly flashes me a thumbs-up.

Nasher asks me to prepare official language that will authorize California cities to proceed under uniform direction on size, color, placement, and application. I call Oliver Gajda in San Francisco with the news and drive over to Burbank to meet my brother Glenn for a celebratory beer.

I expect the next meeting to be a cakewalk. Finally, close to eight years after I had first returned from Europe with a head full of ideas, one would be officially approved at a state level.

---

61 Birk, Mia, *San Francisco's Shared Lane Pavement Markings: Improving Bicycle Safety,* City of San Francisco Department of Parking & Traffic, February 2004.

I'm sitting quietly next to Kelly; he tells me he's run out of ideas but is here "for inspiration."

Nasher reads the proposed language and asks for comments. Everyone is quiet. It looks like my time hanging out with these men is coming to an end.

"As much as I appreciate the study," says Nasher, "I am uncomfortable adopting this as a California standard. This is a radical change, and I want to see it adopted nationally first."

It takes but a moment for his words to sink in. Memories fly to the forefront of my mind: the Portland planning director wiping out four years of bike-parking code work by making it "voluntary," the national Bicycle Technical Committee's blanket dismissal of the blue bike lane markings, San Diego railroad officials' devious tactics to kill the Coastal Rail Trail. Once again, I had been deceived by my own optimism.

Kelly whispers, "Uh-oh, girl, you're losing 'em. Better say something."

I stand up and ask to speak.

"Gentlemen, again, great to see you. Now, I certainly understand Mr. Nasher's concerns. California indeed will be leaping ahead of the rest of the country. Why not? California has always been a progressive leader." I seek the eyes of the panelists, realizing how little I know about these men. I should have done my homework, like Eric Fishman when he wrangled the Bridge Pedal permit out of a similar panel of Oregon men. Do any of them ride bikes? Have I misinterpreted their positive strokes as more than simply a winning contrast to Chris Kelly's weak sales pitches?

Seeing nothing but stony faces, the levity fades from my voice. "You now have a well-executed study showing the sharrow to be effective. Dozens of cities are poised to put these on hundreds of miles of streets with or without your blessing. So you have a choice: adopt the marking with specific guidance on the type, size, color, and placement, or accept the chaos that will ensue as California cities proceed on their own."

The official from AAA nods. "I agree. We've got to get some guidance on this so we can put the word out to drivers."

"Me too," says a mild-mannered state trooper straight out of *Reno 911*.

"No," says Nasher, digging in his heels. "The national committee should lead." He tables the item for future consideration.

Suddenly, the years of carefully researching the sharrow, crafting the study, collecting data, creatively solving problems, analyzing reams of information, writing, editing, finalizing, and presenting the report seem like time wasted, as do the flights to L.A., hours stuck in traffic, elevator rides to the bowels of the building, and time spent explaining myself to a panel of close-minded men. I had fared no better than Kelly, with his unstudied, profit-centered, kooky ideas.

What had once been a fun quest morphs into Dante's—Manuel's—*Inferno*. The question is whether I can find a way out.

⚙ ⚙ ⚙ ⚙ ⚙

"They want you to adopt it first," I explain on the phone to Richard, chair of Manuel's Bicycle Committee. My failure to gain their approval for the blue bike lane experiment had become a running, terse joke between us. It's doubtful that I have much credibility with him. Yet the cards are in his hands.

After a brief conversation, I can't decide if Richard is a fan of the sharrow or a foe of the chaos unfolding in the absence of uniform guidance. Whatever his motivation, he agrees to try to advance it through his committee, but not before he admonishes me again for eschewing the federal process.

"Sorry," I reply. "It really wasn't up to me. The City of San Francisco did not want the additional expense or hassle."

A few months later, the sharrow falls one vote short of his committee's approval. They want to see more studies. I am stuck in purgatory between state and federal committees:

"You go first!"

"No, you go first!"

"Really, I insist, you go first!"

The San Francisco project budget is shot to hell. More than anything I want to complete my mission, but it's slipping away. Oliver is understandably pissed. I really have no clue what to do next.

⚙ ⚙ ⚙ ⚙ ⚙

"Would it help if I fly in to talk to the committee?" asks Richard on the phone from Arizona. He too is disappointed by the negative outcome. If California, a large and influential state, takes the lead, it will help him advance the sharrow at the national level.

"Would you really?" I ask, surprised, exhausted, and delighted all at the same time. I've done my best to no avail. Passing the baton to Richard is definitely worth a try.

Richard testifies that the national committee is much more likely to adopt it if California makes the first move. The California panelists fire questions at him like he's a contestant on *Jeopardy*. He demonstrates extraordinarily intimate and superior knowledge of Manuel's detailed characteristics, rules, and personality traits. He should have won a million dollars, but he will have to settle for my eternal gratitude.[62]

---

62 The shared-lane marking was officially added to the Manual in 2009. For detailed guidance, consult the NACTO Urban Bikeway Design Guide at www.citiesforcycling.org.

Nasher calls for a vote. Again, the panel is silent for a good minute or two, then the AAA representative loudly declares his support. The rest follow suit with a near-unanimous "aye." I swear I can hear Oliver cheering from San Francisco.

Me? I feel not the joy of victory but bone-weary exhaustion. Years of slogging...one state down, one treatment only. What about the rest of the country? What about treatments such as bike boxes, signals, colored bike lanes, way-finding signage? Will we have to fight as hard and long for these as well? Is this what the suffragists felt like, begging men to give them permission to wear pants, to be allowed to participate in crafting their own destiny? I suspect the answer is yes. So be it. Like the right to vote, the right to healthy transportation choices is, without a doubt, worth the fight.

CHAPTER 31

Bicycling Home

The sun beats down on my head unchecked. My helmet acts as a convection oven, but it's the only thing preventing combustion. Forget frying eggs on the sidewalk; one could open a nice little breakfast bar on this blacktop.

We set out early enough, but the cool of the morning feels like a lifetime ago. At 2 p.m. it's a balmy 114 degrees in the shade, for some of which I would give my right arm, a vast fortune, and my virginity. OK, someone's virginity.

Instead, I'm lying in a parking lot by the side of a humongous road just a few tantalizing miles from the finish of the Wildflower Ride near my alma mater, Richardson High School. Does a thick patch of stinkweed a few feet from my face qualify as wildflowers?

Three miles from the finish line, 57 miles under my saddle, I've bonked—an unpleasant combo of Texas heat, cloying humidity pulled in from the Gulf of Mexico, and perhaps my lack of training inside a sauna. Then again, these temperatures aren't meant for man or beast, certainly not those from dreary but lush Portland, Oregon. I close my eyes, click my heels three times and mutter, "There's no place like home, there's no place like home."

Crap, I'm still here. No matter how hard I wish for a transporter machine, SAG wagon, or catapult, I'm stuck.

Having recently won a decade-long battle with severe back pain through an impressive fitness routine, Russell, my buff, hyper-competitive youngest brother, had egged me on, well past my comfort zone.

"Come on, Mia," he had urged. "I've never gotten to ride with you before."

"Gotten" to ride with me? No one in this family has ever *wanted* to ride with me! Where's my *#@$$# brother anyway? Relaxing at the finish line without a thought of me in his head? Pure folly to think I could keep up with him. He left me in the dust 15 miles (24 km) ago. Beating older Sis must be a thrill for him.

So now here I am, in the latter stages of heat-induced mania, giggling madly. "Mom's gonna be really mad when Russell shows up without me...."

"Can I help you?" I open my eyes to a fine pair of Lycra-clad legs. Greg, a hunky guy I was riding with back when the world still made sense, hands me a bottle of Gatorade, a bag of caffeinated jelly beans, and a pack of pick-me-up strawberry-flavored "goo"—like a shot of cake frosting. Tears of gratitude stream down my cheeks.

By the time I feel human again, Greg has vanished, presumably off doing more good deeds. The last few miles I share with other stragglers hugging the side of the road. We pray no Hummer, SUV, or pickup truck driver will mow us down, as we weave and wobble to the finish line.

This unglamorous ride was made possible by Eric Van Steenburg, executive director of the Friends of the Katy Trail. He'd flown me to Dallas to help answer a question posed to him by arts patron Deedie Rose, who, with her warm, lilting Southern accent and blond chin-length bob, reminds me of my stepmother Diane.

"I want to ride my bike from the Katy Trail to my office. What will it take to make that happen?" Deedie asked Eric.

The wildly popular Katy Trail has truly lassoed people's imaginations. In 1997, a coalition of community members and city leaders banded together to preserve the greenbelt along which the former Missour–Kansas–Texas (MKT or "Katy") Railroad traveled through Dallas. They envisioned an urban park featuring a pedestrian and bicycle path set among thirty acres of nature—all in the densest part of the city.

Managed by the nonprofit Friends of the Katy Trail, thanks to 1,200-plus dues-paying members, the concrete bike trail and adjacent soft-surface running path are clean and well-maintained. After surviving the Wildflower Ride, I joined Russell and his wife Gali at a restaurant just off the Katy on Knox Street. Hundreds of people passed by in the hour we drank a bottle of wine and ate a light Italian meal. With more than 300,000 people claiming a home or workplace within a mile (2 km) of the trail, it's no wonder it is packed day and night.

Like most urban trails, the Katy Trail has spurred economic development. Lovely new townhouses and restaurants have popped up in close proximity, and trailside properties sell for 40 percent higher than identical ones just a few blocks away.

This in turn drove away the bad guys. That hasn't stopped the local media from having a field day any time there is an incident, though. One TV station actually referred to the Katy as "a corridor of crime." The reality, the Dallas chief of police said during a press conference, is this: The only reason you hear any stories about incidents on the Katy is because they're so unusual.

The Katy Trail in Dallas

In the first six months of 2008, more than two hundred incidences of crime—including a person getting shot in the face—occurred at high-toned North Park Mall, where big-haired Texas fashionistas drop gobs of cash to accessorize appropriately with their latest spring wardrobe. In the same period, the Katy recorded but one incident: a flasher who was considered art by the passersby until he started to move.

To answer Deedie Rose's question, as Eric tells it, "I knew just who to call."

"A year ago, I was in Portland for a conference," he explains to a handful of key Dallas uptown/downtown movers and shakers who have mobilized in response to Rose's call to action. We're gathered in the office of Angela Hunt, a trim and youthful city councilwoman stylishly dressed in a tasteful, muted fuchsia bouclé skirt and jacket. In addition to four power brokers, we've got a public-works representative, Keith Manoy. A middle-aged man with kind eyes, he reminds me of Morgan Freeman. Behind him is a wall-sized aerial photograph of downtown Dallas and, at Eric's end, a whiteboard and screen.

As Eric begins his presentation, I wave off an offer from Hunt's assistant for weak coffee and nondairy powdered creamer (Portland has changed my coffee standards forever).

"Alta's George Hudson led a walking tour of Portland," explains Eric. "We walked to the Portland streetcar, which took us to a trail along the river and just like that, we were in another world!" Pacing the room like a panther in a too-small cage, he hunches, talks with his hands, and swings his shoulders like a weight lifter posing. Every so often he rakes his fingers through his sandy brown hair for emphasis. A background in communications serves him well in raising funds and pushing forward the Katy Trail.

I'm ready to get out my checkbook.

"Then—get this—the trail took us to an aerial tram spanning a freeway. Apparently, it was built to deal with the traffic problems on the roads leading up to the city's largest employer, Oregon Health & Science University. It was like taking a bubble-shaped glass elevator in the sky. We walked back down the mountain along a nature trail to where we started. It was awesome!"

Eric's personal tour of Portland ended well after dark, standing at a light-rail platform next to a woman with her bike. "Downtown was full of life even then," he marvels. "And then, we got on the train, where the bike hooks were already full! This is what I want to see in downtown Dallas."

Eric introduces me to the assembled group as a relocated Dallas native.

"I'm so happy to be here today. Truly, I'm honored to be part of this exciting project." Helping make Dallas more bicycle friendly makes me giddy. I've always seen Dallas as chock-full of improvement opportunities, but I long ago gave up on the idea that it would ever realize its potential. "Prove me wrong," I silently beg.

Dallas occupies a special place in the history of bikeway planning and implementation, for it was ruled for seventeen years by a unique guy, Paul Winter. On his personal blog, he bragged that he "got rid of the city's only bike lane after fifteen years of trying, and thereby was honored by *Bicycling Magazine* and the League of American Bicyclists' executive director as working for America's 'worst city for bicycling'."

In the rest of the world, a bicycle coordinator's job is to facilitate bikeway development and encourage bicycle use. On Paul's planet, of which he was ruler and sole occupant, the bicycle coordinator's job is the opposite.

"As long as I'm the bike coordinator, Dallas will never have on-street bike lanes," said Paul to a bike-shop owner. Only people confident enough to "take the lane" on busy roads should be out cycling, in his mind.

As a result, Dallas's car-dominant streets sport nothing but a mishmash of numbered "bike route" signs that you're supposed to decode with a huge foldout map last published in 1992. I tried to do this once, and found myself terrified, on busy roads, unclear where the numbers were taking me. Then the signs disappeared. Motorists buzzed by, honking, yelling, "Get off the road!" One hurled a beer can, another spit.

"Oh, Honey, it's not safe riding a bike here," my stepmother Diane soothed. "But you could ride around White Rock Lake." Meaning, you can drive your bike to the only other trail and ride in circles. Which I did, along with a zillion other starved-for-options people.

You reap what you sow; with no bikeways, precious few use bikes for transportation. As of 2008, you are five times more likely to be killed on a bicycle in Dallas than in Portland.

❀❀❀❀❀

"In the next decade we plan to have 30,000 downtown residents. We must make Dallas more pedestrian and bicycle friendly," states Councilwoman Hunt with a serious look on her heart-shaped face.

Like a fish gasping for water, I start gasping for breath. "Whoa," I say. "Hold the phone. Back up a sec. We're in Dallas, right?

I grew up here and come back to visit regularly. In Dallas, you drive. Downtown Dallas is largely a pedestrian-unfriendly pit, with incomplete or obstructed sidewalks, big wide roads, few pedestrian crossings, no shade trees. To me, going downtown means getting lost while trying to find the correct highway.

At my twentieth high school reunion, midnight signaled a transition from the formal party to a bar "around the corner." (In Portland, when we say that a restaurant is around the corner, it's literally a short walk around the actual corner of the actual block on which one is standing.) A car full of whooping, hollering old gal-pals then drove down the highway for about twenty minutes. In Dallas, that's "around the corner."

Saying good-bye to my parents in a restaurant parking lot once, my kids caught a glimpse of a McDonald's playland across the street. We started toward the bright yellow tubes. "Mia, what are you doing?" asked a bewildered Diane.

"Um…crossing the street. Kids gotta get out their *shpilkes*."

"Oh, honey, no no no…not safe. Please, take your car."

Oy.

The Dallas Metropolex is sprawled in all directions. Most Dallasites cannot imagine getting around any other way than driving. With the exception of light-rail and bus-expansion systems, all public works, development and business priorities have been on motor-vehicle movement. Period. End of story.

The people in this room are singing a very un-Dallas-like tune. What is going on?

This "cycle track" in Amsterdam is on a separate level from both motorists and pedestrians.

Given Dallas' notoriously bike-hostile history, my advice to our steering committee is to start small with bike lanes, sharrows, or bike boulevards.

Councilwoman Hunt, fresh from a trip to Copenhagen, strongly asserts, "People will just drive on bike lanes. Cycle tracks are the best solution."

"I don't disagree with you," I reply. "I just want to be clear about the trade-offs. Since cycle tracks are attached to the sidewalk, they take precedence over every driveway and side street. That is going to be a major change for motorists. Also, you need to add in separate bicycle signals at every major intersection, meaning more delay for motorists."

I look Angela in the eyes. "Also, national transportation guidelines don't endorse this kind of innovative design yet, and your public-works department—no disrespect to you, Keith—is not supportive of even bike lanes, let alone cycle tracks."

"Look," says Bill Mabus, vice president of the company building the fancy new Ritz hotel. "We need full separation from motor vehicles."

Translation: "We don't give a rip about the national standards. We've got the money and power to do it right the first time. Got it?"

Angela turns to Keith, "I know that this plan is pushing the limits for y'all. I want y'all to have an open mind, OK? I am confident that you will be able to direct your team toward a 'yes.'" Everyone nods in agreement.

I wish Rob was here in this roomful of permission-avoiding Texans. Must be where I get it from.

I feel something akin to ecstasy, listening to her not-too-subtle encouragement. I take a deep breath and add, "Keith, I grew up here, and I love coming back to visit my family. I see opportunity everywhere. Dallas is ripe for a bicycle plan. Given that y'all have been philosophically and forcefully opposed to any and all bikeway facilities, I'm curious to know your reaction."

"You know, Mia," he says thoughtfully, "it's time for us to change."

"On-street parking will have to be removed on Routh Street." I inform the group. "Parking removal is always a huge challenge, believe me." The battle over Portland's Northeast Forty-Seventh is going to look like my daughter's kindergarten class tug-of-war compared to the full-out battle royal that will ensue on this street of upscale boutiques when we announce the parking/cycle-tracks trade.

"Again," I suggest, "you could start small, by either turning the street into a bicycle boulevard or placing sharrows on the road."

Boots Reader, another upscale-property owner, chuckles. "Sure, I hear ya. But heck, do you know how many parking spaces are out there already? Thousands, maybe?"

"It's time we stopped being so wimpy," he adds. "If we want things to change, we have to change them."

A few months later, the city quietly shifts Paul Winter, on the verge of retirement anyway, to another position. The reign of the ruler of a strange and isolated planet comes to an end.

Over the next year, Deedie Rose's request for a single route morphs into a full network of bikeways and walkways. Whereas the Katy Trail was built on a railroad right-of-way, the Uptown/Downtown Arts Loop, as we name it, will be integrated into the roadway network. Is Dallas truly ready for such a radical departure?

For the answer, Eric and I head to a meeting with Gabriel Barbier-Müeller, Swiss-born developer of high-rise luxury condos predicated on the success of high-density living experiences in the world's most cosmopolitan

---

 **Wherever you are, that's where you start. Tailor solutions to your community's unique needs.**

cities. Two of Gabriel's target audiences are educated twenty- and thirty-somethings who grew up on the urban comedies *Seinfeld* and *Friends*, and retirees attracted to downtown's world-class cultural options. His clients also include former suburbanites who want control of their time. The first resident of the Azure luxury condo tower, for example, traded a 29-mile (47 km) commute for a 9-miler (14 km), putting him in closer proximity to his grandchildren and netting him a larger, hassle-free shared pool.

Iced tea awaits at our meeting with Gabriel, who enters the room with an entourage of female assistants in business suits. I know better than to ask for hot tea this time.

We are allotted twenty minutes to make our pitch, as his helicopter is waiting on the roof to take him to his private jet, which is taking him to Barcelona after a stop at the Olympics in Beijing.

Eric tells his Deedie Rose story, while I hand out maps showing the various streets under consideration. Practically the entirety of one of the streets, Harwood, named for Gabriel's company, is owned by this one man.

"Harwood is a perfect street to connect the Katy to the Arts District," I pitch and pass around photos of bike lanes in Portland and Boulder, and cycle tracks in Copenhagen, Amsterdam, and Geneva. The catch: prohibition of on-street parking. "However," I admit, "there's not enough room for both on-street parking and world-class bikeways and walkways."

The room falls silent as Gabriel considers. His assistants busily text and email on their handheld devices. A hundred degrees outside yet frigid in the room, I hug my jacket close and am sweating nonetheless. There is no doubt that his opposition will torpedo the project.

Then he stands, straightens his suit jacket, and offers his verdict. "Why would we use space on the street to store cars?" His steely, silvery good looks and intensity stop me from mistaking this statement for a real question. "We want the street to be crackling with life. Our residents will be able to walk from the Azure to the opera or a concert at the American Airlines Center. We are not just creating a place to live but an urban *lifestyle*."

Delighted, Eric and I walk back to the Katy Trail office in the scorching sun. Over the next few months, every single stakeholder with whom we meet cheers us on with, "This sounds fantastic. How can I help?" Many agree to either allow the trail on their private property or fund their segment.

Normally I encounter so much resistance. Why in Dallas, Texas, of all places, do I find such a unified and enlightened spirit?

If these can-do, action-oriented business leaders succeed, the rest of us will have no excuses, none at all. Of course, there's nowhere to go but up when you're the nation's worst city for cycling. But, as postulated in the fascinating business book *Good to Great*, it's often easier to go from bad to great than from good to great. I think—I hope—that Dallas will show us that, in a big way.

In 2008, I am again home for a visit and to present the final Katy Trail Arts Loop Plan. The positive feedback from the crowd of almost one hundred lifts me so high, I can barely see the ground. No longer can I deny the evolving attitudes.

After the meeting, I find my seventy-two-year-old stepfather, Tommy, at home in his comfy chair watching the *Blue Planet* series.

"Can you believe the amount of plastic that has been dumped into the nation's oceans?" he asks, tearing his eyes away from the TV to give me a hug.

Eyes back on *Blue Planet*, he continues, "Back in the 60s, we designed a collection system that dumped waste oil and chemicals into the Houston ship channel for a tank farm. The water was so corrosive that it ate the paint off the bottom of the ships, and the chemicals would burn on the surface. This was standard procedure for the industry."

His regretful tone gives me pause. Is this the same man who lambasted my career as freakishly out of touch with reality? I keep quiet as he continues, "I'm not saying I'm proud of it, Mia. The conservationists put so much pressure on the industry to clean up the channel that we spent the next ten years installing pollution control equipment. As a result of that, by 1972 people could fish in the channel."

He gets up and beckons me to follow him to the garage, a place of extreme male organization, with all manners of tools hanging from corkboard pegs. Displayed proudly is a new Marin carbon-fiber road bike.

"What the...? Tommy? This beauty yours?"

"Go ahead—pick it up," he orders. "It only weighs twenty-three pounds."

But that isn't all. Stashed in his welding shop are another bike, helmet, and fingerless biking gloves. They're for me.

My mom beams proudly. "Of all his hobbies so far, this is my favorite." (Tommy's hobbies have included race-car driving, sailboating, remote control minisailboating, and metal sculpting.)

"He's in the best shape of his life. Just look at him!" He rides every night around his Carrollton, Texas, subdivision. The streets are quiet, but to get a workout means going around in circles. He and his biking buds—all men in their sixties and seventies—want long, safe riding options.

"You know, Mia, I used to think you were crazy, but you were just ahead of your time." He hands me a *Dallas Morning News* editorial that reads,

Tommy, always lovable (left), now fit as a fiddle (right)

Most people around Dallas would define "hike" as what happens when you get a bad parking spot. "Neighborhood" means anything within five freeway exits. "Mass transit" is the blob of traffic inching ahead in rush hour. The car culture may be dominant in these parts, but counter-cultural forces are busy trying to entice us out of our guzzlers and onto our feet. The Friends of the Katy Trail, for one, has announced an exciting new project to connect center city neighborhoods and downtown through a network of hike and bike paths. It can't come soon enough.

My mom hugs me, pride in her eyes. "I finally get what you mean about bicycling being so good for the world. It sure is good for Tommy, and that's good for me."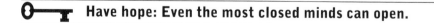

If folks like Tommy are embracing a vision of a healthier world, we've come further than I ever dreamed. And if we can make Dallas into a bicycle friendly place, then, in Tommy's words, "By gawd, I s'pect y'all kin do it anywhere."

Have hope: Even the most closed minds can open.

A Long and Winding Path

Back in Portland, the political winds once again blow in our direction with the election of personable Sam Adams, first to city council, then a few years later to the mayor's office. His chief of staff, Tom Miller, is a daily cyclist, and his transportation policy director, Catherine Ciarlo, is the fabulous former director, of the Bicycle Transportation Alliance. "It's time to be bold," whispers the soothing, tickling, teasing breeze.

Although it's been years since my cubicle-dwelling days, I am deeply involved in the shaping of Portland as a consultant, advocate, and close friend. It would be so lovely to declare victory and call it a day, put our energy into something else—but we can't. We've only scratched the surface of what we can become.

CHAPTER 32

Imagine

Pedestrians and cyclists jockey for position on the too-narrow Sellwood Bridge sidewalk.

Fix the bridges! That was the public's top priority at the beginning of the revolution. Now, fifteen years later, I'm happy to report that we've got bike lanes on the Burnside, wider sidewalks on the Hawthorne, better access to the Broadway, a two-way path on the Morrison, and a perfect pedaling platform, the Steel Bridge Riverwalk. Mileagewise, these puppies are insignificant. In form and in function, though, they make all the difference in the world.

Total bridges needing TLC (not counting the two freeway bridges we get to experience but once a year on the Bridge Pedal): eight. Fixed so far: five. Upgraded, most unfortunately, without bikeways: two. (Both these are owned by the state highway department.)

That leaves one bridge, on the southern edge of town.

My son was so freaked out the one time we biked on the Sellwood Bridge's dinky sidewalk that he is now adamantly unwilling to bike on all bridges. The roadway—narrow travel lanes, no bike lanes, and constant traffic—is equally terrifying.

Like Skyler and me, very few souls brave this adventure more than once. This is not OK, not at all. On the west side of the Sellwood, we've got the Greenway Trail. On the east, the Springwater Corridor. Both slide

215

along in harmony with the Willamette River and happily converge 6 miles (9 km) upstream at the Steel Bridge.

But down here, at the Sellwood, we've got bupkes. It's like a bad relationship building in its dysfunction over time. With each passing year, frustration builds. It's a broken link to the donation page of a charity website, an expensive gold chain with a missing clasp. In other words, what we've got here is a deal-breaker.

Spring turning to summer, warm interspersed with cool, I pedal to Alta's one-story renovated warehouse. Today, I'm dressed to the nines—caffe latte-colored high-heeled sandals and linen A-line skirt, pink cropped corduroy jacket—for a newspaper photo shoot on bicycling fashion. I wheel my new sage-colored Trek Allant into the lobby and am touching up my mascara and lipstick in the handlebar mirror when one of my top-notch former students, the sardonic, sarcastic Rory Renfro, walks over and announces, "Vandelay Industries."

Not bothering to look up, I intone, "Exporter or importer?"

"Both. Bad news. The numbers are too high, my friend."

Now he's got my attention. "What numbers are too high? How high? Are you high?" He's fond of something he calls a "liquor luge," so you never know. I put away my makeup along with my happy party mood.

Until now, the Sellwood Bridge replacement project has gone swimmingly. The firm of CH2M Hill, in contrast to companies like BBS, has treated us with respect. Unlike most bridge, interchange, and roadway projects, on which motor-vehicle space is doled out in spades and then we squabble over the cookie crumbs, community leaders, activists, and politicians stand in unprecedented unison in favor of world-class bikeway/walkways on the Sellwood. More than just a bridge replacement, it's a symbol of a new era in which pedestrians and cyclists are a top priority rather than an afterthought.

My humble assignment has been to estimate future bike and pedestrian demand. It's just like trying to project future car traffic, only for us nonmotorized types. The results will influence the size and character of the new bridge for generations to come.

It turns out that lots of people—thousands, actually—want to bike or walk over the bridge, but won't due to the woeful conditions. Multitudes—eight thousand to twelve thousand on a daily basis twenty years hence—will make the new and improved Sellwood a regular part of their routine.

They wanted the numbers, I gave them the numbers. Apparently, they can't handle the numbers.

"Too high? Too frigging high *how*?" I demand of Rory.

"Don't get me wrong," says Rory, in a tone meant to soothe the ranting. "I don't disagree with you. They're questioning our methodology." "They" meaning various local, state, and federal highway engineers and planners. Even some of the CH2M Hill engineers are skeptical.

Let's see, we compared the Sellwood to our other bridges, looked at twenty years of bike use data,[63] analyzed paths in ten major cities, and factored in destinations, population density, demographic trends, travel patterns, a planned streetcar line, current and future transit use, and planned off-street paths on both sides of the river.

The Hawthorne Bridge carries more than 12,000 daily bicycle and pedestrian trips.

OK, sure, our methods aren't as well accepted as the auto traffic modeling techniques, which always, 100 percent of the time, show that traffic will increase. Beats me why people want to pay for this inevitable bad news.

Here's my experience with traffic modeling. On Tacoma Street, just on the east side of the Sellwood Bridge, traffic models projected that trading a travel lane for pedestrian improvements would cause back-ups. The groovy reality: traffic flowing just fine.

Next up: travel lanes reallocated on 15 miles (24 km) of streets to gain bike lanes. Thumbs up all around.

In response to bicycle congestion, the city doubled the bike lane width on the approaching ramp to the Hawthorne Bridge.

Harbor Drive in downtown Portland, turned into Waterfront Park: Newsmen gathered the day it opened, ready to capture the ensuing gridlock, which never materialized.

---

63 Traffic modeling is based on reams of historical traffic data, coalesced into a document called the ITE Trip Generation Manual. If you want to know how much traffic a McDonald's, school, office building, or church will generate, you look to ITE. In the bicycling world, very few communities other than Portland have historical data. Through Alta's National Bicycle and Pedestrian Documentation Project, more than one hundred cities and three universities are gathering and evaluating bicycle and pedestrian counts, with the goal of creating a complementary bike/pedestrian traffic data manual and companion projection tools.

The I-5 and Hawthorne bridges each shut down for long periods of repair. Folks heard the news of the impending traffic catastrophe, went on vacation, adjusted their schedules, got on their bikes; life went on, and the sky did not fall. Still up there, still blue or gray, depending. So you've got to take traffic modeling, in my experience, with not just a grain but a big pinch of salt.

The projected Sellwood bike/walk numbers are too high? For what? Their imaginations? They should try to navigate through the pedestrians, dog-walkers, joggers, skaters, families, and speed demons on a lovely summer Saturday on the trail leading down to the Sellwood. Or check out the Hawthorne Bridge in the morning commute. A decade ago, we spent $1.2 million widening the sidewalks. Guess what? They're so tightly packed with cyclists, it's borderline unsafe. The projected Sellwood numbers of a generation hence are less than today's Hawthorne numbers.

Based on what I've seen so far, I think bike and pedestrian trips will be way higher than we can possibly imagine. A bridge is a one hundred-plus-year investment, for Pete's sake. Have we learned anything by now? We do it wrong, and we're stuck with it for a long, long time. **O—x**

What was I thinking? That all the world's engineers and planners get this? Of course it's hard for them to imagine droves of people bicycling where no one in their right mind does now. Take a deep breath, girl, come back to earth, and hold your ground.

"Yo, Biff, let's run the numbers again," I say to Rory, whose spiky blond hair appears to be fearfully reaching for the sky.

"Giddyup," he replies, flashing me a thumbs-up. This little hiccup is but another variation on the same old build-it-and-they-will-come song we've been singing for almost two decades. At least this time, we know the chords and lyrics, tune and harmony. One day, I know, we'll be belting an aria as we pedal or walk with 12,000 of our friends across the superb Sellwood Bridge.

That day can't come soon enough, but in the meantime, we've got work to do. The real question is not whether my projection is accurate, but this: What if we build our bridges, roadways, and communities around what we want to achieve? Not how much space can we squeeze out after we've already allocated enough space to perpetuate our driving patterns, but this: How much space should we allocate to ensure that bicycling and walking are safe, comfortable, fun, and normal daily means of transportation? That amount, considerable to be sure, will be precisely perfect.

O—x **Design for what you want to achieve rather than what is dictated by traditional traffic models.**

CHAPTER 33

Redemption in Blue, Part One

"Greetings. My name is Jane Paulson, and I'm an attorney. I'd like to speak to you about being an expert witness for a case in which a bicyclist was injured in a blue bike lane. Please call me back at your convenience."

Uh-oh. Years earlier, when we first began to experiment with colored bike lanes, I had been warned this could happen, that we were risking liability exposure with our non-standard blue lanes. Somewhere in the ether, Manuel is cackling with told-you-so glee.

I ride my bike over to Paulson's downtown office building and take the elevator up to her sixteenth-floor suite. A solidly built woman with a brown pixie cut and Jennifer Capriati face meets me at the elevator with a bottle of water. The facts: A young man was bicycling west on Northeast Broadway. He stuck out his left hand to signal that he was changing positions, and shifted into a blue bike lane that takes you through the complex intersection of North Williams.

He crashed into the side of a right-turning truck. An architectural draftsman, he was unable to work for more than a year due to broken hands and wrists. The police did not cite the driver.

The cyclist hired Paulson to sue the trucking company for negligence. Paulson wants me to help prove that he had the clear right-of-way. In turn, the trucking company is suing the city for a faulty design.

Our ten blue bike lanes have a near-spotless safety record, but it only takes one incident to provoke a lawsuit. Will the voices of doom prove correct? Will the city have to shell out big bucks for our deviant behavior? Or is the liability threat a myth? We're about to find out.

I bike down to the city's offices and find boxes of videotapes, research, and memos documenting the decision-making process. After a few days immersed in the evidence, I bike back to Paulson's office and pin an aerial photo to the wall of a conference room.

"This is a difficult intersection from a bicycle perspective. We've got a right-turn-only lane next to a through/right choice lane at a highway on-ramp. Basically, there is no good place for a cyclist to be."

Paulson nods in agreement.

Originally dismissed as too tough, city staff and the business community eventually warmed to the idea of bike lanes in this corridor. This spot was a real toughie. Drop the bike lane, directed that old nemesis Manuel. This made no sense to us. Drop the bike lane? Here? What does that say to cyclists other than, sorry, you're hosed? How does that help alert motorists to watch out when they turn? But since the city's traffic chief Rob Burchfield is generally a rule-abiding guy, we followed Manuel's direction and dropped the bike lane a hundred feet before the intersection and added a standard Bike Lane Ends sign for panache.

The results, recorded on videotape: cyclists hugged the curb, in exactly the most dangerous spot possible, one after another cut off by turning motorists. One girl seemed paralyzed. She waited at the curb for a gap in traffic, and almost took off twice but hesitated. Finally, she dashed between two cars, nearly getting nailed.

If that's what we get from following the national standards, something's decidedly wrong. Rob's team took immediate action, placing arrows on the pavement to encourage cyclists to merge left across the right-turn lane and to the center of the right/through lane. This way, we hoped, they'd assertively "take the lane," and drivers would stay behind. ⚷

"Watch this," I instruct Paulson. The video, shot on Bike Commute Day, showed a couple hundred cyclists in a two-hour period. Most of the cyclists merged left across the right-turn lane. Better than before, for sure. But they were still on the right side of the second lane.

"Oh, look," said Paulson, pointing at the stream of cyclists on the screen. "That guy got to the middle of the lane."

The one: Roger Geller. Of the hundreds of cyclists, only he, the city's bike coordinator, was confident enough to take the lane.

⚙ ⚙ ⚙ ⚙ ⚙

I must have asked the engineering team fifty times if we could please just eliminate one of the turns. Doug, Rob, Lewis—all normally fix-it, go-to guys—wouldn't do it, not even in the wake of evidence showing bicyclists' preference for hugging the lane edge.

⚷ **Do not let fear of liability prevent you from doing the right thing.**

Any intersection with a right and right/through combination of lanes is awful from a bike perspective. Best solutions: eliminate the right/through lane or separate bikes from turning cars with a bike-exclusive signal.

Fifty percent of traffic at this intersection turns right. Eliminate a turn and traffic would back up for miles, set off an outbreak of measles, and cast bad juju on the Portland Trail Blazers, who play at the nearby Rose Garden arena. We couldn't have that, obviously.

How about a common European solution: a bike-only signal, whereby motorists can't turn when cyclists are proceeding? No, says Manuel, not allowed. But yet, we had a problem, one that could not be solved if we stuck with the lame advice in the beastly book. That's where blue markings came in. Not a perfect solution, but a whole lot better than nothing.

Knowing that this was an intersection needing attention made me want to fix it, not ignore it and hope the problem would go away. So we made a choice. To infinity and beyond! Outside the Manual into a brave new world. The question remained: Did we go too far?

"Yes, I saw the Yield to Bikes signs," the trucker says in his deposition, acknowledging his familiarity with the bike lane on his daily trucking route. Motorists should see a prominent Burma-Shave series of signs, a bike lane, and a bright blue area as they start to turn.

"Did you see the blue markings?" Paulson asks.

"Yes, I did." He understood that he was supposed to yield to cyclists. He had even seen the cyclist, but assumed he was further back when he made his fateful turn.

A month, two months, six months go by. Behind the scenes, briefs are filed, questions asked and answered, and I lose track of the legal process. But I never lose hope.

"I feel your pain," says my colleague Jeff Olson, as he gets ready to bowl a sparkly green fifteen-pound ball. I suspect that a caricature artist would have a field day with the brown muttonchop sideburns that often frame his freckly face. No stranger to the stranglehold mighty Manuel seems to have on our profession, that Jeff. All he wanted, a decade earlier, was a sign to warn motorists to Yield to Pedestrians. This didn't seem unreasonable, given that the good book allowed for signs about Amish horse-drawn carriages, deer crossings, and how to find the nearest gas, food, and lodging.

Jeff smashes a strike with aplomb. Not a moment in our fifteen-year relationship have I felt anything but warmth from Jeff. We both spent our

Left to right, the Alta partners: George Hudson, Brett Hondorp, me, founder Michael Jones, Jeff Olson

early career years involved in transportation advocacy in D.C., and then renewed our friendship at the 1994 ProBike/ProWalk conference in Portland, when the elevator of the Marriott opened and there was Jeff, holding a five-month-old baby. In his role as New York bicycle and pedestrian manager, he was as determined as me to elevate walking and bicycling from toy to treasure. Boldly placing a Yield to Pedestrians sign in the crosswalk seemed like a no-brainer in a state where every single day a not-so-boldly-walking New Yorker got run over. He came to Portland seeking inspira-

In 2009, engineers add a new bike signal to separate motor vehicle right-turns from through bicycle movement.

tion; he left with a friend (me) who would become his business partner. Our annual bowling/bonding ritual isn't perhaps as good—not remotely frequent enough—as the weekly Lucky Lab meetings and hill climbs of my bike-program days, but we'll take it.

I weakly knock down a few pins with a ten-pound ball as we commiserate. Like us Portlanders, forging ahead with European treatments, and like San Francisco, intent on applying sharrows, Jeff and colleagues fought through words and actions for seemingly eons, to no avail. An incensed lawmaker took it a step further by introducing legislation thwarting Manuel's supremacy. But, no, said the voices of doom—deviation will harm the great state of New York. Federal funding will be withheld, ambulance chasers will descend, and the dire doomsday of Y2K will be doubly bad. The governor caved. It took close to another decade of machinations and experiments before New York—and the rest of the country—was able to put up a sign to remind motorists not to mow down their walking compatriots.

It's the eighth frame, and Jeff's beating me soundly. I'm distracted by his long battle and bleakly understanding that the blue bike lane lawsuit could be a key to a much larger question. To what extent are we going to let Manuel and his highway buddies control urban areas striving to create sustainable transportation systems?

My phone rings; it's Jane Paulson. This just in: The trucking company has dropped its lawsuit against the city.

"Really??? Why?" I dance around and wink at Jeff, who shakes his head in amusement.

"Well, I can't say for sure, but it looks like they didn't think they could win." Score! The city's documentation, research, and careful decision-making were enough to dissuade further action. The trucker's company insurance paid for the cyclist's medical costs and offset some of his lost income. **0—x**

Oh yeah! Three strikes in a row seal the deal. It's a cause for celebration, a vindication not just for Portland, but for communities everywhere forging ahead into a bicycle friendly future.

0—x **Carefully document your decisions, base them on best practices, monitor the situation, and make adjustments.**

CHAPTER 34

Redemption in Blue, Part Two

Pioneering traffic engineer Doug McCollum, designer of both standard and blue bike lanes, passes away in 2008 after a valiant fight with brain cancer. For his work and for his support, I am eternally grateful. He had a rare talent for doing the right thing without ruffling feathers. At countless meetings, he explained complex engineering issues in a down-to-earth, understandable way. No matter where you go in Portland or how you get there, you'll be traveling on Doug's handiwork.

At his memorial gathering, I run into the maintenance bureau's retired Roger Talley. He shakes my hand and then reminds me, "I truly thought you were a nutcase then. Do you remember? You wanted me to install all that blue plastic? Blue plastic...man, oh, man, that was funny."

He elbows his wife, who looks on demurely.

"Yes, I remember, Roger," I say, with a tight grin. Knee-slapping, funny stuff, Roger.

He dries his eyes. "Listen, I want to thank-you for all you've done. My wife and I recently bought bikes. We love it! Look at me—I've lost thirty pounds!" And of course, he likes the green (formerly blue) bike lanes, and agrees that they help improve safety.

Why green instead of blue? Over the years, various city officials nationwide took note of the blue bike lanes and began exploring Europe themselves. After numerous requests to federal officials for permission to experiment with color, guidance was given that green would be the preferred color, since blue is reserved for handicapped parking stalls.

I shake my head, not in surprise, but relief. "Thank you," I whisper. "That means a lot, more than you'll ever know." It would mean a lot to Doug too, if he were still with us.

Perhaps a decade from now, the Roger Talleys of the national scene will apologize for their lack of respect. They'll say thanks for all we've done.

Or not.

In the meantime, I'll take Roger's handshake.

CHAPTER 35

Boxes

There's nothing quite like seeing your face on the front page of the newspaper. No, I'm not running for political office or wanted for criminal activity. In August 2007, I make my coffee and unfold the paper to see myself and spunky Sasha, resplendent in a sassy pink furry coat, mounting up to pedal to school. The *Oregonian* article[64] is about my leadership in Portland's transportation revolution, building Alta Planning + Design, and creating the Initiative for Bicycle and Pedestrian Innovation,[65] a new education and research program at Portland State University (PSU).

The article appears as I am nervously peeking out from behind the clouds of two dark and turbulent years. The tragic death of a close friend, the demise of my marriage, and a series of accidents and unraveling friendships had plunged me into a swirling river of pain. I slowly found my way to shore through counseling, music, prayer, writing, tennis, dedication to my kids and work, and, of course, bicycling. Humbled and flattered by reporter Jeff Mapes' complimentary words, I took the article as a sign that we are indeed on the right track.

This is the year of skyrocketing gas prices and a nationwide realization that sedentary lifestyles and lousy diets are causing a level of poor health too costly to bear. Robert Redford's Sundance Channel flies out to feature our bicycling efforts on their *Big Ideas for a Small Planet* series.[66] The *New York Times* touts our $100 million bicycle industry.[67] Officials announce that bicycling is one of the top tourism activities in Oregon, and every major airline magazine celebrates Portland's bicycle friendliness.

A couple years earlier, a skinny young hipster journalist and sporting-goods promoter named Jonathan Maus moved to Portland with a vision: a blog that combines quality journalism with relentless promotion of

---

64 Mapes, Jeff, "Mia Birk: A key spoke in Portland's bike culture," *Oregonian*, August 2007.
65 The Initiative for Bicycle and Pedestrian Innovation is an integral part of the College of Urban Studies. We offer courses for students and professionals and conduct cutting-edge research. For more information, see www.ibpi.usp.pdx.edu/.
66 www.sundancechannel.com/videos/230318497.
67 Yardley, William, "In Portland, Cultivating a Culture of Two Wheels," *New York Times,* November 2007.

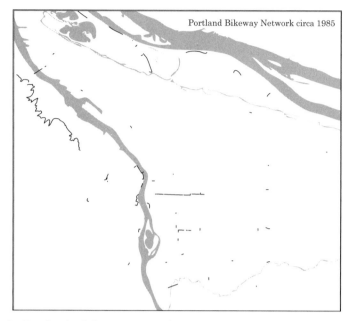

The wiggly line in the left corner is a former logging road in a large park, beautiful but minimally usable from a transportation standpoint.

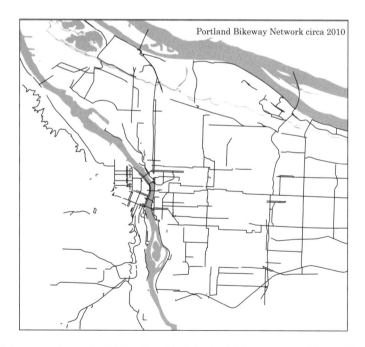

By 2010, approximately 300 miles (480 km) of bikeways facilitate bicycle transportation.

everything bicycle. "Sure, it's a great idea," taunted a friend, "so great it will earn your family two cents and a spot living in a hippie van down by the river." Maus ignored the jab and birthed his dream: bikeportland.org. Those of us working on the utilitarian side of bicycling come to realize that thousands are crazy into mountain biking and cyclo-cross, road, and track racing. By 2007, Jonathan's sizzling pace produces five to seven daily articles on new bike shops and businesses,[68] school-related biking activities, political

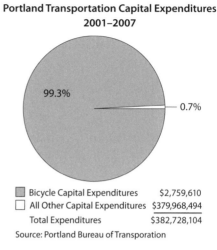

Portland Transportation Capital Expenditures 2001–2007

99.3%

0.7%

■ Bicycle Capital Expenditures	$2,759,610
□ All Other Capital Expenditures	$379,968,494
Total Expenditures	$382,728,104

Source: Portland Bureau of Transporation

battles, and non-stop bikin' fun.[69] Tens of thousands across the nation follow his every word. Slowly, it seems, the mainstream news community is waking up to the fact that this quirky form of transportation and recreation is the real deal.

In the space of a generation, for the cost of but one measly mile of urban freeway, Portland has developed a 300-mile (482 km) bikeway network.

On the rise steadily for fifteen years, bicycle use skyrockets to levels no one can ignore. Close to 18,000 people ride across the downtown bridges every day, making up 16 percent of vehicular traffic.[70] With a Bridge Pedal's worth of people traveling by bike every day, no longer do we need to celebrate a few hundred diehards. Heck, 10,000-plus people cycle the World Naked Ride[71] annually. I'm told it's liberating. I'll take their word for it, because my clothes are staying on (in public). ⚷

⚷ **Collect data, estimate and project usage, measure your success, and report back.**

---

68 A few notable examples: Portland Pedal Tours, Icycle Tricycle, Soup Cycle, Chris King Precision Components, and B-Line Sustainable Urban Delivery.

69 Various groups and individuals can be credited with panoply of fun bikey events, which include unicycle and bike polo, a Pedal Potluck Picnic, the Easter "Bunny on Bikes" parade, Zoobomb (drunken crazies on teeny tiny bikes bombing down a 12 percent grade hill from the zoo), Kidical Mass (a variation on Critical Mass involving kids and families), Move By Bike (whereby friends convene with cargo bikes and trailers to help move your books, boxes and furniture), and two-hundred-plus events each June during Pedalpalooza.

70 Upwards of 18 percent of Portlanders, as high as 28 percent in some neighborhoods, bicycle to work at least some of the time. See www.portlandonline.com/transportation/ for statistics and citations.

71 One of 4,000 annual bike-related events, races, rides, and tours offered by a long list of organizations. See "Bicycle-Related Business Growth in Portland," June, 2006 and "The Value of the Bicycle-Related Industry in Portland," September, 2008. Studies by Alta Planning + Design.

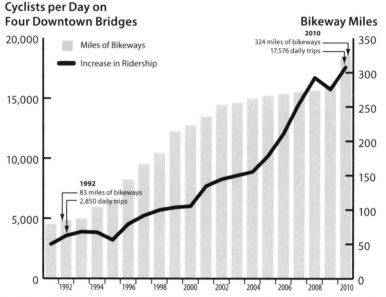

As the City of Portland expands its bikeway network (vertical bars), bicycle use is steadily rising.

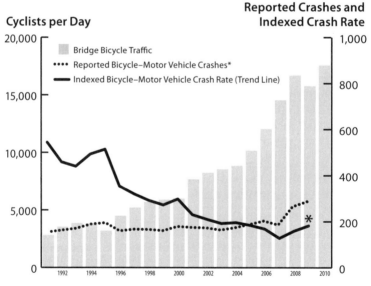

Extrapolated from peak period counts. "Crash Rate" represents an indexing of annual reported crashes to daily bicycle trips across the four main bicycle bridges.
*2008, 2009 Reported Bicycle–Motor Vehicle Crashes data reflects increased crash reporting requirements.

At the same time, the number of bicycle–motor-vehicle crashes is holding steady and the indexed bicycle–motor vehicle crash rate (solid line) is plummeting.

In the same period, the indexed bicycle–motor-vehicle crash rate plummets, mirroring trends in Europe, San Francisco, and Seattle showing that the more people cycle, the safer it becomes.

We're floating on a feel-good cloud of positive statistics and media attention, when suddenly, the party crashes down to earth.

Brett Jarolimek, a thirty-one-year-old art student, bicycle racer, and Bike Gallery mechanic, glides down the steep hill of North Interstate. A truck driver overtakes him and makes a sharp right turn across his path. There's no way for Brett to slow down in time, and he slams into the side of the truck. A couple of weeks later, Tracey Sparling, also an art student, goes straight on a green light and is crushed by a right-turning cement truck. The loss of these two fine people brings the year's number of bicyclist fatalities to a record six. A decade gone by, yet it's 1997—the mournful year of Keren Holtz's death—all over again.

Commissioner Adams directs city staff to respond quickly. An in-depth analysis reveals the "right hook" to be involved in about 10 percent of crashes.[72] Surely a design solution exists, Adams insists.

Of course there is. Been talking about it for years. It's all over the bicycle friendly cities of Europe. We've been champing at the bit to pull it out of our toolbox for more than a decade. But hey, you've heard it before, and you're hearing it now: It's not in the Manual.

The bike box is an intersection safety treatment to prevent bicycle/car collisions, especially those between drivers turning right and bicyclists going straight. Envision a big bright red (or blue or green) box on the road with a white bicycle symbol inside. You have to be asleep to miss it.

If you're driving and have to stop at the red light, the box is in front of you and you can't turn right on red. This dramatically reduces conflicts with pedestrians in crosswalks and bicyclists in the bike lane. Waiting bicyclists are directly in front of you. When the light turns green, they clear out first. Boldly and clearly, the bike box states: vulnerable road users take priority.

Roger and Rob quickly ready plans for fourteen intersections. It's bike box time.

---

72 Greg Raisman, City of Portland: "9.5 percent of bike crashes are right hooks. However, you are approximately three times less likely to have a serious injury or fatality in a right hook when compared to any of the next five most common crash types for bikes. So, they're more frequent, but tend to be less severe."

The bike box: a mainstay of bicycle friendly European cities

The site of Tracey Sparling's death is an intersection like a thousand others. Hundreds of times a day, a cyclist rides up in the bike lane and waits at the red light. If you're in a motorist blind spot, though, like Tracey was, you're in trouble. How can we blithely ignore that when we're driving, we cannot clearly see what we might hit? When will the auto industry—or when will we force them to—redesign trucks and cars to eliminate blind spots?[73]

Thousands turn out for a protest rally of collective frustration. In the crowd are not just angry cyclists, though. The chief of police mounts the podium to offer her support, then announces that, from here forward, bicycle–motor-vehicle crashes will be analyzed in a new light. Why? Many

---

[73] The City of Portland held a series of events to increase cyclist awareness of truckers' visibility limitations. They added "If you can see this sticker, I can't see you" stickers on their large fleet of trucks. On the dashboard sits placards with recommended routes that avoid streets with a heavy prevalence of bicyclists. Let's do this nationwide. Trucking companies, AAA, transportation departments: Let's all band together and get our fleets of trucks and armies of truck drivers better equipped to handle this new era in which bicyclists and pedestrians are part of our daily existence.

police officers unwittingly place blame on the cyclist for their mere presence on the road, thus absolving the bad-behaving motorist of responsibility. No more, she says.

For the burden of safety must be squarely placed on the more dangerous vehicle operator. Yes, of course, cyclists need to do our part. But drivers, we've got to hang up, stay sober, keep our hands on the wheel, slow down, focus on what we're doing, and yield to more vulnerable road users. Period. Here's a hidden truth: Like train conductors who become traumatized after they unintentionally end lives, if you smash into, run over, or get smashed into by a pedestrian or cyclist, it messes you up whether it was your fault or not.

The sadness at Brett's memorial service permeates deep inside me. A thousand people sway in sorrow. From the back of the room, I watch the slides and absorb the testimony of his friends and family. The sadness of my own tough years bubbles to the surface, and I'm crying not just for Brett, but for my own mistakes and losses. So badly do I want to break through Manuel's cold hard box so that never again will I have to attend a memorial for a young person whose death could have been avoided.

Without a doubt, bike boxes will help. But yet, if we don't get federal approval, they will remain like the blue bike lanes, a Portland experiment languishing within our borders.

Not a week goes by without a community leader from Albuquerque, Akron, Astoria, or Austin asking me about colored bike lanes, bike boxes, bike signals, and the like. On all these treatments, we seem to be getting nowhere fast.

I remember Richard, the Arizona engineer who came to the rescue when the sharrows were stalled in California. Would he help again? Perhaps... but only if, I suspect, we play in his sandbox, by his rules.

Permission...forgiveness...Forgiveness...permission...What to do?

"OK, Richard," I whisper to myself. "I give in."

"Rob/Roger," I email. "Please consider doing this as an official Federal Highway Administration experiment. So many jurisdictions are begging for the bike box to be added to the Manual."

"Do you know how much it will cost?" Rob wants to know. Local jurisdictions must bear the cost of the study, ranging from $25,000 to $150,000. Is this the best use of limited taxpayer dollars?

Cities across America are creating higher quality on-road bikeways. Clockwise from top left: Broadway bike lane near Times Square; protected cycle track in San Francisco; intersection markings in New York City; shared bike/bus lane in Minneapolis; and a two-stage left turn box in Portland, Oregon

"Good news, my friend," I offer. "Have you heard about the Initiative for Bicycle and Pedestrian Innovation?" Our new research institution quickly rounds up funds for data evaluation.

I pat myself on the back. Yes! Finally, we will shepherd one of these techniques through the federal process! Once again, my optimism proves pathetically naïve.

"Much to have heartburn about," notes an email from one of Richard's fellow officiators. "Does it bother anyone else that PSU has an Initiative for Bicycle and Pedestrian Innovation? That suggests that we'll be seeing a lot more new treatments being tested. How long before Portland has eliminated any semblance of uniformity from their traffic control?"

"Portland's attitude seems to be: 'We're doing it our way, and you can take it or leave it,'" notes another. "Also, the 'Institute for Innovation' could be a serious long-term issue if this pattern continues.... If FHWA endorses what Portland's done so far, it could have serious long-term impacts on the entire MUTCD experimental process. Also, what if the 'bicycling community' embraces the Portland results in spite of (or because of) FHWA's rejection of the 'experiment'?"

And those are the nice ones.

They don't like the concept, research methodology, or researchers. We get not one shred of respect for the progress we've made, the expertise we've gained, the leadership we've shown. They want us to delay, rework, and come up with three times the money.

Intertwined on the list of critics is the country's small but vocal anti-bikeway fringe, folks like Paul Winter in Dallas who insist that bike lanes, cycle tracks, bike signals, bike boxes, and the like are the devil's work. In their minds, the only folks who should be cycling are those confident enough to "take the lane."

Here's what we know: In communities with few or no bikeways, a tiny number—less than 1 percent of the population—of strong and fearless men cycles. In communities

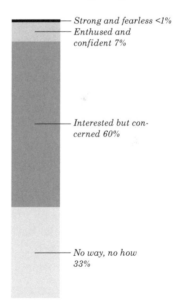

Strong and fearless <1%
Enthused and confident 7%

Interested but concerned 60%

No way, no how 33%

Breakdown of cyclist types (courtesy City of Portland Bureau of Transportation; other cities have corroborated this typology through surveys and focus groups)

235

like Portland, where we have invested in bike lanes and boulevards, about 6 to 8 percent of the population has responded enthusiastically by integrating cycling into their lives for at least some trips. Approximately a third of the population is not interested or able to cycle. That leaves a pretty big chunk—around 60 percent—who want to bicycle, think it's a good idea, and are interested, but are highly concerned about safety and will not in any way, shape, or form start cycling unless we invest in low stress, protected bikeways. The choice is clear: invest in bikeways and get more people out cycling, or don't, and retain cycling as an elite sport of a privileged group of adrenaline junkies. ⚬━⚊

I suppose the negative reaction on the anti-bikeway blogs is to be expected. What is unexpected is an editorial in *Adventure Cyclist,*[74] a bicycle-touring magazine, blaming Portland's bike lanes for Tracey's and Brett's deaths. Why would a wonderful organization whose sole mission is to promote bicycle tourism publish this fact-free, flame-throwing column? Loyalty to a long-time contributor? Sensationalism to increase sales? Remember, I remind myself, all news about bicycling is good news, and Roger's excellent rebuttal[75] will help expose the columnist's extreme unprofessionalism.

Taking stock: So far, we've got delay, derision, and disrespect. I don't get it. Portlanders are grateful; the vast majority of bikeway professionals, thrilled. Finally, an American city is installing a technique our European counterparts have long found to be effective.

But that's not all.

A California-based traffic engineer, Fred Stickler, calls the sales-hungry *Portland Tribune* (a semi-weekly paper) with the dish. Portland is innovating! It's straying outside the Manual! The *Tribune* runs a front-page story questioning the green bike boxes' legitimacy.

On local blogs, Stickler posts inflammatory emails encouraging people to get injured in a bike box so they can sue the city. He tries to recruit a local lawyer (an old friend and colleague) to join his crusade. In this he fails, but manages to rope in a young lackey, Brian. Stickler directs Brian

---

⚬━⚊ **Design your bikeway network not for those who are already cycling but for those you would like to attract.**

---

[74] Schubert, John, "Portland's Agony: Two Cyclists Died as a Result of Poorly Designed Traffic-Control Devices," *Adventure Cyclist,* April 2008.
[75] Geller, Roger, "Portland's Pleasure," *Adventure Cyclist,* April 2008.

An added benefit of the boxes is that they keep motorists out of the crosswalk.

to file Freedom of Information Act requests; city staff waste dozens of hours responding to these requests, attacks, and media stories.

"It really hurt to see Brian out there, fanning the flames before the news cameras, saying that the things we had done to make the city more bicycle friendly were responsible, rather than the truck driver who ran over Brett," says one of Brett's friends. "Brett would have hated that."

Not satisfied with his troublemaking, Stickler then files a complaint against Rob to the state engineering board.

Now it's personal.

Rob's wife, Wendy, shares my birthday. She's a garlic farmer extraordinaire, speedy soccer player and one of my favorite people on the planet. Skyler adored her so mercilessly when she was his preschool teacher, he would have happily traded me in.

Rob hired me—an unknown from D.C.—based on a one-hour interview. He gave me the opportunity of a lifetime. Not a day goes by that I don't feel grateful for it. He supported my European research tour, covered my ass when I occasionally tipped the forgiveness/permission scale, and brought me back from my darkest hour during the bike-parking code debacle.

Like many traffic engineers, he's a bit introverted and quiet, dodges the spotlight and prefers to play by the rules. Yet he's taken our fair city to the highest levels of cycling and safety thus far seen in the United States.

Why on earth would Stickler file a complaint against Rob? Like many federal committee members, Stickler sees strict adherence to the Manual as being of utmost importance. He's deep inside the Borg, and disconnected from reality. Resistance is futile. Deviation not tolerated. You will be assimilated.

Perhaps I'm ascribing to him malice rather than simple incompetence. Or perhaps he's Casey, an oversized, freckled, big-haired cheerleader who would raise her hand to tattle that I had failed to say the prayers broadcast—in full defiance of Supreme Court rulings separating church and state—over the public junior-high loudspeaker. "You're going to hell," she whispered to me, then stole the jacket I had bought with three months of Big 'D' Donuts earnings.

Whatever his motivation, he stepped well over the line when he impugned Rob's reputation.

Rob and I may be getting older, but we can still climb the hills.

We set off one afternoon in a dewy mist. Silence reigns as we ascend under the willow trees now devoid of rustling leaves. We crest at the Fairmount Loop and chase each other through one, two, three 3-mile (5 km) laps. Fury is our fuel.

On the fourth lap, I slow, spent. Rob pedals up beside me, and we ride side by side another half-loop in a companionable quiet. The road is wet, and the drizzle steady, but we are oblivious.

"Rob, why don't you join the national committee? Please? Then they would hear from you directly and understand what we're doing."

"Mia, they can call, email, text, snail-mail, telegram, Twitter, or Facebook me. I'm not hard to find. If they want to know what we're doing, all they have to do is ask. Me, I have a job to do: make the City of Portland the best and safest place it can be. I can't justify taxpayer time or money for two trips a year to D.C. to sit and listen to them diss us."

I apologize profusely for my role encouraging the city to apply for federal approval. Just because bike boxes have not made it through two decades of impossible *Indiana Jones* mazes, traps, snake pits, and burning oil does not mean they are unsafe or unworthy. Transportation professionals want to know not just what has made it through the challenging federal rubric but the day-to-day, on-the-ground, nuts-and-bolts of successful urban cycling systems.

"This sandbox is no fun," he sighs, the dew shimmering off his now all-gray beard. Goodness knows, we've got enough like-minded friends. Colleagues in Seattle, Berkeley, Cambridge, Tucson, and Chicago are all defying Manuel with progressive bikeway treatments. New York City is blowing us away with their bold reallocation of roadway space to pedestrians and cyclists and use of color, bike boxes, and signals. Their reaction to the hornet's nest Portland stirred is a) what can we do to help, and b) phew, thank goodness we didn't put ourselves through that!

"True enough" I agree. "True enough."

We're quiet for a moment, two old friends mulling, churning, our thoughts weaving, bobbing, and dancing in the steam of our breath. A wispy thread, like a memory strand pulled from Professor Dumbledore's mind, takes form. It's mine, it's his, it's ours.

Rob and I look at each other. It's a Vulcan mind-meld, no words necessary. We can both see the solution hovering right in front of our faces.

We know what to do.

Less than a year later, we launch Cities for Cycling,[76] a coalition promoting best international practices in urban cycling. Our goal: Shine a light on the full depth and breadth of progressive solutions. Nothing in my twenty-year career has been this easy. Every official we approach says, hell yes, we too have been frustrated with the federal process. Sign us up!

Portland Mayor Adams and Catherine Ciarlo take the lead, followed by New York Mayor Bloomberg and his powerhouse transportation director Janette Sadik-Khan and city officials from Chicago, Boston, Seattle, San Francisco, Minneapolis, Washington D.C., Austin, Philadelphia, Cambridge, Berkeley, and more. National advocacy groups—Bikes Belong and the League of American Bicyclists, among others—jump into our sandbox without hesitation. And in March, 2011, we e-publish the first edition

---

Take leaders on a ride in a bicycle-friendly community like Portland, Boulder, Fort Collins, Minneapolis, New York City, Davis, or Vancouver, B.C.

---

76 For more information of the Cities for Cycling project of the National Association of City Transportation Officials, see http://nacto.org/cities-for-cycling/.

of-the groundbreaking NACTO Urban Bikeway Design Guide,[77] spotlighting twenty-one top-notch bikeway design treatments with photos, schematics, 3D renderings, and rich detailed guidance.

I welcome all of you, even Fred Stickler and the like, to come ride with us one of these days. One caveat: come only if you are willing to open your eyes to a world that is changing for the better.

The green bike boxes are working well, as expected. Will they prevent all future right-hook crashes? Probably not. Of course, we'll never know. But I do know this: If we do nothing, then that's what we will get.

---

[77] http://nacto.org/cities-for-cycling/design-guide/

CHAPTER 36

The Gift

At the Cleveland High School track on a warm day in early fall, six-year-old Sasha is learning to ride a bicycle without training wheels. She's tried twice before, in front of our house and at the park. Both times, she couldn't get her balance, veered off course, and crashed. Since then, no amount of cajoling, bribery, or firmness got her to try again.

Until now. Today, she is determined. Coming up at school in a couple of weeks is our bikeathon fundraising event: the Tour de Ladd. Nothing like a little peer pressure to spur action. I tell her that it's no problem if she can't ride. Training wheels are fine, and some kids are going to ride scooters or be cheerleaders. She puts her hands on her hips and cocks her head to the side. For a second, I can see her as a teenager. She sneers, "I am *so* not going to scooter, Mom."

Her bike is baby pink with coaster brakes and pink and purple handlebar streamers. Its name, painted in sparkly purple cursive on the downtube, is Mystic.

I run alongside her, hand on her back, and let go. She loses her balance and crashes, legs entangled with the bike. I get her up, brush her off, and wait for her to stomp off in frustration. Instead, she picks up the bike and declares she's ready to rock and roll. She crashes again, but is slightly less entangled than before. Third time, she leaps to the side, inelegantly but effectively. A few times later, she can stop herself without crashing.

I've invented a little cheer: "Sasha is a biking girl, Sasha is a party girl. Go go Sasha!" She stares straight ahead with

Trailer-bikes are a great way to transport children. Sasha loves hers!

alligator eyes and a determined frozen grin, biking a little further, gaining control and balance. Speedy Skyler slows, encouraging, "Sasha, just keep going…don't stop…and pedal faster! You're doing so great! Much better than me when I learned to ride!" For an ultracompetitive kid like him, one who rarely lavishes affection on his kid sister, this is high praise indeed.

Sasha makes it around the track one whole time. I'm jogging alongside her, singing my goofy song. At the end of the field, a practicing squad of high-school cheerleaders joins in the celebration. As she pedals by, they do cartwheels and yell, "Gooooo, Sasha Rose!"

She skids to a stop, both feet on the ground, gets off, balances the bike on its kickstand, and sashays with confidence to the water fountain. My heart is bursting with the pride of one who has just given her child a priceless gift: freedom.

It's a drizzly day in early October when we cut the ribbon on the first Tour de Ladd. Our quarter-mile (0.5 km) course of temporarily car-free streets will be not an ultra-test of strong legs and spirit, but of tiny legs and big smiles.

October is pretty reliable for dry weather, but the weather gods are not cooperating. No matter. It's just rain. The Tour de Ladd is on.

We've got three hundred bikes lined up on the covered basketball court. The kindergarteners line up to go first. The cheerleading section practices, "Pedal to the Metal! Go Ride Ride!" Two police officers offer safety tips by bullhorn.

Abernethy Elementary is just a normal neighborhood school. We have no special immersion program, just a solid curriculum and a group of dedicated parents.

OK, maybe we're not just a normal school.[78] About fifty percent of our kids bike or walk to school regularly, thanks to years of dedicated Safe Routes to School (SRTS) efforts. In this, we are quite different than most of America's schools. Although Portland's been doing some form of bike/walk-to-school activities since the 1990s when I was cajoling school district officials and principals to put in bike racks, the recent surge of activity comes under the national SRTS program, thanks to Earl Blumenauer, Senator Jim Oberstar from Minnesota, and a pint-sized organizing dynamo named Deb Hubsmith from Marin County, California. With more

---

[78] Complementing our focus on fitness is an equally strong healthy food fetish. The Garden of Wonders is our base for science education, and the Scratch Kitchen provides locally grown (some from our garden), freshly prepared meals. Is it any wonder the Abernethy kids are such good learners? No empty carbs and sodas for these little bodies.

"Fit kids learn better," insists Abernethy Principal Tammy Barron, a huge sup-porter of Safe Routes to School and the Tour de Ladd, pictured here.

than 160 U.S. representatives and senators working together in the bipar-tisan Congressional Bike Caucus, Earl is no longer a lone wolf howling livability to the wind.

SRTS takes a "Five E" approach: engineering (physical infrastructure improvements to help make bicycling and walking safer); education (bicy-cle and pedestrian safety courses); encouragement (events and activities); enforcement (of laws intended to slow motorists around schools and get them to yield to pedestrians); and evaluation (to determine the success of the effort).[79]

For three years I managed Portland's pilot SRTS program and have been involved in other efforts in California, Montana, Maine, and Mis-souri. In Portland's twenty-five pilot elementary schools, we increased levels of cycling and walking to 38 percent of school-commute trips. Once resistant Buckman Elementary became one of our shining stars. But now I'm just a mom, carrying on the good vibes with the Tour de Ladd.

---

[79]   For more information, see www.saferoutesinfo.org/ and www.saferoutespartnership.org/

"Cyrus was a nightmare," John tells me, as I adjust the helmet of his developmentally disabled son. This is one of the things I'm most proud of: In preparation for the Tour de Ladd, we've gotten our whole school properly fitted with helmets.

Cyrus has a fairly complex set of issues requiring an ever-evolving regimen of drugs and medical appointments. One thing for sure: He is highly prone to emotional volatility. By fifth grade, Cy's condition was compounded by a ballooning weight problem caused by a combination of metabolism-affecting drugs and inactivity. In this, he mirrors close to fifty percent of our children nationwide.[80]

But then an amazing thing happened: Cy won a brand-spanking-new mountain bike in our SRTS raffle and learned how to ride. Since he started biking to school, his weight has dropped and his moods mellowed. Often their family rides turn into an adventure. They stop for fresh, locally grown food at the farmers' market. They run into friends, or stop to snack on juicy wild blackberries. They catalogue all the wildlife they see—hummingbirds, butterflies, beavers, nutria, red-winged blackbirds, and robins.

"Bicycling saved us," declares John. Earl would be so proud. Cyrus gives me a big smile and heads off to find his bike. ⊙━ᴛ

⊛ ⊛ ⊛ ⊛ ⊛

The skies are a misty shade of gray but hold back their spittle. Dapper City Commissioner Nick Fish cuts the ribbon, then speeds off. Surrounded by kindergarteners on teeny-tiny bikes, he's in his trench coat and dress shoes on my silver and black step-through-frame Trek T80 Navigator. (Later, his staff will tease him mercilessly about riding a girlie bike.) The street is lined with a hundred screaming parents and teachers. A couple of guys on super-tall bikes—handmade by fusing two bicycle frames together—entertain the kids, while police officers ride along, a calming presence for the wilder boys.

In the lunch line afterward, kids bounce up and down. "This is the best day ever!" proclaims one fifth grader. I peek in at Sasha's first-grade class. Half the kids have their heads on their desks, resting, worn out... happy.

⊙━ᴛ **Find at least one short driving trip per week—to the store, school, restaurant, park, or friend's house—and switch it to foot or bike.**

---

[80] Data from Centers for Disease Control: www.cdc.gov/obesity/data/trends.html

CHAPTER 37

Patience and Faith

In the field of planning and design, the greatest measure of success is seeing your ideas realized. In Portland, my daily travels provide that validation and make me wildly happy. But as a planning consultant, I've had my doubts. We can't just write a work order and restripe the road, or make a phone call and get a crew out to fill a pothole or install a bike rack. We come in at a certain point in the project or program, whether it's the initial planning, feasibility, design, or implementation. We get involved in a community, meet some amazing people, struggle through challenges, then wrap things up and move on.

What happens to the plans we write, I often wonder. Is anyone pushing them forward? Are they sitting on a shelf? Are people using the trails we've built?

One sunny afternoon I head to the mountains to find one community's answer. For way too long, the primary attraction of the little town of Government Camp was the public restroom, where skiers and boarders stopped on the way up to the ski resorts. Then, a decade ago, property owners decided that being a poop stop wasn't good enough. They wanted something better. To pay for that something, they would tax themselves. Step #1 in their vision: a system of world-class biking/cross-country ski trails for both transportation and recreation. Right up my alley.

For about a year, George Hudson and I drove up here weekly, meeting with property owners and residents, hiking through the forest, wading through streams. At one public meeting, a group of menacing snowmobilers tried to hijack the plan. I calmly explained to the roomful of down-parka-and-heavy-boots-clad paratroopers, "Snowmobiles not only render cross-country ski conditions miserable, they destroy the pristine quiet beauty of the backcountry with noise and belching fumes. And don't even get me started on gas-powered leaf blowers. What's wrong with raking? Go home, people, go home."

OK, I didn't actually say that. Six years of getting yelled at in public meetings in Portland taught me a few things.

What I actually said was, "Folks, please. I understand you are upset. We have been hired to do a plan for nonmotorized ski and mountain bike trail improvements, not snowmobiles. The Forest Service is planning a separate snowmobile plan to come later."

We had a lengthy stare-off while I wondered if I was going to have to fight my way to the door. Then they trooped outside to rev their engines.

Eventually, we forged a plan to both stimulate the local economy and provide balanced transportation options.

I drive down Main Street slowly, taking in the new brick sidewalks, decorative street lights, hanging planters, banners, and new storefront facades, the realization of the second part of their vision. Kathleen Walker, a dark-haired U.S. Forest Service official with shoulders so square and tight they cry out for a massage, stands next to her pickup truck by the bike-rental shop. As the representative of the area's largest landholder, she was at the center of it all during the Trails Plan process. Now she's taking me on a tour so I can see firsthand the results of our work.

"Holy cow, Kathleen! This looks amazing!"

"Oh yes, it sure does," she acknowledges with a Lauren Hutton gap-toothed smile, then launches into an Ellen DeGeneres flat-toned monologue. "So you know there's all this money sitting in the urban renewal fund and Dick Kohnstamm—you remember Dick—he proposes that a couple hundred thousand should go to upgrading the grocery store, which of course he owns, so then Charlie Wessinger—you remember Charlie, owner of Summit Resort?—he's like, man, I need some money for my pet project, which is only fair given that Kirk Hanna—you remember Kirk, owner of Ski Bowl?—is getting more than a mil for Collins Lake development stuff like roads and sidewalks and

Government Camp Main Street, a far cry from its former status as a pit stop

whatnot...." Oh, the delights of small-town politics!

As she talks, we walk our bikes just a bit up the hill behind Main Street. It's a glorious September day; Mount Hood still resplendent in its gray summer nakedness.

"Ready to ride?" she asks at the trailhead.

"Always!"

My rented mountain bike handles the bumps of the packed dirt trail just fine as I follow Kathleen's solid teal-shirted back up and down the gentle slopes. Although I have a fraction of a tad more than zero mountain-biking experience, I am at ease enough to let my mind depart from the task of staying vertical. Cedar and hemlock trees creak in the wind. A red-crested woodpecker

Off-road trails in beautiful places are another piece of the puzzle in attracting people to cycling.

rhythmically pecks a snag up ahead, and a chipmunk burrows in a rotting log.

Kathleen stops after a couple miles on what looks like a wooden raft straddling a trickling stream, where ten young Americorps volunteers are on break next to a pile of hoes, axes, picks, and shovels. A couple smoke cigarettes; the others stretch and chat. For the past few summers, they've been removing trees and debris, digging out trenches, installing drainage pipes, bridging streams, and packing tread. Their motto: "You gotta break a few eggs to make an omelet."

Kathleen introduces me as a trail-planning consultant. The reaction, in stark contrast to my family's long-ago confusion and sympathy, is awe-struck enthusiasm.

"They pay you for that?" a young man asks. He means not that my job is unworthy, but that it's wicked, way cool, and could he come work for me, please? (Go to a progressive sustainability-oriented college, young man, and study landscape architecture, planning, or engineering. Then we'll talk.)

After three hours of pedaling, I realize that I am in the presence of *The Incredibles'* smart, tough, ferociously motherly Elastigirl, who can stretch and mold around obstacles that arise in her path. One trail had to be adjusted due to the Federal Wilderness Act, another due to the presence

247

of a wetland, a third due to local politics. Kathleen's toolbox is overflowing with solutions.

We note a tiny stream next to the trail. "It's like putting a finger in a dike here," laughs Elastigirl. "Wherever we hit water, we build a trench or install a pipe, and water pops up somewhere else." She makes a note of the spot so she can mobilize a volunteer crew.[81]

"It's a perfect task for city-dwellers. Small stuff like this, not too far of a hike in, make 'em feel like they're contributing, which they totally are, because we sure appreciate their help."

Too many people, when faced with even one obstacle, shut down and give up. The highway department told her, no, you can't put in a signal to cross our miserable, fast-moving, highly dangerous highway (Manuel won't allow it, of course), and no, you can't have any money to build a bridge or tunnel.[82] Most others would have given up, shut the project down. Elastigirl defiantly brought the trail right up to the highway.

"Five years, ten years, whatever; eventually, they'll give in."

From 6,000 feet high, I absorb yet another lesson: patience and faith. Whether we're talking about changes at the national or local level, it takes time and commitment for good ideas to take root. A decade for changes to be conceived, massaged, solidified, funded, and implemented is the norm, not the exception. The good people of San Diego, California and Pasadena, Texas, may not yet have built their bikeways, but at least they've got a plan. What it will take to build all the bikeways, walkways, and trails across the country is exactly what they've got up here: leadership, quality staff, motivated residents, and money, which they raised all on their own. **0━⊤**

The results: a thriving little Cascadian-themed town laced with 10 miles (16 km) of popular, easy-to-use off-road trails. Add these to the more than 5,000 miles of bikeways and walkways Alta staff have achieved across the country, and the 40,000 miles or more in the pipeline. Bit by bit, we're creating a more healthy, sustainable, livable future.

0━⊤   Have patience, persistence, and faith.

---

81 The fabulous International Mountain Bicycling Association helps communities worldwide build and maintain mountain bike trails while stewarding the land. For more information, see www.imba.com.

82 The highway department did widen the one existing bridge with an extra travel lane and sidewalks beautifully decorated with copper relief panels etched into brick light posts. Myself, I would have left out the extra lane but included bike lanes. This bridge, however, is located in the middle of town and is not a substitute for the much-needed crossings on each end of town.

"Still gotta put up some more signs, adjust the map, do some advertising," admits Kathleen. "I took some serious flack for this one." She points to a sign hammered about 10 feet (3 m) high on a tree that reads: "Maggie's Trail. Built thanks to the Clackamas County Urban Renewal Fund and the Government Camp Trails Plan."

Apparently, allowing the crew boss to name the trail after his dog pissed off some folks, especially after he named a second one after his deceased mother, Lucy, may she rest in peace. I can only laugh at the competing, backstabbing, self-serving, tattletaling ski resort owners' reaction to a trail being named after a government official's dog.

Kathleen shrugs protectively, "Yeah, well, Bruce has been working his ass off for this community for twenty years." Not a bad way to acknowledge his contribution.

"Come back this winter," she encourages. "You like to cross-country ski, right? You'll love the trails when they're under snow."

Yes I do, Kathleen, and yes, I will.

A bouquet of flowers to you, Government Camp, for following through on your dreams.

And for all those other dreams, those trails not yet built, lives not yet improved, choices and chances not yet realized, I offer a tool kit of solutions and an endless reservoir of hope. A more healthy, safe, and livable future is within your reach, I promise.

CHAPTER 38

Joyride

It's a lucky person who finds the perfect career at a young age, sticks with it, and spends an obsessive amount of time just about every day for twenty years, so far, in a state of joyous decision-making, networking, creative problem-solving, mentoring, learning, and giving. The world is full of jobs that feed our bellies but not our souls. Somehow, I found this strange and wonderful path from which I empower people and transform communities, one pedal stroke at a time. If you had told me, when I was a fifteen-year-old miserably trying—and repeatedly failing—to pass the parallel-parking part of the driver's test so I could be a teenage soccer mom, "Yo, Mia, you're going to be the queen of bicycles," I would have doubled over in hysterics, spewing Diet Coke out my nose.

The path looks like a mosaic that is constantly being formed and reformed into new patterns, each one unique, each one perfect. The pieces of the mosaic are deliciously beautiful moments and people, ideas, and opportunities.

When I was a young girl, I was in a hurry to get to what I saw as real life, where I could make a difference. Even now, I struggle to be patient, for I want the world, the entirety of it, to be the place it can and should be. But after two decades of this, one thing is clear: Sustainable change takes time, and in the meantime, life, if we're lucky, carries on one day, one hour, one moment at a time.

Right now, I'm watching a steady stream of pedaling, walking, smiling, laughing, talking, weaving families on North Willamette Boulevard, once a battleground over bike lanes. It is our darkest moments that teach us our greatest lessons, no? The fireman's shocking behavior—threatening certain death—taught me to see our own officials' fears as a harbinger of the larger public's. After testing the delay that speed bumps actually cause fire trucks, we got clear on which streets would be eligible for bumps. A primary fire response route, Willamette would not be one of them, but hundreds of miles of neighborhood streets would. With the fire department no longer in opposition, we then rallied enough support from the neighborhood and city council to mark the bike lanes. Willamette became a premier bikeway enjoyed by close to six hundred daily cyclists. 0—T

My humble volunteer job for the afternoon is "Intersection Superhero." I've embraced my mission: Keep cars off the road. My bright red cape will serve to warn frustrated, clueless, or maybe curious motorists that I'm serious about my job.

"Hello, sir!" I'll say with a smile and thank-you for understanding. "Willamette is closed to motorized traffic until 4:00 p.m. As you can see, we've got quite a fun ride going on today." I'll hand him a map and show him which streets to use.

"Thank you!" he'll say, and comment that it sure looks fun and he hopes to do the next one.

Alas, my heroic skills go untapped. This 8-mile (13 km) car-free "Sunday Parkways"[83] course has been well publicized and marked. Either the whole neighborhood is out walking and biking, or they've figured out another way to get where they need to go. So, instead of disarming wayward motorists with charm, I flit around like Tinkerbell sprinkling pixie dust on friends: Bike Gallery owner Jay Graves, busily pumping tires and lubing dry chains, Rob and Wendy Burchfield, and Women-on-Bikes leader Janis McDonald, dressed like she's ready to do a polka dance.

My dear friend Linda Ginenthal, helmet-free, long salt-and-pepper hair flowing down her back, bikes up and gives me a big hug. These fun-filled Sunday adventures are part of her program to reduce drive-alone trips. Lovely Linda's Transportation Options[84] group was the outgrowth of the bicycle program downsizing years ago. It took a few years for them to gel, but when they did, my-oh-my did they gel in style.

Want information on bicycling, walking, or transit? No pressure.

Yes? No problem.

Within a week, a cheerful, fit, healthy-looking man or woman bikes over, rings your doorbell, and hands you a tote bag with your customized bike, walk, or transit map, coupons for a helmet or bike lock, free stuff (umbrella, bike bell, pant leg strap, etc.), and schedule of upcoming neighborhood fun. Then, 9 to 13 percent of you shift some of your trips from driving to biking, walking, or transit. That's a real, honest-to-goodness bargain at thrice the price.

0—T **No matter what obstacles you encounter, keep going.**

---

[83] Sunday Parkways, aka, car-free Sundays, aka *Ciclovias*, was inspired by the indefatigable Gil Peñalosa, executive director of Walk and Bike for Life and brother of Enrique, the former mayor of Bogotá, Columbia. For more information, see www.walkandbikeforlife.org/.

[84] For more information, see www.portlandonline.com/transportation/.

Linda and I cheer on a group of ten pedaling a many-bike fused contraption called the Millipede, chat with kids from the Asian-American Center, and stop to get water from the good folks at a booth promoting evangelical crusader Luis Palau. It's the ultimate everyone-is-welcome party. If I were a politician or ice-cream vendor, I'd be all over this like flies on molasses.

"You did it, girl!" I call out as she waves buh-bye. I know how hard she's been working to raise funds, corral volunteers, and inform the neighbors that their streets will be car-free for a day, and please, pretty please with sugar on top, give it a try: bike or walk for today, just one day, this day, but maybe, if you like it (and you probably will like it), you'll do it again another day, then another day after that, and soon you'll be part of the daily platoons of happy pedaling Portlanders.

Families enjoy Sunday Parkways' safe, festive atmosphere in droves.

I escort through the crowd one dude in an old Ford Chevy pickup who apparently didn't read the sixteen flyers dropped on his doorstep, missed the lawn signs, and failed to clue in when volunteers put up barricades and his best-selling author neighbor, Joe Kurmaskie, aka the Metal Cowboy, raised a tent in the street and attracted a crowd of admirers and crazed children. Other than that, my intersection seems to be under control, so I decide to check out the 8-mile (13 km) course.

A police officer waves me through a busy intersection.

"What do you think of this?" I ask.

"Impressive," he states cheerfully. "'Course, lots of folks ride bikes around here. Just glad we can help make it safe."

"Probably also happy to get paid overtime, eh?" I wink, flutter my cape, and fly on 'til morning. Good lord, wasn't it just yesterday when a roomful of officers walked out on my feeble attempt to influence their bicycle law enforcement approach?

After six hours of successfully protecting my intersection from security breaches and still buzzing from the positive energy of 20,000 safe, happy people, I stash my cape in my wicker handlebar basket and put my flowery sage-colored helmet back on. Why can't it be this way every day?

Sometimes, the path is there, but we can't find it or even see it. Our eyes, hearts, and minds are simply not open wide enough. It took me a while to find it, after all, coming all the way from Texas. Once my eyes were opened, though, I couldn't go back. Forty thousand eyes opened today. They're on the path now, along with Roger Talley, my stepfather, Tommy, and all the skeptics-turned-cyclists I've encountered over the years.

On my ride home I am struck by how far we've come. Each challenging bike lane, path, boulevard, and bridge made its way through obstacles and opposition to a place of undisputed success. Even those once-nasty stretches of industrial highway are solidly rideable now.

Not one of these existed fifteen years ago. We've come such a long way.

And yet, we've still got such a long way to go. In the far-out, hilly, and suburban parts of the city, the barriers are many, bikeway opportunities less obvious, and bicyclists scarce. We're not done yet, not by any stretch of the imagination, and the Portland Bicycle Plan for 2030 tackles these areas head-on.

I turn onto Lincoln, the once-congested street that perfectly embodies the spirit of how communities can reclaim and rebalance the space beneath their feet. For every three or four cyclists, a motorist slowly navigates the two-wheeled parade. Penny-pinching students mix with high-income fitness freaks. They are fresh-air lovers, speed-seekers, free thinkers, Lycra-clad Lance-wannabes on expensive bicycles, youthful twenty-somethings on single-speeds, gorgeous forty-something moms toting two or three kids, middle-schoolers dangling an oboe or backpack from their skinny shoulders. We may not be in Copenhagen, but I sure do like how it feels.

Four minutes of spacing-out zen climbing a short but steep hill gets my blood pumping, until I crest and glide home.

Two months later, it's our street's turn. Even better than the daily weave of cyclists and motorists will be a nonstop stream of humans devoid of metal boxes. Heaven is about to descend in my front yard.

At 9:00 a.m., the barricades go up. An eerie, delicious combustion-free silence fills the air. Boyfriend Glen and I drag brother Bruce's old grill from the backyard to the driveway. Not a great grill, with about half the burners working right, it's probably not worth the hundred bucks he charged me, the scammer, but functional nonetheless. Like magic, a couple of colleagues show up unplanned and ask if they can help.

"Sure!" I instruct. "Open the fridge carefully—seven hundred hot dogs stacked in there like a Jenga tower—and fill up the cooler in the driveway. Thanks so much!"

Around noon, a quartet of highly talented bluegrass musicians sets up a sound system in my front yard. They pick and harmonize through "Brown-eyed Kentucky Girl" and on to "I Ain't Broke but I'm Badly Bent." Like fireflies attracted to a light, people stop until a swelling, dancing, swaying throng singing along to "Shenandoah River" occupies two-thirds of the street.

I wander the crowd, pushing Glen's grilled beef, turkey, and tofu dogs on friends, neighbors, and strangers alike. My son and his pals eat until their stomachs hurt.

"Hi, Mia!" exclaims neighbor Frances, another happily transplanted Texas gal. "How much?"

"They're free." I smile.

"Why are they free?" she queries. "They're charging a buck a dog just up the road."

The twelve car-free miles are one humongous block party. Some guy's dragged a pool into the middle of the street. Other offerings include Samba classes, mask-making, and food. Entrepreneurs along the route sell ice cream, postcards, and soft drinks.

Top to bottom: Me handing out hot dogs; Sunday Parkways organizer Linda; and our thank-you card to the City of Portland for this amazing day

255

A friend informs me that she's just seen Sasha up the street selling lemonade. I dropped her off at Catherine's earlier; it didn't occur to me to be concerned about her roaming without my permission or knowledge. When I was her age, the whole neighborhood was our exploring ground. Today's kids can't leave their backyards without an escort. Fear of getting snatched by a stranger, which almost never happens, and of getting hit by a car, which is also quite rare, as well as our habit of driving them everywhere, has robbed our children of something essential.

This day, Sasha experiences a delicious few hours of freedom. From then on, she insists on walking herself to the bus stop and to close-by friends' houses.

"Mom, I'll be fine," she asserts. Let me be a kid, loosen up the tether, stop worrying. OK, Sasha, I hear you loud and clear. Go, play, sell lemonade, laugh, explore, live it up.

"No, really," Frances insists, curious. "Why would you buy all these hot dogs and go to all this trouble and all you ask is for us to sign a thank-you card?"

Why? Because I am surrounded by excellent people, including Glen, who has been happily turning weenies for four hours under a roasting sun. (For the record, we gave away six hundred.)

Why? Because this is awesome. Thousands of people are on my street, moving their bodies, smiling, engaging, connecting, showing that yes, we can integrate bicycling into their daily lives. Because we started talking about car-free streets two decades ago, and here, right now, is its manifestation—public space put to its highest and best use: helmet-unnecessary, yield-only, pollution-free, community-building, laughter-filled transportation recreation innovation. ⊶

"Enjoy," I say to Frances, and hand her, wrapped in a bun, a weenie bit of my gratitude.

⊶ **Open your streets to people on foot or bike and celebrate every success. Most of all, enjoy the ride!**

Transforming Communities and Emporing People, One Pedal Stroke at a Time

1. Look beyond the bike: Bicycle transportation succeeds best when combined with investments in compact development, transit, and walking. Engage in and support various efforts to help shape your sustainable community.

2. Key human elements: strong local political leaders, effective community advocates, and well-trained and supported city staff. With one or two, you can make some progress, but it is the combination of all three that is the recipe for success.

3. Develop and adopt a robust, visionary, comprehensive bicycle transportation plan. Use the planning process to engage your community in a deep conversation about the future of transportation.

4. Develop a network of bikeways that is connected, comprehensive, and gets people from where they are to where they want to go. It should be a combination of off-street paths, on-road separated bikeways, and low-stress neighborhood greenways and must appeal to a wide variety of ages, cycling skill levels, and trip purposes.

5. It's not just the bikeway infrastructure, it's the attitude. Embrace the role of encouraging people to bicycle as part and parcel of the way you do business.

6. Get your traffic engineers on bike as a regular part of their job.

7. Start with the low-hanging fruit: easy-to-implement projects.

8. Court the media and don't freak out if you get negative press. It's important to get 'bike' in the public consciousness.

9. Set aside at least 1 percent of your transportation budget to get the ball rolling.

10. Adopt "Complete Streets" policies and/or legislation, then execute! Unenforced policies and plans that sit on shelves gathering dust are worthless.

11. Backlash is normal. Expect it, prepare for it, but don't back down. Changing built infrastructure and deeply ingrained habits is really hard stuff.

12. Look to the world's best cycling cities for planning and design guidance.

13. Work hand-in-hand across bureaucratic boundaries to create complementary off- and on-street bikeways.

14. Iconic, highly visible, albeit costly off-road urban pathways are worth the investment. Garner funding via grants, partnerships, local funding, tax measures, hook, crook, and creativity. The more you invest, the more your community will reap the benefits of active transportation.

15. Top priority: Upgrade bridges and pinch points.

16. Institutionalize care of bikeway facilities into daily maintenance practices.

17. Fully integrate bicycling with your transit system through low-stress bikeways to stations, storage at stations, and provisions for bikes on transit vehicles.

18. Build relationships with local leaders and take them on rides to see the good and bad and to envision future possibilities.

19. Retrain officials throughout every facet of government to understand the needs of people on bikes.

20. Integrate requirements and incentives for bike parking, showers, and lockers into building codes.

21. Train developers, architects, and all staff involved in building permits, planning, development, and design.

22. Encouragement key #1: Celebrate bike commuters with events and contests.

23. Encouragement key #2: Invest time and effort in the personal touch—one-on-one mentoring (aka personal travel-planning programs or individualized marketing programs) to overcome resistance and mental barriers.

24. Tie your network together with bikeway signage noting destinations, mileage, and time.

25. Whenever you ride, be courteous, obey the law, and smile and wave at any motorist who shows you the slightest shred of kindness.

26. Foster community groups to recycle and reuse bikes for the good of underprivileged youth.

27. Send thank-you notes to public officials who support bicycle transportation.

28. Don't let weather challenges dissuade you from creating bicycle-friendly infrastructure.

29. Encouragement key #3: Hold mega-fun, car-free community events, which are a wonderful way to connect people with public space and open their hearts and minds to bicycling.

30. See the bicycle as a tool for empowerment and social change, not just sport or transportation.

31. Encouragement key #4: Focus on women! When women and children ride in significant numbers, then you know you're making progress.

32. Put away the Lycra for short trips; embrace cycle chic.

33. Encouragement key #5: Integrate bike safety education into schools and invest in comprehensive Safe Routes to School programs. Start now.

34. Face the naysayers with solid research and facts.

35. Understand all sides of an issue, then look for and create win-win solutions.

36. Fight just as hard to avoid car-exclusive, bike-hideous roadway, bridges, and interchanges as you do to create something new.

37. In the suburbs, focus on building off-street paths and shifting short trips in neighborhoods to bike or foot. Let go of the focus on the long, hard-to-impact journey-to-work trip.

38. Use the shared-lane marking (aka, sharrow) where the speed differential between cyclists and motorists is low, to advertise neighborhood greenways or to fill in short gaps. Detailed guidance on the sharrow at http://nacto.org/cities-for-cycling/design-guide/.

39. Wherever you are, that's where you start. Tailor solutions to your community's unique topography, urban layout, demographics, and growth patterns.

40. Have hope: Even the most closed minds can open.

41. Design for what you want to achieve rather than what is dictated by traditional traffic models.

42. Do not let fear of being sued prevent you from doing the right thing. (It rarely happens, and you'll be fine if you follow key #44.)

43. Carefully document your decisions, base them on best practices, monitor the situation, and make adjustments as necessary.

44. Collect data on the number of people on bikes, estimate and project usage, measure your success, and continually report back.

45. Design your bikeway network not for those who are already cycling but for those you would like to attract—those interested in bicycling but concerned about safety and desire low-stress bikeways separated from motor vehicle traffic or shared in low-speed conditions.

46. Take leaders on a ride in a bicycle-friendly city like Portland, Boulder, Fort Collins, Minneapolis, Davis, or Vancouver, B.C.

47. It starts with us: find at least one driving trip per week—to the store, school, restaurant, park, or friend's house—and switch it to foot or bike.

48. Have patience, persistence, and faith.

49. No matter what obstacles you encounter, keep going.

50. Open your streets to people on foot or bike and celebrate every success. Most of all, enjoy the ride!

A Step-by-Step Guide to Turn Your Town into a Bicycle Friendly Community

Reprinted courtesy of the League of American Bicyclists

Here are the steps you can take to bring bicycling improvements to your town.

1. ***Check out the Bicycle Friendly Community Overview Presentation.***
   Download the presentation at www.bikeleague.org/programs/bicyclefriendly america/communities/bfc_overview09.pdf. As you review the presentation, you'll see that all types and sizes of communities and the nation as a whole can be positively affected by increased bicycle accommodations, education, and promotion efforts. Whether decisions that affect your bicycle planning, infra-structure, education programs, encouragement and enforcement efforts occur in a township, town, borough, city, or county level, the BFC program can help frame the discussion with your decision makers.

2. ***See what Bicycle Friendly Communities are up to in the annual Bicycle Friendly America Yearbook.***
   Get inspired by great ideas, simple solutions, and innovative programs in Bicycle Friendly Communities across the United Statews in this yearly publi-cation. See the latest at www.bikeleague.org/programs/bicyclefriendlyamerica /bicyclefriendlyyearbook/index.php and contact the League for hard copies—info@bicyclefriendlycommunity.org.

3. ***Evaluate your community with our bicycle friendly Community Quick Scorecard.***
   Take a few minutes to complete this quick scorecard to see how your com-munity stacks up in bicycle friendliness. The scorecard allows you to take an objective look at your community to determine if it already has the basic foundation for a Bicycle Friendly Community. View the scorecard at: www.bikeleague.org/programs/bicyclefriendlyamerica/communityscorecard/.

4. ***Review the application yourself to see how bicycle friendly your com-munity is today.***
   Is there a written policy on maintaining bicycle-safe streets? Is there a bicycle advisory committee and/or a bicycle coordinator? These basic resources can

be vital to a town's ability to respond to bicyclist's needs. Highway engineers often will not change their practices unless written policy tells them to do so. A bicycle advisory committee is a good structure for getting such new policies written and formally proposed. Having someone on staff designated as bicycle coordinator can be crucial in achieving these measures. (Remember, it is a cardinal rule in every bureaucracy that any task not specified as someone's job is a task that will never get done.) Please note that only applications submitted on-line will be accepted.

5. Plan your strategy for pitching bicycle friendly improvements.
Obviously, if the mayor is a ride leader in the local bicycle club, your strategy is simple—show her or him the program materials! Most communities will take a little more work. First, you must identify the decision makers responsible for the policy changes you seek. In big cities, the mayor's office would typically delegate responsibility to the city's head of transportation or public works. In a smaller town, there may be a full-time city manager that reports to a citizen city council. In any event, you must make some calls to determine who needs to be persuaded before you can set out to persuade them. Next, find one or two bicyclists who have some influence with the decision maker. If you're lucky, there is a local government official who is an avid cyclist. Without such a person, identify the most visible bicycle dealer in town and the leader of a local bicycle club. Ask around and find support. If you find a bicyclist who is already known and trusted by government leaders, your work will be much easier.

6. Gather support.
Ask for a letter recommending the Bicycle Friendly Community program from any organization that might be inclined to support better bicycling. The local bicycle club is a natural first choice, but local environmental groups, civic organizations, businesses, and others will tend to cooperate if you make it easy enough for them. Draft the letter for them so they know exactly what you need to minimize the amount of work you ask of them. The Bicycle Friendly Community program frames positive change for bicyclists into the form of a "yes or no" question to a political leader: "Will you support this program?" Politicians hate to say no to anyone. They especially do not want to say no to an organized group of people. And it's not likely they will want to say no to many different groups. Find clubs, shops, and other bicycle-affiliated groups in your area at: https://members.bikeleague.org/members_online/members/findit.asp.

7. Call your government official and request a meeting.
Attend with your best spokesperson and copies of the letters of support with you to the meeting. Talk about the benefits of the bicycle improvements you desire, as well as the benefits of a Bicycle Friendly Community designation.

8. Ask for something specific and try to get a specific commitment.
A good starting point is to ask if the person will submit the application for Bicycle Friendly Community status. Another good ask is how long it will take to designate a bicycle coordinator. One way the city can show its support for building a Bicycle Friendly Community is by adopting the Action Plan for Bicycle Friendly Communities. This sets the goal as a city resolution or proclamation without the potential worries of going directly for applying. You could also propose working with the new coordinator on implementing the other

bicycle friendly criteria items (such as convening the bicycle advisory committee, proclaiming Bike to Work Day, developing bicycle-safe engineering policies, etc.). Be specific in your requests and, if the official raises concerns, ask him or her to be specific. Following the meeting, write a thank-you memo that spells out your understanding of what was agreed to. See the Action Plan here: www.bikeleague.org/programs/bicyclefriendlyamerica/communities/images/action_plan.pdf.

9. Follow up and follow up (and follow up).

Lack of persistence is the downfall of many a bicycle advocate. Motivated people motivate elected officials and their employees. If you raise an idea and then don't pursue it, they grow suspicious about just how important that idea is to you. So many people are clamoring for their time and attention, they will forget if you make yourself forgettable. Keep calling back and keep going back. Commit to the result and make it happen!

For additional information on creating change in your community, these organizations can be of great assistance:

Alliance for Bicycling and Walking: www.peoplepoweredmovement. org/site/. The national umbrella organization for the nation's bicycling and walking advocacy groups.

Alta Planning + Design: www.altaplanning.com. Creating active communities where bicycling and walking are safe, healthy, fun, and normal daily activities.

America Walks: www.americawalks.org. The national umbrella organization for the nation's pedestrian advocacy groups.

Association of Pedestrian and Bicycle Professionals: www.apbp.org. Please join in exchange for useful information, a Listserv, and professional development courses.

Association of American State Highway Transportation Officials (AASHTO) Guide to Bikeway Facilities: With a new guide forthcoming, this is a good starting point for basic bikeway planning and design.

Bikes Belong: www.bikesbelong.org. The national advocacy arm of the bicycle industry.

Cities for Cycling: www.citiesforcycling.org. A project of the National Association of City Transportation Officials (NACTO).

City of Portland Bicycle Program, **Smart Trips and Safe Routes to School Program**: www.portlandonline.com/transportation. Research, presentations, and plans galore.

First Stop Portland: www.pdx.edu/fsp/.A Portland State University program to develop itineraries for and host out-of-town delegations (meetings, speeches and tours).

Initiative for Bicycle and Pedestrian Innovation, Portland State University: www.ibpi.usp.pdx.edu/. Come to one of our excellent courses on pedestrian and bicycle planning, design, and implementation!

Institute for Transportation and Development Policy: www.itdp.org

International Mountain Bicycling Association: www.imba.com

League of American Bicyclists, Bicycle Friendly Communities Program: www.bikeleague.org/programs/bicyclefriendlyamerica/. Learn how to make your community or business more bicycle friendly.

Manual on Uniform Traffic Control Devices: mutcd.fhwa.dot.gov/ Part 9: Traffic Control for Bicycle Facilities addresses bicycle traffic, mutcd.fhwa.dot.gov/pdfs/2009/part9.pdf.

National Association of City Transportation Officials (NACTO) Urban Bikeway Design Guide: nacto.org/cities-for-cycling/design-guide/. The fabulous NACTO Urban Bikeway Design Guide (2011) provides photos, 3-D renderings, details, requirements, research and other information for design and implementation of treatments such as colored bike lanes, shared-lane markings, advance bike boxes, bike signals, signage, and other progressive bikeway design techniques.

National Complete Streets Coalition: www.smartgrowthamerica.org/ complete-streets.org

National Pedestrian and Bicycle Information Center: www.pedbikeinfo.org/

Rails to Trails Conservancy: www.railstotrails.org/index.html. Excellent information on development of trails.

Safe Routes to School Clearinghouse: www.saferoutesinfo.org/

Safe Routes to School Partnership: www.saferoutespartnership.org/

Streetfilms.org: A superb collection of short films about various aspects of bicycle friendly communities and culture.

Q&A WITH MIA BIRK

You faced a lot of obstacles as Portland's bicycle coordinator. Just reading about them raised our blood pressure! What kept you motivated to press on?

Every challenging battle was mitigated by the awesome stories of people starting to bike, getting fit, changing their lives for the better. Plus, we (remember, it wasn't just me alone—I was working with a team of terrific folks) were/ are 100 percent solid in our commitment to bringing bicycle transportation to Portland and beyond.

I am blessed to be friends with activists fighting for many changes—from getting toxic chemicals out of baby bottles to cleaning up our water supply. It's all hard, meaningful, productive work.

Giving up then was not an option, nor is it today. We are not just fighting for a bike lane here and there. We are engaged in a larger struggle for a healthier planet for our children and generations to come. It's an honor to have been able to build a career on this, to work side by side with a bunch of great people doing this great work.

Life is short; I'm intending to contribute as much as I can in the time I'm fortunate enough to be on this planet. And I'm going to leave it in better condition than when I got here if I have anything to say about it.

The wheel-and-pony shows you used to explain cycling to the community made for some good stories. It must have been nerve-racking to face these audiences, some of which were quite hostile to the idea of bicycle transport. Why did you choose this approach?

The City of Portland has an extensive history of involving the public in decision-making. This can make for maddeningly slow (and sometimes scary) processes, but on balance ends up creating better, longer-lasting outcomes, as evidenced by the many good facets of our city. My bosses at the time had had positive experiences conducting outreach for concepts such as traffic calming and light-rail, so the bike-oriented outreach made sense.

These days you work as a consultant on cyclist/pedestrian issues in cities around the world. Is there a city you see as the next Portland?

A bunch of cities are full-steam-ahead doing incredible things very quickly. These include New York City; Long Beach; Minneapolis; Seattle; Washington, D.C.; Chicago; Philadelphia; Fort Collins; St. Louis; Jackson Hole; and Vancouver, B.C. There's probably another two hundred cities making great strides all across North America.

What was/is the most effective way to humanize cyclists for drivers?

The one-on-one approach—cajoling and charming colleagues and friends to give it a try. Bike-commute challenges and celebrations. Big, game-changing, eye-opening events like Portland's Bridge Pedal, Sunday Parkways, and other such Ciclovias (car-free events). Connecting community to the many joys of bicycling through repurposing used bikes to needy families. Empowering women through bike maintenance classes and rides. Modeling that you can look fashionable while on a bike; it's not all about Lycra and speed. And starting Safe Routes to School programs. Many aggressive drivers get awfully tame around kids. All in all, the more we get motorists to ride bikes at least part of the time, the better it will be.

What do you see as the biggest obstacle to turning any city into a cycling city?

Political will.

Your children are also cyclists. Were they always enthusiastic about traveling by bike? What setup did you use to get them around before they could ride on their own?

My son, Skyler, hated the helmet when he was little, so that made for some miserable rides in the trailer or bike seat, both of which we used. My daughter, Sasha, is pretty much always happy, so she was fine with however we transported her. Each was on a trail-a-bike for a while. Now my son (age twelve) rides my old Trek 1420 road bike. He likes it because it's speedy and light.

Working as a liaison between cyclists and motorists isn't an easy job—both groups often see the other as threatening. What was the best way to defuse this tension? Is there anything you think cyclists can do to make drivers understand them better, and vice versa?

The tension is still there, although in my neighborhood it's gotten way better. I think this is because so many people around here now bike—so chances are, when you come up to a stop sign and that motorist waves you through even though the car has the right-of-way, that driver is a cyclist at least part of the time.

I think all of us can behave better, no matter how we get around. Let's all take a pledge to do, shall we? Ready?

When I am driving, I pledge to drive slowly on neighborhood streets. I will be patient and calm, especially around bicyclists. I will scan for and stop for pedestrians, always. I will refrain from talking, dialing, texting or otherwise messing with my cellphone, as well as anything else that takes my attention away from the road. I am pleased to see cyclists on the road, and I hope to get on my bike for my next trip.

When I am riding, I will not blow traffic signals. I will look for and yield to pedestrians. I will stay in the bike lane (if there is one and it is safe to do so) or over to the right to the best of my ability. If you behave aggressively toward me, I will repeat to myself, "Serenity now, serenity now," rather than flipping you off or confronting you. I will smile and wave thanks whenever you offer me the slightest bit of courtesy, because I know it can only help to be gracious to you, whoever you are.

One of the most inspiring moments in *Joyride* is when the city of Dallas hires your company to help them make the city more friendly to cyclists and pedestrians. Your experience in Portland makes you think that's impossible—but everyone is completely on board and things like cycle tracks are suddenly on the table. Do you see this happening in other cities these days?

Yes, I sure do. The Dallas story is personal, since I grew up there, but is meant to represent all the large auto-oriented cities taking their first steps toward a more bicycle friendly future. That interest and confidence in bicycle transportation is growing, as evidenced by my company's growth, even in this down economy. And it's also evidenced by the increased competition we face; large engineering and planning firms all now have bike/pedestrian specialists on staff, and compete against us for even the smallest projects.

Near the end of the book, an old friend tells you he used to think you were crazy but now realizes you were just "ahead of your time." What do you think of that statement? Has the time come for transportation cycling to be more than just a crazy idea?

That was my stepdad, Tommy, whom I adore. He's in good company with dozens of old friends and family who thought my work promoting bicycle transportation was silly at best. Follow-up story: Tommy was at the dentist, and the person working on his teeth started telling him about this lady on the radio from Portland, Oregon, who was talking about making Dallas more bike-friendly. Tommy just about spit up with joy—it was me! Nowadays, very few people react with derision or amusement; rather, they say things like—"I wish we could bike." "I've been to Portland/Copenhagen/Amsterdam and it's so cool that so many folks bike." "We sure need you here..."—stuff like that.

Given your line of work, there's probably only one way you can answer this question, but do you believe the United States can match Europe in terms of the percentage of the population that cycles?

Yes and no. (Is that what you expected?) We are relying on a carrot approach by providing bikeways and encouraging people to bike. Europeans do that (often with higher degree of separation) but also use economic strategies to shift people to more sustainable means of transportation (biking, walking, transit). I think we can definitely match the better European cities if we are willing to create higher-quality bikeways and make it more expensive to drive. Otherwise, no.

Can you suggest one thing that cyclists can and should do to promote bicycle/pedestrian friendliness in their community?

Raise money to send a delegation of key city officials to Copenhagen or Portland or Boulder, Colo. Portland's already-enlightened traffic engineer, Rob Burchfield, said the week he spent in Amsterdam and Copenhagen was the equivalent of fifteen years' worth of conferences and trainings. He already was on board conceptually, but experiencing it in real life brought it home for him.

In Portland, we host tours almost every week for transportation officials, politicians, civic and business leaders, and advocates through Portland State

University's First Stop program. There's no better sales pitch for bicycle transportation than a ride on a lovely summer day.

Tell me about the *Joyride* tour.

The year after the publication of the first edition of *Joyride,* I visited fourteen states and three Canadian provinces, gave some sixty presentations, participated in events, Skyped into meeting rooms, led webinars, delivered a TED talk, wrote essays for my blog (www.miabirk.com/blog) and other publications, and learned to tweet. Every time I would start to whine about the impact of the travel and relentless correspondence on my health and family, I would receive another heartfelt email or note about how my words and stories inspired the sender. So I would buck up and go pack another bag.

The tour started at TREK World in Madison, Wisconsin, where I discussed with hundreds of bike retailers why and how to get involved in—even lead— their community's efforts to become more bicycle friendly. (It may seem obvious that bike retailers would want to expand their market by attracting new riders, and many successful retailers do engage in these efforts, but many come to it through their love of bicycling as a sport, not an understanding of the power and potential of bicycling as a means of transportation.) From there I was in Las Vegas, Bellingham, Seattle, Indianapolis, Bloomington, Calgary, Toronto, Vancouver, B.C., Washington, D.C., Tucson, Syracuse, Ithaca, Schenectady, Chattanooga, Richmond, Philadelphia, Billings, Denver, Fort Collins, Boise, Nampa, and a handful of towns in North and South Carolina. Why these places? In each, a local advocacy group, government, or university (or all three) sought inspiration and input to help get them to the next level.

In Calgary, my visit helped push over the top a bold, visionary new bicycle transportation strategy. In Bloomington, the public works director gained an understanding of the concept of bicycle boulevards and accelerated plans for new bikeways. In Toronto, advocates depressed by a downturn in political support sighed in relief when they learned that Portland too went through such a phase. In Syracuse, the city's transportation planner got inspired to walk the talk and get out and cycle more. Seattle's staff and advocates took heart from my stories of painful backlash. A group of dynamic women in Tucson used me (with permission, of course) to kick off a health-oriented advocacy campaign. Engineers in Fort Collins gained detailed guidance toward the creation of separated on-road bikeways, while trail proponents in muggy Richmond celebrated in the aftermath of my trip thanks to a new city commitment to on-street bikeways. These are just a few examples.

All in all, it was a year on the frontlines of the battle for the future of North American transportation. I'm pretty sure this will be the focus of my next book. Stay tuned!

ACKNOWLEDGMENTS

Joyride grew out of my bicycle and pedestrian planning course lectures at Portland State University. Thank you to Ethan Seltzer and Jennifer Dill, in particular, who invited me in and embraced a vision that led to the creation of the Initiative for Bicycle and Pedestrian Innovation (IBPI). With every course, research project, and continuing education class, we raise the bar a little higher. Joyride proceeds are directed in part to the IBPI, as well as a number of other nonprofit organizations working to create healthier, safe, clean, and green communities nationwide.

Deep, heartfelt thanks to my expansive, complex, wild, and wonderful family, for all that I am and all that I have, as well as to my superstar posse of friends.

Glen: Timing is everything, as we both know. For all that you bring to my life, I am eternally grateful.

To my colleagues at Alta Planning + Design: Thanks for your support and understanding, hard work and numerous contributions.

To the incredible cast of Portland heroes, both past and present: Earl, Jay, Rob, Doug, Lewis, Rich, Roger, Jeff, Linda, Janis, Barbara, Jerry, Catherine, Rex, Jonathan, Rick, Rich, Karen, Charlie, Rod, Brian, Scott, Teresa, Vic, and many more...you have inspired the nation. Thanks to the many colleagues who reached into their memory banks to corroborate, inform, correct, or sharpen my recollections and research. Beyond Portland, a special shout-out to Andy, Cara, Oliver, Jon, Ben, Randy, Charlie, Dan, Peter, Charlie, Michael, Deb, Sharon, Kit, Cong. Oberstar, John Burke, and all the rest: You know who you are, you mavericks, you daredevils, pushing the envelope, never slowing in your persistence to create a better world for generations to come.

Special thanks to Joe Kurmaskie, aka The Metal Cowboy, for his guidance, support, and help in shaping the narrative and bringing the stories to life.

To my colleagues and friends at the various nonprofit organizations of which I am a part, and to my clients and friends around the globe, I hope *Joyride* helps us all spread the love.

For all those we have lost from senseless, unnecessary crashes: You are not forgotten.

Finally, this book is for anyone and everyone, wherever you are, who recognizes that bicycling and walking are—or should be—a part of our daily lives. Enjoy the ride!